FOOD CITY: VANCOUVER

Food City: Vancouver

The Delectable Guide to Finding and
Enjoying Good Food in Vancouver
and the Lower Mainland

ANGELA MURRILLS

POLESTAR
BOOK PUBLISHERS

Polestar Book Publishers acknowledges the ongoing support of The
Canada Council, the British Columbia Ministry of Small Business,
Tourism and Culture, and the Department of Canadian Heritage.

Cover design by Jim Brennan.
Interior illustrations and cover art by Bernie Lyon.
Printed and bound in Canada.

Canadian Cataloguing in Publication Data
        Murrills, Angela.
        Food city
        (The City series)
        ISBN 1-896095-47-X

        I. Grocery shopping — British Columbia — Vancouver. 2.
Diners and dining — British Columbia — Vancouver. 3. Grocery
shopping — British Columbia — Lower Mainland. 4. Diners and
dining — British Columbia — Lower Mainland. I. Title. II. Series: The
city series (Victoria, B.C.)
HD9014.C33B75 1998641.3'009711'33   C98-910615-2

Polestar Book Publishers
P.O. Box 5238, Station B
Victoria, British Columbia
Canada   V8R 6N4
http://mypage.direct.ca/p/polestar/

In the United States:
Polestar Book Publishers
P.O. Box 468
Custer, WA
USA   98240-0468

5 4 3 2 1

Acknowledgments

This book couldn't have been written without the generous assistance of all the chefs, restaurateurs, suppliers, store owners, writers and everyone else whose names appear in these pages. Special thanks (in more or less alphabetical order) to: Karen Barnaby for telling me all her secrets; Dawn Boxall of FarmFolk/CityFolk for, time after time, connecting me with the right people; Christina Burridge and Sandra Furch of the B.C. Salmon Marketing Council; Janice Buxton; Ian Cowley and Cate Simpson-Cowley; Sid Cross; Martin Dunphy, a fellow fan of hot sauces; Henry Fowlds of the Australian Trade Commission; Jessie Horner; food consultant and mycologist Bill Jones for sharing his favourite food stores; Judith Lane, concierge extraordinaire who cheerfully Told All; to John Levine for directing me towards Vancouver's many wine clubs (and revealing his favourite spots in Richmond); Murray McMillan, *Vancouver Sun* Food Editor; editors Rhonda May of *CityFood*, Beverley Sinclair of *The Georgia Straight*, Jim Sutherland of *Vancouver Magazine* and Cameron Nagel, publisher of *Northwest Palate*, where bits and pieces of this material were originally published; Annie Moss of Wild West Organic Harvest Co-op for linking me with organic food stores far and wide; Larry Garfinkel, Cathy Moss and Alvin Wasserman for setting me straight on delis; Mary O'Donovan, Market Co-ordinator at Granville Island Public Market for providing me with a list of all the special seasonal treats available; fellow scribe Tim Pawsey who, when I couldn't for the life of me remember the name of the cheese guy behind Capilano Mall, couldn't remember either — but at least knew someone who would; to Ruth Phelan of the *Vancouver Sun* Test Kitchen who figured out exactly how many recipes are in the Edith Adams Kitchen; to Joan Seidl, Curator of History at the Vancouver Museum who let me spend a pleasurable afternoon rummaging through old cookbooks; to Barry Stickels of Doug's Fine Meats; and to Laura Vandriel. Special thanks to Stephen Wong for walking me around Chinatown and answering my idiot-level questions, and to Stephanie Yuen for helping me take my first fumbling steps in Chinese translation.

Finally, thanks to Marg Meikle for instigating this project. All I said was, "Gee, now you've done *Dog City: Vancouver*, someone should do a food version..." And thanks to her husband Noel MacDonald, fountainhead of arcane facts. A big thank-you to James Barber who, busy urban peasant though he is, took time to write the introduction, and to my editor Lynn Henry who kept me calm when I was way past even the most pessimistic deadline.

Above all, thanks to my husband Peter Matthews (who took most of the photos) and my daughter Kate, my best-beloveds who cooked for me, tolerated phone calls at unseemly hours and in general gave me the bastion of love and support without which writing a book is a pretty lonely business. Thanks guys.

To everyone who lives to eat (rather than vice versa).

Food City: Vancouver

PREFACE

Look at it this way: if we get to live out our alloted span of three score years and ten, plus a decade more because we're ultra-conscientious about not eating too much salt, fat or other nasties the medical establishment is currently railing against, that means (the years when Mom is cooking not included) a grand total of close to 65,000 meals. What an extraordinary opportunity to explore the world of food.

In Vancouver, we do have a world of food to explore. The Italians, Greeks, British, German, Chinese, Japanese and people of other nationalities who have moved here have all brought their favourite foodstuffs along with their luggage. I live in Kitsilano, not a particularly ethnic neighbourhood. Yet, within five minutes' walk I can find poppadoms (both full size and cocktail size), Vietnamese spring-roll wrappers, Chinese sausages, feta cheese, Iranian rosewater and a dozen kinds of olives from around the Mediterranean. On top of that, Vancouver has the warmest climate in Canada. Vegetables and fruit flourish locally, and they all come fresh to our tables — not just cabbages and carrots, but blackberries as big as thumb-joints, pink, white and yellow oyster mushrooms, and dozens of different salad greens.

But it's not just ethnic diversity and access to produce that makes Vancouver such a terrific food city. It's the passion we have for what we cook, and the energy we spend on tracking down what we need. Raiding the supermarket is obviously the easiest way to buy your food, but few of us do. Instead, we get up early on a Saturday to be first at the market, drive halfway across town to pick up the perfect wedge of Camembert, call the butcher to make sure he's got lamb shanks in stock, or sign up for a weekly home delivery of organic produce.

The pages that follow do not contain an exhaustive list of every butcher, every baker and every candle-nut seller in and around Vancouver (that's what the Yellow Pages are for). It's not a cookbook in the conventional sense, either. There aren't teaspoons of this and microdots of that. Instead, you'll find recipes that a neighbour might tell you about: "I make this really great dish with eggplant..." That kind of recipe. Nor is this a book of restaurant reviews, though you will find a list of places where you can go and have good food and a good time. If there's something common to them all, it's value. That can mean the Vietnamese lunch that sets you back all of eight bucks for two. Or the save-up-for-months-and-worth-every-cent dinner at Bishop's or Lumière. In short, this book is an entry into foods, places and experiences that you may not know about.

In one way, writing *Food City:Vancouver* was enormously frustrating. There were so many facts, so little time. Every piece of information revealed three or four more trails to follow. A phone call to one of my favourite butchers, Jackson's on 4th Avenue, led to a 20-minute conversation with Brian Jackson as he reeled off recipe after recipe (they're all in the book). Other serendipitous things happened, too. A baker I know told me how he made this bread and that bread and then, just as the conversation was winding up, added "Oh, and at Christmas time I make gingerbread earrings!" Rambling around Chinatown one Saturday morning, I found what must surely be the ultimate fusion dish at the Streamland Bakery on Keefer Street — a tuna danish.

In my quest for ethnic foods for homesick immigrants, I did eventually track down Mrs. H.S. Ball's chutneys from South Africa, and Lucozade — the traditional British remedy for when you're feeling a bit under the weather — but I never did come upon New Zealand Hokey-Pokey ice cream. If anyone out there knows where it is, please let me know.

I hope you'll have as good a time using *Food City: Vancouver* as I've had writing it. I hope, too, that it will prod you to become a culinary explorer yourself. Wander down that side street. Poke your head inside that intriguing store. Ask the fishmonger how he cooks his clams. Go out there and make your own discoveries in this most marvellous of food cities.

Enough words: let's eat!

— *Angela Murrills*

INTRODUCTION

by James Barber

Everybody eats — some of us with passion, some without. There are fastfooders, who fill their stomachs with the same apathy as they fill their cars with gas; there are the gourmets who do it for social status without ever really liking it; and there are the plain down-and-dirty gutsers, who eat, no matter what they eat, with curiousity and joy, with the awareness that something new, something marvellous is always around the next corner.

I learned to cook in France — not the glossy magazine France of tall white hats in fancy restaurants, but the French countryside in wartime, when food was short and anything with leaves, feathers or fur was considered edible. A chicken stupid enough to roost overnight in a tree was almost sure to wake up next morning in a stewpot, maybe with potatoes, or just as likely with dandelion roots or chestnuts off the trees, to be eaten later in the day with a salad of weeds from the hedgerows. Going for a walk meant continually evaluating: Could we eat that? Or this? Shall we try? I quickly learned the thrill of accidental discovery, but, more important, I learned not just to look but to listen. Finding food was important, but equally important was finding out what to do with it. Luckily, there was almost always somebody to give a hint.

Food foraging in North America today is more exciting than all those years ago in France. Our hedges are markets and small stores. And we still listen: we hear about the woman in Abbotsford who raises chickens on nothing but organically grown vegetables and the Romanian guy who grows 37 varieties of tomatoes, and we get ideas from TV, radio and magazines. But the really important source of interesting food is always the "network" — the rumour, the gossip, the experience: "We've got the best sausages we've ever had at Columbus Meats"; "Ginger on broccoli is really great"; "J.N.Z. Meats on Commercial — no nitrates." The problem is that most of this information comes when you're having a good time. Perhaps you're eating with people, or talking about food, and you always mean to write it down but you never do because you can't find your notebook — and even if you could, you think you might look silly.

Angela Murrills' book is a series of notes you never made. I've known Angela for years. I've cooked with her, eaten with her, foraged back lanes and shopped with her. She was always the one who wrote it down. I wish I had.

STOCKING THE KITCHEN

Any camper will tell you: It's possible to make a decent meal using nothing but a battered old fry pan and a can opener. On the other hand, the better the tools, the easier it is to cook — and the more you'll enjoy it. A solidly built saucepan and fry pan, and a couple of razor-sharp knives, are all you need to start. Once you discover what you really like to cook, you can buy the kind of dishes you're most likely to use: enamel-on-cast-iron dishes that go from stove-top to oven to table if you're a one-pot wonder; the best wok you can find if you like to whip up a stir-fry four nights a week; sturdy whisks if you're known for your sauces. Or maybe all three.

A rock-solid chopping block is essential. Now that researchers have confirmed that wooden blocks are perfectly safe, we can feel comfortable about using an age-old tool that was always far nicer to work on than any white plastic substitute. Buy the largest you can afford: chopping onions on a board the size of a frisbee is the fast route to insanity.

Every cook has their favourite tool. I lived without a microwave oven for years. The one we own now is second-hand, cost $50 and is superb for warming up coffee or last night's leftover Chinese takeout...but cook with it? Where are the smells? Where is the sizzle? Now, a food processor — that's different. Separate me from my 20-year-old Cuisinart and you're mincemeat. Chopping parsley, crunching bread crumbs, making ice chips — I've subjected it to severe abuse over the years and its motor continues to thrum away. I'm also a strong advocate of the "Braun wand," a hand-held gadget that turns a mixture of vegetables and stock into a delicately smooth soup in 20 seconds.

If you're known for your chicken vindaloo, you might want to pick up a coffee mill and use it exclusively for spices, or track down a pestle and mortar made of marble. Big wire strainers are a must for draining pasta or steaming vegetables. A top quality vegetable peeler and a good cheese grater will preserve your good humour and your knuckles.

Think of the satisfaction to be had in chopping a shallot into tiny dice or cutting a tomato into paper-thin slices. Remember the slow sensual ritual of stirring a pot of soup as it burbles gently on the stove. Preparing food ought to be a thoroughly pleasurable experience — and with the right tools, it can be.

COOKWARE STORES: Tools and Supplies

Vancouver is blessed with a huge number of kitchen stores. Here are some good places to start if you're after that perfect pot or the ideal casserole dish. Kitchen drawer gridlock alert: some of these stores carry gadgets galore.

COQUITLAM:
Cookshop
1300-2929 Barnet Hwy • 464-6266
(see also: Vancouver)
Top name cookware — Calphalon, All-Clad, Chantal from Germany, Opa from Finland — and others, including Look non-stick cookware from Iceland. If you're short of space, look into their solid maple prep tables/carts which can accommodate a goodly number of utensils and dishes.

LANGLEY:
Bon Chef Kitchen Store
6339 200th St. • 532-7993
Knives and spices but no table linens. This is strictly stuff for the kitchen. The 60-foot wall of gadgets includes the entire Norpro line from the U.S., who also make the Krona cookware carried here.

NEW WESTMINSTER:
House of Knives
476 East Columbia St. • 522-7735
Twelve branches in lower mainland shopping centres. Victorinox knives from Switzerland, Henckels (in different grades) and Wusthof Trident from Germany. Gadgets, too — such as Omessi brand garlic peelers, and oil and vinegar cruets from Czechoslovakia.

NORTH VANCOUVER:
Basic Stock
3-3069 Edgemont Blvd. • 990-7274
(see also: Vancouver)
Known for Cuisinart cookware, Cuisinart food processors, bakeware, stainless steel gadgets, dishes and linens. This is also the place for KitchenAid stand mixers, up to five quarts, in lots of colours.

That Restaurant Look
Rack of lamb with roasted winter vegetables, a sumptuous chocolate pâté with fresh mango coulis, even the same old meat-loaf or take-out Chinese — everything looks better on a large, white, wide-rimmed plate. Twelve inches is the restaurant size.

VANCOUVER:

Acme Plating & Silver Shop

1530 West 6th Ave. • 733-3317

When your copper fry pan starts to show its age, here's the place to get it relined. You can also bring in worn-out silver-plated flatware or serving pieces.

Atkinson's

1501 West 6th Ave. • 736-3378

Spring cookware in copper or stainless steel from Switzerland, as well as china, flatware, crystal (including the world's classiest and most expensive scotch glasses) and linens.

Basic Stock

2294 West 4th Ave. • 736-1412

2150 West 41st Ave. • 261-3599

(see also: North Vancouver)

Casa

420 Howe St. • 681-5884

Villeroy & Boch oven-to-tableware that ties in with dinnerware. Fabulous dishes from Portugal, Italian majolica, lots of table linen made in Canada or imported from Europe and India. Boxing Day blow-out is worth waiting for.

Pass the Salt

Here's an idea worth stealing if you want to put on a bit of a splash: Save large shapely oyster shells and serve salt in them.

Chocolate Mousse Kitchenware
1553 Robson St. • 682-8223
Stock is geared to a West End clientele so you'll not only find Henckel knives and soft-handled Good Grips utensils, but plates, cutlery, table linen and cookbooks too.

Cookshop
555 West 12th Ave. • 873-5683
(see: Coquitlam)

There is no love sincerer than the love of food.
— George Bernard Shaw

Drinkwater and Company Fine Cookware
4465 West 10th Ave. • 224-2665
Known for top-of-the-line cookware such as Le Creuset. Bargain-hunters wait for the Paderno sale in October. This store is particularly known for special orders. Want a spaetzle maker or a beautiful kettle that actually works? Anything they can find, they'll bring in. A bonus, if you get on their mailing list, is Anne Drinkwater's chatty and informative newsletter.

Intrex Trading Inc.
222-8599
Rick Downie imports commercial-strength copper pots and pans from France and sells them direct. The Cupronil brand comes from Normandy and is made of solid copper with a stainless steel lining and cast-iron handles. Prices average $150 for a fry pan or $350 for a sauté pan with lid. Downie can also bring in a vast range of professional-quality tools such as stainless steel garlic presses and sugar density meters.

Kitchen Corner
2136 West 4th Ave. • 737-1871
1684 Commercial Dr. • 254-3739
2686 Granville St. • 739-4422
Dishes, cookpots, baking pans, glasses, baskets. You've never seen so much stuff — and all of it cheap.

Lightheart & Company
535 Howe St. • 684-4711
375 Water St. • 685-8255
No cookware but lots of wonderful platters and bowls. Doulton, Royal Worcester, Spode, Gien and Artichaut

from France and the largest selection of Portmeirion's botanical garden pattern in North America. The Water St. location is mostly giftware.

Market Kitchen

#2-1666 Johnston St., Granville Island • 681-7399
Cast-iron cookware, copper cookware, All-Clad cookware and more. Lots of specialty bakeware and hard-to-find items like madeleine forms and savarin rings. Check out the Vancouver-made Darcy oven-to-table pottery.

Ming Wo Cookware

23 East Pender St. • 683-7268
Nine other locations.
Opened in 1917, the Pender St. location is still my favourite. Tons of cookie cutters, good quality zesters, butter paddles, curlers, graters — plus pots, pans and a vast selection of woks. If you're on the hunt for those intricate Chinese vegetable cutters and garnishing tools, here's the place.

Puddifoot's

2350 West 41st Ave. • 261-8141
Atlas and Kuchenprofi pots as well as the cheerfully coloured Emile Henry line. Also a good place to stock up on restaurant-quality large white plates and large plain wine glasses.

WEST VANCOUVER:

Tools and Techniques

250-16th St. • 925-1835
Cindy Evetts sells Calphalon and other good quality cookware lines, plus useful gadgets such as terra cotta brown sugar savers, bright-coloured pasta spoons, Good Grips vegetable peelers, B.C.-made glassware and hand-painted pottery. Get on her mailing list and you'll receive lively newsletters with recipes, and details of cooking classes and new products.

Inside Ming Wo Cookware

Problem:

Buying new flatware has left you flat broke and you still need to put plates on the table.

Solution:

Take a run around Chinatown, where you'll find blue and white plates, bowls and platters galore for very little. Feel free to mix and match patterns.

BECOMING PROFESSIONAL:
Restaurant Supply Stores

Now that open kitchens are fashionable in restaurants, we can see what goes on behind the scenes. While kitchens at home are becoming increasingly multi-purpose, a commercial kitchen is still strictly business. This stands to reason: If a chef is pushing out 50 plates of prime rib an hour, the last thing he or she wants is French country kitchen ambience.

While you may not necessarily need a walk-in freezer or a potato rumbler — a gadget that peels potatoes — plenty of restaurant equipment can work just as efficiently in a regular kitchen. A bonus: The equipment you buy from these specialized stores is meant to be banged around, dropped and thrown at the wall by temperamental chefs. It is, in a word, sturdy.

A couple of notes: "Smallwares" are exactly that — the little necessities like plates, glasses and sugar shakers. Also, while these stores will happily sell to keen amateurs, the hours they keep aren't necessarily regular retail hours. Calling ahead may save you going out of your way unnecessarily.

BURNABY:
Nella Cutlery Inc.
5327 Lane St. • 451-7865
Sells Victorinex, Swibo from Switzerland and their own Nella brand of knives, as well as slicers and grinders.

DELTA:
Cassidy's
10207 Nordel Court • 930-8233
(see also: Vancouver)
Browsing for commercial-quality stoves and fridges? Head for the Delta location. Otherwise both Delta and Vancouver showrooms carry pots, pans and "anything in a restaurant or bar that you don't eat or throw away" which means plates, glassware and — exclusive to Cassidy's — Dudson chinaware, considered the best in commercial-grade china. Figure around $100 for a dozen dinner plates. The Keg, Milestones

and White Spot are some of the major restaurants who shop here.

LANGLEY:

A-1 Food Equipment
8-19739 56th Ave. • 533-6590

The stoves are $2500 but they last. Also available: fryers, convection ovens, flippers, turners, stainless steel and aluminum pots and pans.

VANCOUVER:

Alternative Uniform Designs
1392 East 3rd Ave. • 255-7477

Geared to professionals but the snappy designs and styles — such as chili-printed pants and berets — appeal to amateurs too. A popular wedding gift is the chef and sous-chef set personalized with the happy couple's names.

Cassidy's
68 East 7th Ave. • 874-5143
(see also: Delta)

Dunlevy Food Equipment
5 East 5th Ave. • 873-2236

Stoves, fridges and "we're big on reconditioned appliances." A good source for smallwares. White china dinner plates are under $30 a dozen.

Fabrications Inc.
22 East 5th Ave. • 290-4478

If you're seeking a permanently spot-free tablecloth, here's the spot to find it. This company sells mostly to hotels and restaurants such as Joe Fortes, the Bread Garden and Montri's, but they'll happily let you purchase one of their wipe-clean plastic tablecloths. Patterns include florals and geometric prints.

O'Grady Westcoast Food Equipment
717 East Hastings St. • 254-1325

Cooking pots, ranges and ovens, including the Zesco line which is exclusive to this store in Vancouver. No smallwares.

Designer China
Sunflowers, chilis, fruit or fauna? Use Crankpots Ceramic Studio to paint your preference on a platter or bowl. (555 West 12th Ave. in City Square, 871-0302.)

Paragon Food Equipment
760 East Hastings St. • 255-9991
Basic appliances — some locally made by Polygon Metal Works — plus about 4,000 different kinds of smallwares. It's impossible to come out without a classic diner sugar shaker.

Polygon Metal Works
290 West 3rd Ave. • 873-6661
If your search for the perfect oven has been fruitless, Polygon can custom-make you a stove, range hood, countertops or cabinets.

Russell Food Equipment
1255 Venables St. • 253-6611
Equipment and smallwares.

The Used Food Equipment Centre
34 East 2nd Ave. • 873-9981
Ranges and fridges, mostly from restaurants that are updating or have bitten the dust.

Specialized Equipment:

MAPLE RIDGE:
Chocolates by Grace
11951 224th St. • 463-3767
Home chocolate makers will find 400 varieties of plastic moulds, ranging from hockey sticks to animals, flowers and fruit. The most unusual is a mold shaped like an aspirin. They can also create your corporate logo in chocolate.

SURREY:
Scoop-n-Save
13472 104th Ave. • 585-2888
Anything to do with birthday or wedding cakes. Little statues, sugar flowers, the lot. Also thousands of chocolate moulds.

VANCOVER:
Tin Tin Market
236 East Pender St. • 801-6002
Good for utensils and intricately carved wooden

moulds that the Chinese use for making cakes but which could double as butter moulds if you want to do a major Martha Stewart number at your next dinner party.

Tinland House Ware
209 East Pender St. • 608-0787
A great selection of strainers, restaurant-quality steamers, pots and big white dinner plates. Stock up on squeezie bottles here: yellow and red for mustard and ketchup, and clear for everything else.

Chef's Tip
"Be sure to add enough salt to pasta, potatoes or vegetables when you cook them. It's so important."
— Michael Noble, Diva at the Met

THE AGA COOKER

Owning one of these cast-iron giants takes commitment — they weigh up to 1290 pounds (as much as a quartet of football players) and take a day and a half to install — but any Aga user will tell you it's worthwhile. As Cathy Kipp of New Westminster, B.C., explains: "It's like having this big, fat, beautiful empress in the kitchen who exudes this motherly warmth." An Aga costs about the same as a small car does, but to its 150,000 owners worldwide, this British-made cooker isn't merely a major appliance, it's a cozy, comfy way of life.

The Aga was invented 75 years ago by Dr. Gustaf Dalen, a Swedish physicist and Nobel Prize Laureate who, blinded in an accident and confined to his home, realized how much time his wife spent in the kitchen. Dalen put his wits to work and came up with the Aga, a cooker that could handle several dishes simultaneously.

Decades pass but the Aga stays the same, still built from solid cast iron, still cooking by radiant heat and always "on." A single burner unit keeps ovens and hot-plates at the right temperatures to roast a turkey, bake a soufflé, make toast or cook pasta, all at the same time. Owners sometimes dry their jeans over the towel rail and, on chilly Yorkshire farms, newborn lambs are occasionally put in the cozy warming oven.

Aga owners include Martha Stewart, Dustin Hoffman and Paul McCartney. Writer John Updike calls it "an object of reverence" and, in England, any novel that revolves around contemporary village life is an "Aga saga."

Locally you can buy Aga through Alpine Appliance Installations (727 Kilkeel Place, North Vancouver, 980-8889)

Burning Desires

In their restaurant kitchens, chefs can cook on the cream of the cream of stoves. At home, it's a different matter.

Michael Noble, of Diva:"The stove is electric. I'd love to have gas."

Robert LeCrom, Executive Chef, Hotel Vancouver:"I use an electric stove. On my boat I have an alcohol-fueled stove."

Andrew Skorzewski of Rainforest Café cooks on "a 20-year-old electric stove with two burners that work, and an oven that's 75 degrees hotter than it says — and I hate it. But I *can* cook on two burners and with an oven that's too hot."

Richard Zeinoun and Lisa Gibson of Habibi's cook on an electric stove — by choice."I find it's more convenient," says Zeinoun,"and I think you can control it better. In the old school, nobody would accept that."

KNIVES, POTS AND PANS: Who Uses What?

Michael Noble of Diva at the Met uses a combination of knife brands. "The Henckel full set is my basic set. I'm also quite partial to the Trident knives. I find them very comfortable to use. Once, when I was a very poor cook in Switzerland, I bought a Victorinex filleting knife in the market in Berne."

At home, Noble uses Farberware cookware almost exclusively. How he came to acquire it is a story in itself. "When I was working at Chartwell I used to take the bus home to Steveston at 11 p.m. The bus had the same driver each night. He was a keen cook and we'd talk about food. When he moved to a smaller house, he gave me his Farberware. I have Lagostina as well." Adds Noble, "I don't cook much at home."

Made by the same company that manufacturers the famed Swiss army knife, Victorinex is the brand of choice of Robert LeCrom, Executive Chef at the Hotel Vancouver. "I've used them for as long as I can remember. The wooden-handled ones, not the plastic."

Vikram Vij of Vij's uses nothing but Henckel knives, a brand also favoured, along with Trident, by Carol Chow of the Beach Side Café. "They're a tiny bit more expensive but they keep a good edge."

"Knives?"Andrew Skorzewski of Rainforest Café admits to an eclectic collection. "I don't have two of the same brand. My Goldhamster is my favourite. It's hard steel, beautifully designed and balanced, a real chef's knife. I bought it from Puddifoot's and it's a joy to use."

INGREDIENTS

Imagine taking some freshly cooked pasta — any kind, long, curly or wide. Now toss it with the cheapest olive oil you can find. Then toss it again with dried parsley flakes from a jar at the back of the cupboard and a sprinkling of pre-grated orange cheese from the cardboard cylinder behind it. Dump it on a plate. On the side put a couple of slices of mass-produced white bread. Shred iceberg lettuce into a bowl and top it with bottled dressing. There's Meal Number 1.

For Meal Number 2, you take the same kind of pasta, drizzle it with a little extra virgin olive oil and add some freshly snipped Italian parsley (that you keep in a jar of water so that it's always crisp and beautiful). Pull out that wedge of real Parmigiana from the fridge, grate a little of it over the pasta, then toss everything together so that all the flavours have a chance to get friendly. In the centre of the table goes a loaf of crusty bread from the local baker. Fill the salad bowl with crunchy greens. They don't have to be a "gourmet" mix of arugula, radicchio and mache — though that's nice; they could simply be the leaves of a locally grown butter lettuce. Either way, over the salad goes a vinaigrette you've just whisked up from some more of that olive oil, wine vinegar, freshly ground pepper, salt and a smidgen of Dijon mustard.

Meal Number 2 you can serve to yourself and your friends with your head held high. The first meal is one you wouldn't serve to a dog. The idea is simple: Good ingredients — authentic ingredients — are at the heart of wonderful food.

THE CONDIMENT CUPBOARD:
Spices, Seasonings and Herbs

Twenty years ago, spices usually stood in a row like soldiers along the back of the stove. Oregano for the lasagna and spaghetti sauce. Garlic powder for the garlic bread that went with both of them. Cinnamon for cinnamon toast. "Poultry spice" for sprinkling over roast chicken. And that was it, basically.

Chef's Tip

"Use a few ingredients. Never more than one main spice. If it's ginger, stay with that and use nothing else."
— Robert LeCrom, Executive Chef, Hotel Vancouver.

Today, it's not uncommon for keen cooks to have as many as four dozen seasonings toppling out of the kitchen cabinet. Juniper berries for marinating game. Spanish and Hungarian paprika. Black mustard seeds for made-from-scratch curries, and yellow mustard powder for potato salads.

Buying spices in little glass jars is so expensive that we're reluctant to throw them out when they begin to lose their potency. Buying spices in bulk means they're cheap enough that you don't feel like a wastrel when you ditch that half jar of cinnamon that's lost its "oomph." Buying dried herbs the same way makes sense, too — and for the same reason. Use fresh herbs whenever you can — they really do make a difference (and they look pretty too). Chives, basil, tarragon, mint — you'll find an ever-growing selection at your supermarket. Sometimes, buying a herb connects you directly with the country that grew it. The bunches of dried Greek oregano at the Parthenon Supermarket are tied by hand with small pieces of checked fabric. La Grotta del Formaggio carries Sicilian oregano on the branch. At the Punjabi Market, you'll find pungent fresh curry leaves.

If the pantry seems fuller than it was five years ago, it's hardly surprising. We've also bumped up the number of condiments we use routinely. Today's chutneys do more than sit on the side of your plate of chicken vindaloo. They often earn their keep as a basting sauce. Chinese sauces — black bean, hoisin and char siu — make stir-fries a thing of the moment. As for vinegars, do a head-count and you'll likely find half a dozen on your shelves: red wine, white wine, balsamic, rice vinegar, apple cider vinegar and maybe a raspberry or strawberry vinegar. Oils are the same: you'll probably find Canola oil, olive oil (and probably extra virgin olive oil as well), sesame oil for Asian dishes and even mustard oil if you're hot on Indian food, or walnut oil if you can't get enough of authentic French salads.

Regular salt, sea salt, kosher salt. Black pepper, white pepper and green and pink peppercorns. Of course you need them all — and here are some places that can help you add to your collection.

Secrets of Saffron

Sacred dye, alleged aphrodisiac and soother of nerves, saffron is appreciated as much for its joyful sunny colour as its clean, slightly medicinal, taste. It comes from the mauve-petalled crocus sativa and it's the most expensive spice in the world, largely because it takes the stigmas of 1700 flowers to yield 25 grams. Essential in paella, classic in risottos and bouillabaisse, saffron adds subtle flavour to Indian pilaus and desserts, too. In Cornwall, at Easter, it's stirred into sweet bread-like saffron cake. In fact, at one time, such quantities were grown in England that a town was named after it: Saffron Walden in Essex. Here's how to use it: Soak the tiny strands in warm water till it turns dark orange, then add to your dish. It's expensive, but a pinch packs a punch. You'll find the best prices in Iranian grocery stores.

Grow Your Own Sweetener

Stevia is an attractive, easy-to-grow herb that yields a substance over 200 times sweeter than sucrose.

NORTH VANCOUVER:

Everything Garlic

Lonsdale Quay Market • 988-0003

They're not kidding. Garlic au naturel and garlic in every possible shape and form: sauces, pickles, dressings, even garlic shampoo, unscented. Garlic potato chips. "It's chic to reek" T-shirts.

Ann Kirsebom/The Toast of the Town Cuisine Ltd.

987-9187

Teacher and caterer Kirsebom is known for her Tequi-Lime BBQ Sauce. You'll find it at The Pepper Pot, The Queensdale Market, Peter Black Butchers, Edgemont Gourmet Meats — all on the North Shore — and in the summer at the East Vancouver Farmers' Market (see page 212).

SURREY:

A Taste of Heaven

Fraser Heights Village Centre • 408-1603

3 108th Ave. • 588-7171

While this store does sell pastas, coffees, teas, chutneys and jams, many customers come here just for the hot sauce. Fifty varieties from Mexico, South Africa, Barbados and the West Indies, including Brain Damage, Endorphin Rush, Cyanide, two limited edition hot sauces packaged in coffins and Chilemania, which is made especially for the store in the U.S. Periodic hot sauce tastings; samples are usually on hand. The adjacent restaurant serves hot wings made with your favourite sauce.

TSAWWASSEN:

Big Don's Homemade Pickles

943-2501

Don Schultz makes bread and butter, beet, mustard and dill pickles, as well as green tomato chow chow, corn relish and cucumber relish. They're all terrific, reasonably priced — and his net profits go to charity. Once the pickling season gets underway, i.e. around September, you'll often find Schultz at the East Vancouver Farmers' Market (see page 212). Otherwise give him a call.

VANCOUVER:

Blackberry Hill Farm

1879 Powell St. • 258-7437

Chris Hoekstra makes jams, preserves, marmalades, chutneys and relishes which she sells at Granville Island Public Market a couple of weeks a month. Hoekstra is also famous for her luscious fruit pies — blackberry-apple, rhubarb-strawberry, apricot-strawberry and the like. In summer you'll see them at the East Vancouver Farmers' Market and the Coquitlam Farmers' Market. Wednesday through Friday you can buy them from her small Powell Street store. Other days by appointment.

The Epicure's Cupboard

5633 West Boulevard • 264-8200

Only Canadian and American food, and almost all West Coast from small producers. Taste treats galore include their best-selling Roasted Garlic and Onion Jam made by a local company, The Butler's Finest. For diet-watchers, the store also carries the Oregon-made Gloria's line of sugar-, salt- and oil-free chutneys and sauces. Jams, marinades, oils, mustards, grilling sauces — and many more ways to fill your shelves.

A Passion for Peppers

www.apassionforpeppers.com

515-7484

Jo-Anne Dooley and Linda Morrow sell incendiary hot sauces by mail. They also host periodic "Hot Lucks" where you might taste anything from a habanero popsicle to a blow-the-top-off-your-head bowl of chili.

Dollar Bag Cookery

Just because a red pepper has one little brown spot doesn't mean it's inedible. Here are some uses for all those veggies that hide out at knee-level at Granville Island and outside your favourite produce store:

- Red, yellow and green peppers: cut in narrow strips, add one sliced onion, sauté together until tender-crisp. Remove and keep warm. Add strips of chicken breast to the pan and brown on either side. Add the vegetable mixture. Toss together. Instant fajitas!

- Halve limes and lemons, squeeze them and freeze the juice for margaritas (limes) or cooking (lemons).

- Remove the soft bits from eggplants. Cube the rest and fry with onions, garlic, ginger, cumin and coriander. Add a little water, cover pot and cook gently till tender.

- Tomatoes. Purée them, skin and all, and freeze in baggies for fresh-tasting pasta sauce in the winter.

- Really mushy mangos: mush them to a pulp in the blender and thin with chilled yogurt and water for the ultimate summer drink.

HERBS: Parsley, Sage, Rosemary and Thyme

Such little leaves — and so much power to add flavour to a dish. Where would we be without herbs? Not that long ago, the only choice around was the dried variety, which quickly lost its pungency. Today you can buy living herbs at the supermarket or fresh-picked nosegays of mint and dill at the produce store. Best of all, if you have a sunny windowsill you can line it with pots of your favourites — and just clip them when the mood strikes.

Quick Grow-Your-Own Salads
Arugula grows like a weed; re-seed every 10 days for constant crops. Cilantro provides foliage and homegrown coriander seeds. Peppery cress seeds from Earthrise Garden Store can be sprouted on a clean damp washcloth.

LANGLEY:

Elysia Herb Farm
23519 Old Yale Rd. • 534-5118
Fresh-cut herbs in season and large quantities of basil in July and August. Also seasoning mixes, herbal vinegars, teas, preserves and chutneys such as mint or apple-lovage. Phone ahead.

Twin Oaks Herb Farm
4533 232nd St. • 530-9589
Raised beds full of huge herbs and five large greenhouses filled with smaller pots — at least 200 varieties in all, with special emphasis on scented geraniums. Besides sage, oregano and other familiar herbs, you'll find citronella, fleabane and arnica. Dried herbs are available in the cooler months.

SURREY:

Easy Acres Herb Farm
12063 64th Ave. • 596-8485
A great place to start planning your herb garden is Steve Hoffman's stall at Granville Island Public Market. March through June, it's chock-a-block with living plants. Unusual herbs like angelica and Vietnamese coriander. Numerous types of sage, thyme, mint, oregano and basil. Other times of the year, you can buy them direct from his farm.

THE HERB GROWER

Even on a chill March morning when a meringue-like topping of snow still garnishes B.C.'s coastal mountains, Heather Pritchard's Vancouver herb garden is bursting with signs of spring. Tender new shoots of feathery bronze fennel are showing around last year's dead growth; the tarragon and chives are thriving. "And look," says Pritchard, pointing at an out-of-the-way corner, "the lovage has seeded itself."

Enthusiasm knows no bounds when you're as much of a herb lover as Pritchard is. Parsley, sage, rosemary and thyme? They're only the start of it. As she points out, it doesn't take long to become addicted to the magic and mystery of herbs. When Pritchard took over the herb garden at the co-op where she lives, she admits she knew nothing. Today she teaches classes, spreading the word about herbs' versatility and reminding her students that, unlike many garden denizens, they are both beautiful and useful.

Starting a herb garden is easy, says Pritchard, although, like all forms of gardening, the climate dictates what will thrive. On the mild West Coast, many herbs survive through the winter; in colder climates, snow can act as a protective blanket. For the home gardener and cook, the early appearance of herbs is only part of the joy of growing them. "You have to wait for August for tomatoes to ripen," says Pritchard. "But you get mint in May." And in warmer regions, lemony sorrel often grows year round.

As co-founder of the Glorious Garnish & Seasonal Salad Company, which is widely credited with introducing unusual herbs and "gourmet" salads to Vancouver chefs, Pritchard works with green stuff on a daily basis. More than 75 varieties of herbs grow at the 10-acre farm, which is not open to the general public. Most of them find their way to farmers' markets (see pages 210-213) or on to food-lovers' plates at the Metropolitan, Pan Pacific and Waterfront Centre hotels, as well as top Vancouver restaurants like Villa del Lupo, Raincity Grill and Bishop's.

For the novice grower who just wants a few leaves to enliven an omelette or salad, Pritchard has wise and encouraging words: "Start with herbs that you

Chef's Tip

"I keep whole basil leaves in the freezer in a jar for when I don't have fresh basil around. Cooked, it's fine."
— Barbara-jo McIntosh, Barbara-Jo's Books to Cooks

want to eat," she advises. "Plant chives — you almost can't kill them — and they multiply on their own." Peppermint or spearmint will take over your garden; it's better to control them in a container. On the coast, lemon balm is so prolific, "it's almost like a weed."

As Pritchard points out, herbs can be savoured at different stages in their life cycles. Fresh oregano will add an authentic touch to a Greek salad. Dried, its flavour becomes even more intense. The flowers, leaves and seeds — both immature and mature — of dill all can be used. The delicate blossoms of sweet Cicely are ornamental in a garden and make a delightful garnish, says Pritchard, while the green seed pod can be eaten like a candy. She also suggests preserving summer's scents by incorporating herbs in pot pourri. Other options are to freeze herbs or to infuse them in vinegars, "purple basil or chive flowers are particularly attractive and flavourful."

However small your outdoor space, it's big enough to support a few herbs. "They can be grown in pots on balconies, patios — anywhere you can put a container," says Pritchard. "They also make lovely hanging baskets. Start with a few herbs and, as you grow confident, you'll want to expand." Parsley, dill and sweet marjoram all grow easily from seed, as does coriander — another good "starter" herb. Its leaves are better-known as cilantro, a vital ingredient in many ethnic dishes. Its dried seeds have a completely different taste. Among the many varieties of basil, the Genovese sweet basil is the best kind for pesto. It's a real sun-lover, says Pritchard. "At the farm, we protect it with a cloche even when it's warm. It helps keep the moisture in." Another tip? "Cut it right back — and that goes for many herbs."

Whether you plant seeds (wait till May), buy bedding plants or beg mint cuttings from friends, it's not hard to get started. And, come July, as you sit in the sun sipping a frosty glass of chilled lemon balm tea or gathering scented geranium leaves to perfume a custard, you'll ask yourself only one question: How come it took so long to get hooked on herbs?

Preserving the Harvest

Try drying those excess Spartan apples or banana peppers (and, come October, wild mushrooms) in a dehydrator. Soft fruits can be made into leather. Smoosh them up in the blender, strain off excess juice, sweeten if necessary, spread the purée on a lightly oiled cookie sheet and dry in a low oven — or your dehydrator.

Turn basil leaves into a pesto base, then freeze in ice cube trays. Defrost for a mid-winter taste of Tuscany. (Add the Parmesan when you use it.)

Scented geranium leaves can be dried to go in your tea, or layered in sugar to use in cake and cookie recipes.

Steep blackberries in vinegar warmed almost to boiling, then strain them out three days later for a potent addition to salad dressings.

PRODUCE:

Green (and other coloured) Stuff

Dark red strawberries that leave trails of juice down your chin. Lettuce leaves so crisp they crunch when you bite them. The first asparagus of the season. Fruits and vegetables? We're spoiled here in Vancouver.

Nowadays, any supermarket can fill your cart with produce that our grandmothers hadn't even heard of. Tomatillos and bok choy, daikon and chocolate-coloured bell peppers. Canadian Superstore has an especially good selection of Asian produce.

Some areas are better than others for veggie-holics. Mid-Kits residents benefit from some of the best deals around. Competition is the explanation. Between Macdonald and Blenheim you'll find at least four places to pick up your veggies. Barring Westpointe Produce (which still offers good deals on organic vegetables), prices tend to be similar. Those who can accept a few bruises and scratches on their aubergines will find ripe pickings among the dollar bags.

Trawl your way along Commercial Drive and you'll leave with a basket crammed with peppers and plums. And there's no better place than Chinatown for phenomenally fresh Asian greens.

Apples

Supermarket apples tend to look great on the outside but taste like a mouthful of Kleenex. Apples don't have to taste like this; for proof, nothing beats a buying trip to an old-time apple orchard.

ABBOTSFORD:
Thorncrest Farms Apple Barn
333 Gladwin Rd. • 853-3108
Take the kids to one of the Applefest weekends in September.

Lettuce Begin

Greens don't necessarily require Fraser Valley acreage. Lettuce and arugula do nicely in containers, provided the pots are big enough, says Mary Ballon of Territorial Seeds. "A lettuce plant needs a six-inch pot to itself. Edge it with nasturtiums or Lemon Gem marigolds if you want to make the whole thing edible." Judicious doses of water, a well-balanced organic fertilizer and sunshine — though lettuce can handle partial shade — will help your harvest grow. Sow seed now, then at three- to four-week intervals for steady salad pickings. Ballon's suggestion for neophytes: the Super Gourmet Salad mix of five varieties. For a catalogue, call 482-8800.

If you have time on the weekend, why not do your grocery shopping at local farms? Most are concentrated in the Fraser Valley and few things are more pleasant than driving around its country roads, gathering food as you go.

A couple of pointers: If it's summer, stash the cooler in the trunk to keep your produce field-fresh until you get home. Take a map, too. Roads in this part of the world don't always follow a grid system. If you have one, bring along a cell phone. That way you can call ahead to check if someone's around. Bring a picnic too. Cafés are few and far between. Besides, nothing beats a sandwich in the open air and just-picked berries for dessert.

ALDERGROVE:
Annie's Orchard
4092 248th St. • 856-3041
More than 30 varieties to choose from.

LANGLEY:
Dave's Orchard
5910 216th St. • 534-9979
This longtime farm (it's been growing apples for over 50 years) offers about 40 different varieties.

MATSQUI:
Soeten Farm
R.R.1, 35075 Beaton Rd. • 820-8752
Certified Organic apple orchard grows Elstar, Boskoop and other varieties.

SARDIS:
Aslan's Apples
46985 Bailey Rd. • 858-3631
Further afield but in addition to fruit they sell fresh-pressed apple cider and hand-crafted dried apple wreaths.

Berries

For deepdown flavour, you can't beat local berries. Picking your own is the most fun and best value. Remember: with any U-pick farm — or farm in general — it's important to call before you go to check that the berries are ripe and ready. Early morning is the best picking time. In hot weather, berries quickly get grey fuzz on them, so plan to eat them soon after you get them home or freeze them for jam-making when the weather cools off.

Places to pick include:

ALDERGROVE:
Krause Brothers Farm
6179 248th St. • 856-5757
Strawberries, raspberries, blackberries, blueberries, also corn, cucumbers, artichokes and a variety of other local vegetables and fruit from the Okanagan.

LANGLEY:
Driediger Farms
23823 72nd Ave.   •   888-1665
Strawberries, red and black currants, raspberries, blueberries, gooseberries, Okanagan fruits, corn, potatoes and peas.

Already picked berries can be found at:

ALDERGROVE:
Cherry Jubilee
2017 272 St.   •   856-5844
More than one chef recommended the Montmorency cherries from this orchard in Aldergrove. Advance orders recommended, and a must for the Morello sour cherries.

DELTA:
Bissett Farms
2170 Westham Island Rd.   •   946-7139
Raspberries, black currants, red currants, blueberries, gooseberries, tayberries (a blackberry-raspberry cross) and marionberries (a loganberry-blackberry cross).

LANGLEY:
Carriage House Farm Blueberries
22822 88th Ave.   •   888-0863
Flavourful, sweet berries sold from a heritage farm.

LINDELL BEACH:
Bertrand Creek Farms
1385 Frost Rd., Lindell Beach   •   858-5233
Raspberries, blueberries, red, white and black currants, gooseberries, Saskatoon berries and blackberries. Also hazelnuts from which they make a truly sinful chocolate-hazelnut spread. Check out the fruit wines, too.

MATSQUI:
Blueberry Springs
4272 Gladwin Rd.   •   853-9507
Raspberries, blueberries and strawberries.

Pick Your Own Strawbs

For deep-down flavour, locally grown strawberries leave those big California hulks in the dust. Grab them while you can. U-pick is the most fun and best value. Check the classifieds in the *Vancouver Sun* for places and prices. Look under Food Products/U-pick.

Early morning is best and berries go mouldy fast, so plan to eat them soon after picking or freeze them for jam-making down the road. Places to pick include: Krause Brothers Farm, 6179 248th Street, Aldergrove (856-5757); and Driediger Brothers Farms, 23823 72nd Avenue, Langley (888-1665). Already-plucked berries can be found at: Bissett Farms, 2170 Westham Island Rd, Delta (946-7139); and W&A Farms, 17771 Westminster Hwy, Richmond (278-5667). Call before you go.

Fresh blueberries

Soapberries

This Native Indian delicacy usually gets whipped into a froth (with copious amounts of sugar) to make Indian ice-cream. Some people gather the berries and make syrup. If you want to know where to buy it, as well as jams and jellies made from huckleberries, choke cherries and Saskatoon berries, call Alice Adolph, 872-2797.

RICHMOND:
Richmond Country Farms
12900 Steveston Rd. • 274-0522
Certified Organic blueberries.

W & A Farms
17771 Westminster Hwy. • 278-5667
Strawberries and assorted vegetables.

General Produce

VANCOUVER:
Famous Foods
1595 Kingsway • 872-3019
The original bulk food store. A tremendous range of grains and spices, dried fruit, dried vegetables, nuts and baking necessities. "Sea salt and olive oil too," adds food consultant Bill Jones. "The deli and meat counter features reasonably priced cheeses and locally smoked meats and seafood."

Norman's Fruit & Salad
1604 Commercial Dr. • 251-5159
Produce with a Tuscan bent. Rapini, fennel and "Italian lettuce" – radicchio. In late summer you'll find peppers galore – round, long, red, yellow, big, small and all a tremendous inspiration to the pickle-maker. Jam- and chutney-makers, take note: In high season, dark purple plums and plump Roma tomatoes can be staggeringly cheap.

New Apple Farm Market
2856 West Broadway • 739-6882
Quality and prices so good that at least one chef buys supplies there for his restaurant.

Santa Barbara Market
1322 Commercial Dr. • 253-1941
Great selection, good prices and top quality. Numerous chefs shop here. As with any produce store on The Drive, this one's especially strong on the vividly flavoured fruits and veggies that are favourites in Italian cuisine.

J.B. Hoy
2171 West 41st Ave. • 261-3533
Tiny, perfect baby squash, extraordinary cherries, greens beans that appear to have been chosen one by one. Top-notch fruits and vegetables from a Kerrisdale store that's been there for eons. See "The Greening of Vancouver," page 37.

Mushrooms

LANGLEY:

Western Biologicals
25059 50th Ave. • 856-3339
Bill Chalmers sells a small amount of fresh oyster, enoki, shiitake and shimeji mushrooms, along with grow-at-home mushroom kits which, in most cases, let you produce a crop in a couple of weeks. Call ahead first.

Farm Fresh Guide
Langley Chamber of Commerce
530-6656
Planning an afternoon tooling around farms in the Langley area is easy with this comprehensive guide. Call for a free copy.

Fraser Valley Farm Fresh Produce Guide
530-4027
A terrific free guide to dozens of farms where you can buy direct from the producer. The region covered extends south to Ladner, north to Pemberton and east as far as Agassiz.

Specialty mushrooms

Vegetables

Fair enough — that zucchini plant you grew did take over the garden, but remember how flavourful all those zucchinis were? Anyone who has ever grown their own vegetables is spoiled for life. You can't beat the taste of a just-picked carrot or peas right out of the pod. The following farm stores will bring back the memories.

ABBOTSFORD:

Wisbey Veggies
40326 No. 3 Rd. • 823-4617
"We grow almost everything in the veggie dictionary," say Bruce and Joy Wisbey. Corn, peas, beans... pumpkins, too.

Yellow Barn Country Produce
4066 Interprovincial Hwy. • 823-6733
Seventeen different types of sweet corn and 14 kinds of potato, as well as lots of other vegetables.

CHILLIWACK:

Forstbauer Natural Food Farm
49350 Prairie Central Rd. • 794-3999
Certified organic produce. They also sell, through a co-op, at farmers' markets around the lower mainland.

Assorted vegetables at an outdoor market

MISSION:

Twin Creeks Farm
9310 Stave Lake St. • 826-2728
Naturally grown vegetables raised without pesticides, herbicides or chemical fertilizers. Vegetable gift baskets, too (order in advance).

SURREY:

Mary's Garden
15821 40th Ave. • 576-9297
Garden fresh vegetables picked daily. Specials available in the fall.

THE "GREENING" OF VANCOUVER

by Diane Clement, Tomato Fresh Food Café

Vancouver has truly become a "global market" for fresh produce. We've come a long way.

In the early 1970s, when I opened my cooking school, specialty produce markets were few and far between. Leafy lettuce, Boston and romaine were the extent of our salad greens. Who had heard of mesclun greens, wild mushrooms or baby vegetables except the major hotel chefs? Fresh herbs were a rarity, unless you grew your own.

Visits to the Asian markets in Chinatown or the local farm markets in Richmond were our only choices for a true market shopping experience. Today, Chinatown's markets are still bustling with activity but, unfortunately, most of Richmond's farmlands have become suburban developments.

Small neighbourhood market/grocery stores have continued to prosper. Along Commercial Drive, produce markets are as busy as ever, with stalls laden with seasonal fruits and vegetables from B.C. farms and from around the world.

One of my favourite market/grocery stores in Vancouver, and a landmark for over 65 years, is the family owned and operated J.B. Hoy's in Kerrisdale. Run by Girlie Koo, husband Allen and sons Ted and Bob, Hoy's now caters to the grandchildren of their first customers. The same dedication and friendly service continues. Their produce, from B.C. farms and imported specialties, is the choicest. As more and more restaurants appeared on the Vancouver scene in the 1970s and '80s, chefs would drop by Hoy's to purchase the "perfect avocado." The Koos would disappear into the back of the store and return with avocados ready to eat that day. The "Avocado Club" became the name of the circle of chefs and regular customers who requested the "perfect avocado." In fact, when well-known Vancouver chef and restaurateur Barbara Gordon opened a restaurant in Toronto, she named it "The Avocado Club."

In 1973, Vancouver's Mayor Art Phillips, and his visionary council and city planners, cut the ribbon

A-a-ahsparagus

Binge when they're at their best and cheapest. Rinse stalks thoroughly (they can sometimes be gritty), snap off the ends, tie in bundles and steam just until they droop ever so slightly ("crisp-tender" is what you're after.) Add melted butter, of course — or soy sauce, orange or lemon juice for variety. Otherwise, cool to room temperature then dip, stalk by stalk, in a simple vinaigrette. Fingers or forks? Who cares. Chopsticks are better if you cut asparagus Chinese style (as James Barber does) then stir-fry with thinly sliced ginger and speckle with sesame seeds.

Navel Lore

The smaller the navel of an eggplant (the little dimple at its bottom end), the smaller the seeds inside. Male eggplants have little navels.

Mashed Potatoes

Comfort food personified. Cook potatoes till pierce-able then mash with a fork or hand-held beater. Fold in butter, sour cream or buttermilk according to taste and waistline, and season with salt and pepper. S-mashing additions: onion chunks or garlic cloves simmered and mashed with the spuds, or carrots or squash for a sunny hue. Try folding in a dab of wasabi mustard as they do at The Five Sails.

on an exciting inner city environment — False Creek and the Granville Island Market. Vancouver's "heart of the city" was born. Granville Island quickly became the place to go, whether to shop for the latest recipe ingredient, or just to browse, stop for coffee and watch the boats drift by. Today, Granville Island is recognized as one of the best public markets in the world. It's the "pulse" of cosmopolitan Vancouver.

Organic to hothouse — you name it! Privately owned and operated organic and hothouse farms have become the most exciting produce commodities of the 1990s. As B.C. consumers become more and more concerned about our environment and what we eat, organic farms and hothouses are on the rise. Farmers are providing restaurants, specialty markets and people at home with superior safe produce.

BC Hot House has gained national and international success for the superb quality of its tomatoes, butter lettuce, peppers and cucumbers, grown without pesticides. In Japan, the BC Hot House tomato is gaining in popularity — so much so that, in Okayama City, there is acually a bank called "The Tomato Bank" with their own tomato mascot, tomato cheer and uniforms with tomato logos. Tomatoes, with their anti-oxidant properties, represent "power" and particularly appeal to the new generation.

Meanwhile, organic farms such as the Glorious Garnish and Seasonal Salad Co. in Aldergrove, provide organic produce to most of Vancouver's top restaurants. The owners, Susan Davidson, Heather Pritchard and Dave McCandless, pull up with their truck, open the trunk to a painter's palette of exotic greens, edible flowers, fresh herbs and garnishes. The dynamic trio works closely with several other organic farmers in the lower mainland so they can offer a more diversified product line, one which offers everything from rainbow tomatoes to baby vegetables.

Having travelled throughout the world as an olympic athlete, and as a chef, cookbook author and restaurateur, I can honestly say that the Vancouver produce markets are among the best. As a Vancouverite, I am proud of the achievements of the farmers and market owners over the past decade — and their future couldn't look brighter.

MEAT

Get to know your local butcher. That's the biggest secret to buying the best possible meat. A good butcher lives by his — it's mostly a male thing — reputation and it's more than his name is worth to sell you anything less than the best.

Hamburger, New York steak, a leg of lamb — most of the time, we stick to a few tried and true favourites chosen from whatever's out there in the showcase. But don't be led astray. Just because it's not in his window doesn't mean your butcher can't get hold of calves' feet for that authentic French soup stock you're planning to make, or a rib roast large enough to feed an army. Reputable butchers have access to practically every part of a cow, sheep, pig, chicken, duck, rabbit or ostrich and it's no skin off their nose (if you'll excuse the expression) to add two pounds of foie gras or ten pounds of lamb shanks to the order they phone in to their wholesale supplier.

Your friendly local butcher can also make your life easier. He will cube meat for you if you ask him, bone that lamb leg you're planning to put on the barbecue, and suggest particular cuts depending on whether you want to grill a hunk of beef or simmer it slowly for hours in the oven.

Mary Had a Little Problem
Barbecuing a whole lamb makes feeding a crowd easy. To track down the main ingredient, talk to your butcher. Many get whole lambs from their wholesaler, then cut them up into various cuts.

LANGLEY:

JD Farms Specialty Turkey Store
24726 52nd Ave.   •   856-2431
Debbie and Jack Froese's free-run turkeys feed on an all-vegetable diet and receive no medications or antibiotics. About eight pounds at Easter, they're up to 20 pounds by Christmas. The Froeses also sell turkey wings, drums, legs, thighs, sausages, breast roasts, stew, pies, turkey lasagne and turkey burritos. They grow pumpkins, too.

RICHMOND:

Broadmoor Meats
110-10111 No. 3 Rd.   •   277-1160
This store in Broadmoor Mall used to be Quality Meats of Kerrisdale on West 16th Ave. Excellent quality, nice service — and they deliver to Vancouver.

Horse meat

Fresh and frozen horse meat can be found at Best Bi Foods (4610 Earles St., 439-8855).

Heringer's Olde Fashioned Quality Meats

190-12251 No. 1 Rd. • 274-6328

Calling Chad and Karen Heringer's place a "butcher's store" doesn't do it justice. "If someone asks for it, and it walks on four legs, we can normally do it," says Chad (an example: the top sirloin of beef with a lamb leg and pork tenderloin wrapped inside that they put together for one customer). Specialties include game, double-smoked bacon from Chad's grandfather's recipe, eight types of chicken cordon bleu, chicken fajita mix, turkey pesto sausage and rosemary boneless turkey thighs. Everyone who works here loves to eat and cook; one employee is a former chef. The Heringers cater especially to people who don't have time to cook. At Christmas you can buy gravy, stuffing and cranberry sauce with your turkey. Try the deli roast beef cooked with 15 different herbs, cabbage rolls, antipasto or salad dressings.

SURREY:

Grandmaison Beef Farm

5175 184th St. • 576-8318

Their organic beef is grown the "old-fashioned way," say farmers Al and Louis Grandmaison. Grain from Alberta and Saskatchewan is milled at the farm and fed to the cattle along with corn silage grown on the land. Specialty stores in Vancouver carry it. Though most of the Grandmaisons' business is freezer orders of custom-cut sides of beef, you'll always find smaller cuts for sale at their farm — mostly frozen, some fresh.

South Seas Enterprises

201-7750 128th St. • 596-7731

Lamb, goat, chicken, duck and beef, all at bargain prices.

VANCOUVER:

Apollo Poultry

1678 Commercial Dr. • 254-2511

Chicken wings, chicken thighs, chicken legs, chicken breasts, both boned and au naturel, and whole broilers and roasters. Ducks, too.

Arctic Meats
1714 Commercial Dr. • 255-1301
One of the oldest names in the city, Arctic Meats is known for its pork, free-range chickens and corned beef made from an old, old recipe.

Columbus Meat Market
1645 Renfrew St. • 253-2242
People come from across town for butcher Eugenio Masi's l'arista: a boned loin of pork seasoned with garlic, black pepper and fennel from Masi's own garden. Hot or at room temperature, it's great. So are his homemade spicy or sweet Italian sausages, and meaty veal shanks for osso buco.

Doug's Fine Meats
4870 Mackenzie St. • 261-7838
Doug Stickels' homemade bangers are worth the schlepp to Mackenzie Heights. We favour a 50/50 mix of the regular pork variety and the spicy Italian kind — and about a half-dozen apiece. Try his fiery Portuguese or the slightly tamer Creole. Ready to sling on the barbie is butterflied and marinaded lamb leg, "lamb doodads" — a loin chop stuffed with seasoned ground lamb — or pork cutlets marinated in a mild curry sauce.

Dressed to Go
Granville Island Public Market • 682-5811
Lovely free-range chicken for cooks who want to start from scratch. Tons of prepared chicken dishes, too: honey Moroccan chicken and Cajun drumsticks.

Falcone Brothers Meat Market
1810 Commercial Dr. • 253-6131
A popular source on The Drive of hot, medium, mild and liver sausage, all made by Joe and Pasquale Falcone. Veal and rabbit, too.

Jackson's Meats
2214 West 4th Ave. • 733-9165
(see Jackson's on Granville)

Foie Gras
You'll find this high-end delicacy brought in from Quebec, fresh or frozen, at Hills Foods (109-3650 Bonneville Place, Burnaby, 421-3100). The deal is cash and carry, and a minimum $100 purchase (which needn't all be foie gras). Persuading your local butcher to bring some in for you is simpler but costs more. Size and colour affect price, as does grade. Extra — about 1 1/4 to 1 1/2 pounds — or #1 are preferred by restaurants, while #2 and #3 are ideal for terrines. Cooking foie gras is simple, says Mark Hills. Sauté it swiftly in butter, then deglaze the pan "with whatever spirit you have handy — port, sherry, wine — and that's about it."

Jackson's On Granville
2717 Granville St. • 738-6328
Founded in 1911, Jackson's is part of Vancouver history. Now the third generation runs the stores. Ads on the wall bring back the days when lamb chops cost 49 cents a pound. The quality is excellent. Jackson's is also famous for its fancy meat preparations. The Turkey Royale, says Brian Jackson, "is virtually boneless except for the wings. The drumstick cavities are filled with pork tenderloin, the thighs with smoked Irish cured ham, and the breast cavity with pheasant meat, Oxford-style pork sausage meat and chicken breast." It takes about three hours to assemble and the store has sold as many as 120 in a Christmas season, not just to locals but out of province too. Less known is their "mock duck of lamb" — lamb shoulder stuffed with seasoned lamb meat and shaped to look like a brace of ducks. Jackson's is famous for their Irish hams too. Naturally cured for 28 days in sea-salt brine (with maple syrup added), they're smoked at low temperature over a secret mixture of hardwoods. The result? A ham that's smoky, moist and naturally sweet.

Jackson Meats on West 4th Ave.

Polonia Sausage House
2434 East Hastings • 251-2239
Close to 50 varieties of fresh and dried sausages made on the spot. They're best known for their ham-garlic sausage, Ukranian sausage and European style ham. Fresh meat is sold here too.

Polonus Old Country Sausage
4286 Fraser St. • 872-1521
Banger heaven. About 50 different kinds of sausage, all at good prices.

Chorizo

Q: Where do El Patio and La Bodega get their chorizo?
A: John's Meats (5453 Victoria Drive, 321-3567). Ask for "El Patio" chorizo.
P.S.: Caterer Lesley Stowe says it's the best in town.

Rid of the Red Chicken and Seafood
8626 Joffre St. • 540-2210

Mostly wholesale, but they do sell retail. Free-range chicken and — despite the name — other meats, too.

Save-on-Meat
43 West Hastings St. • 683-7761

Carnivores willing to venture to the wild side of town will uncover extraordinary deals here. Look for the candy-pink neon pig . Pig's feet, back fat and bacon ends may not turn your gastronomic crank but the rockbottom deals on better-known cuts such as veal shank and leg of lamb definitely will.

Shaughnessy Fine Meats Ltd.
2233 West 41st Ave. • 266-6911

Known for their Alberta beef, which is aged a minimum of 21 days on the premises, and also their pork with crackling. Local Fraser Valley lamb from Walnut Hill Sheep Farm in Aldergrove is also very popular, and available throughout the year, including fresh lamb kidneys and saddle of lamb.

South Seas Enterprises
195 East 26th Ave. • 872-7399

If you want lamb or goat meat to make an authentic curry, this is the place to come, and one of the reasons why Fijian, Indian and Greek people flock to this particular butcher. The other reason? Low prices.

Tenderland Meats
Granville Island Public Market • 688-6951

Magnificent roasts, beef pre-cut for stir-frying, tandoori chicken kabobs — all top quality.

Vancouver Community College
250 West Pender St. • 443-8351

This is a great place to find meat, beautifully cut (instructors are looking over the shoulder of the students) and well-priced. If you're pining for a giant rib roast or a saddle of lamb, they do special orders. Freezer orders, too. If you have an entire lamb or pig on your hands, they can portion it into chops and roasts, provided it's been federally inspected.

Corned Beef

Not the blocky kind that comes in a can but the real thing. "Easy to cook," says Bernie McDougall of Broadmoor Quality Meats in Richmond, who usually has kosher corned beef brisket on hand. Prepare to buy three pounds minimum — it shrinks a little. Pop it in cold water, bring to a boil, discard the water (and some of the saltiness), cover with water again, season with bay leaves and garlic, and simmer 2 to 2 1/2 hours, depending on size. Dry the beef with paper towels, spread with Dijon or hot English mustard, broil for a few minutes to glaze and firm it up for carving — on the bias, of course. Serve with cabbage wedges and boiled potatoes. Leftovers can be sliced and frozen for sandwiches.

Free-Run, Free-Range,
What's the Diff?

A chicken or turkey described
as "free-run" has the run of the
barn. A "free-range" bird is free
to roam all over the farm.

Bang-er On

In a hurry to cook your
sausages? Bring a pot of water
to the boil and simmer them
for four minutes, then brown
them on the barbecue, says
Robert Goodrick of The British
Butcher Shoppe in North
Vancouver (see page 78).

Eggs and…

Double-smoked bacon from
Armando's (Granville Island
Public Market, 685-0359).

Meat from the Farm

You *can* still buy chickens, turkeys or Sunday roasts
from the farmer who raised them.

ABBOTSFORD:
Rockweld Farms
34221 Townshipline Rd. • 859-1199
Their specialty chicken is fed organically, which means
no medication or meat meal in the feed. A lower
protein feed and a longer growth period results in
leaner, more flavourful meat.

LANGLEY:
The Little Red Barn
554 256th St. • 857-9494
Shelly and Allan Cross raise roasting chickens, turkeys
(ready at Thanksgiving, Christmas and Easter), beef,
pork and lamb, all hormone- and medication-free. The
chickens and turkeys must be reserved. Everything
else is first come, first served at their monthly sale.
Get in touch and the Crosses will fax or e-mail you
information. Pick up some of their free-range eggs,
too — you'll even find huge double-yolkers sold by
the dozen.

Thomas Reid Farms
5050 244th St. • 856-5050
B.C.'s first certified organic chicken. Call before going.

MOUNT LEHMAN:
Campbell's Pheasantry
7902 Satchell St. • 856-4375
Pheasants have a pleasant time of it here as they lead
a free-range, non-medicated and antibiotic-free life.
Available whole or specialty cut.

SURREY:
Run-Down, Walk-Up Farm
9043 184th St. • 882-1278
You can buy a lamb whole or have it cut up any way
you want from Bob McCroskey, whose farm got its
quirky name because it's on a hill.

FAR FROM THE MADDING COW

by Jamie Maw

My most intimate confessions include an unholy love for beef. The preferred manner of preparation is on the bone – roasted prime ribs take on a flavour like no other. Pity my English friends, who come from the natural home of roast beef – they can no longer buy it on the bone for fear of mad cow disease.

Prime ribs must be aged a full lunar cycle so that they walk into the pan on their own. My pulpit is a convected DCS gas range, although any oven that can get hot, really hot, will do. Start the roast at 500 degrees. Sear for 10 minutes and reduce heat to 350, just until the roast gives up its surface blood – the signal for medium rare. Do it twice and you will come to know the smell of a crusted beginning, a pink middle and the taste that has no end.

In the wintertime, I serve up the roast in a trinity of mashed potatoes and a most excellent wine-laced gravy, with a lashing of garlic and herbes de provence. I roast young carrots alongside – just until they caramelize in their own sugar – and dress them with a crunch of matchstick fennel.

When the weather warms and the westerly begins to push the waves in the bay, I call up Brian Jackson, whose family has operated a robust butchery in Kitsilano since 1911. I ask him for a sirloin steak, "deep cut" and three inches thick. Trimmed, it will weigh three pounds and have at least a month of age on it. We let the steak come up to cool room temperature, coat it in olive oil and shower it with a rough grind of black pepper. Only Philistines put barbecue sauce on good beef – it masks the flavour, steams the meat and its sugar will char long before the beef is cooked through.

When grilling a serious piece of beef – or a butterflied leg of lamb – there are only two pieces of equipment worthy of the joint venture. One is a Weber kettle grill with at least 10 pounds of real charcoal ignited with a heating coil, never a chemical starter. The other is a good quality gas grill, preferably re-rigged for natural gas. You need a box that means

Stuff that Sausage

Making fillings for homemade sausages isn't the problem. Food processors make all that chopping easy. But then what do you do? While you can form long skinny patties out of the mixture, it's not the same thing as making sausages. Most good butchers can order sausage skins through their wholesaler. The problem is quantity. You may end up with enough skins to girdle the globe. A better idea is to find a butcher who specializes in sausages and ask him to sell you a metre or two.

Secret Revealed

The Russian restaurant Rasputin gets its giant Ukranian sausage at Polonia Sausage (2434 East Hastings St., 251-2239).

business, that will hit at least 600 degrees, and, as importantly, that will quickly recover the temperature once the beef hits the fire. Most propane grills lack confidence and will steam a big cut of beef, imparting an airline flavour and texture. Even a good aged piece of beef will come off a weak grill tougher than a Revenue Canada auditor. If you are equipment challenged, the delicious way out is to grill one and a quarter inch rib-eyes.

Grind on some kosher salt just before grilling. Grill the steak five minutes, tong it 90 degrees west and grill four minutes more with the lid closed. Flip the steak, grill for five minutes. Turn it 90 degrees again and grill it until it gives up its blood. Remove it to a cutting board and let it rest for at least 10 minutes. Carve it against the grain and on the bias. Dish up a bowl of "Grandfather's Homestyle" horseradish, an excellent product made in Surrey and available locally at Caper's Market. Serve the beef with scalloped potatoes, oven-roasted bosc pears finished with a generous nugget of Gorgonzola, and a pre-Mussolini Brunello — and tell someone you adore them more than life itself.

When I go out to eat beef in Vancouver, I have only one destination in mind. Yes, I love Pino Posteraro's biftecca fiorentina at Il Giardino, but I'm more likely to be seduced by his lobster fettucine. And at Piccolo Mondo, Stephane Meyer's filet mignon — caught napping in an all-day reduction of Barolo and thyme, and partnered with a kiss of fried marrow — will surely induce bliss, too. But when the big-boy craving overtakes me and the butcher is closed, I always go downtown to Hornby St. — to Hy's Encore. In a town with a limited history, I can get it in chunks at Hy's. Leafing through some old *Dick Maclean's Guide* magazines recently, there was an ad for the Encore, circa 1963. The proprietor, Hy Aisenstat, a short fat man replete with trademark stogy, is standing before a silver serving dish, pouring cognac over a game bird. The caption beneath reads, "At Hy's, no tern goes unstoned."

I love this aging roué of a room: by day a den for Howe St. brokers doing deals, by night lit dim; part retro-cheek, part a place where gentlemen of a certain stripe might entertain their nieces without fear of disapproval or interruption. The crowd crosses lines — a sprinkling of celebrities toasting their good fortunes, some tourists happy they've wandered into the party, some gen-Xers who like to take their martinis and beef with a dash of irony. But everyone takes their steaks seriously, from the polished waiters who have seen it all but cheerfully reserve a little extra for you, to the griller, whose sole calling is to render a piece of Canada AAA beef precisely to your mood.

A tough day calls for a tender steak. You may smooth its delivery even further with some well-made drinks — a Bourbon Manhattan springs to mind — or a wine list that prizes formidable reds before all else. We always start with the Caesar salad, prepared tableside by Peter with a raft of extra anchovies. I will order the 18-ounce New York, just before medium rare, Eva the filet. We will have baked russets with the fixings, brought to the table in a stainless steel, Ike and Mamie condiment service. And we will share the creamed spinach and then shortly groan.

When the food and drink have had their way with us, I will look over to the corner table where Hy used to hold court. I can swear that he is here tonight, reciting set-piece anecdotes — with crusty beginnings, pink middles and, unfortunately, ends. Now I see the contrails of his cigar smoke twining upwards with the smoke from Jack Wasserman's cigarette, next to the big drinks that are always half full.

Offal? No way.

Don't wrinkle your nose — kidneys are delicious if you treat them gently. Beef and pork innards cost less but lamb or veal kidneys are easier for beginners. Halve them lengthwise, cut out the centre core — the bit that looks inedible — and thinly slice what's left. Melt some butter in a fry pan, sizzle kidneys briskly on either side and team with eggs and bacon for a proper British breakfast. Supper options: cook them French style, deglazing the pan with a dash of red wine. Adding grated lemon peel and Marsala turns them into Italian rognoni trifolati. Either way, serve garlic mashed potatoes alongside to sop up the juices.

SEAFOOD: Bounty from the Sea

Why don't we eat more fish and seafood in Vancouver? Good question. Grilling or pan-frying a piece of cod or salmon is a lot faster than putting on the pasta pot for the umpteenth night in a row. Mussels and clams are just as quick. Wash them, chuck out any that are open — a sign that they've met their maker — put them in a pot with a dribble of wine, beer or plain water, and some chopped onions, garlic or herbs, or all three. Slap on the lid. Turn up the heat. Eat as soon as the shells open.

Once you're comfortable cooking shellfish, move on to Dungeness crabs. I think they're sweeter and tastier than lobsters — and they definitely cost a lot less. Chinese markets invariably have the best prices. Ask, and you can usually have them cut up into manageable pieces for a stir-fry. If you want to eat them whole, here's what to do:

Seafood in Chinatown

Cart them home alive and put them in the fridge. When you're ready to eat, bring lots of water to a boil in the biggest pot you own — a canning pot is about the right size for a couple of crabs. Drop them in quickly, clamp on the lid and set the timer for 12 minutes. Fish them out, crack them and serve them with melted butter, lemon wedges and plenty of bread to sop up the juices. If you're a first-timer at crab-eating, the best advice is to eat whatever looks like crabmeat and chuck the rest. The greenish gunk inside the crab tastes good, too.

Any fish store worth its salt sells only the very freshest fish (or best quality smoked fish). Here are some likely places to land a good one:

ABBOTSFORD:
Silver Brook U-Catch
1364 288th St. • 856-2298
"It was th-i-i-is big, honest!" Land your own rainbows from the trout pond. They supply rod and line, you pay for what you catch. The longer the fish, the more it costs. In 1998, two 21-and-a-half inchers were caught.

BURNABY:
T & T Supermarket
147-4800 Kingsway • 436-4881
(see also: Richmond; Vancouver)
Stunning selection of live fish and seafood. When local prawns are in season, they rarely get any better than here. Unlike most fish stores, you can serve yourself clams, mussels and other bivalves. Dungeness crabs sometimes available at a rockbottom "special" price.

LADNER:
Superior Fish Market
5229A Ladner Trunk Rd. • 946-2097
Salmon is caught from the market's own fleet of four boats. This large store also sells halibut, cod, clams, mussels — all from the West Coast — as well as imported sea bass, Digby scallops and other favourites. Locally smoked salmon too. If you've a fisher in your family, check out the angler-specific embroidered sweat-shirts and T-shirts.

NORTH VANCOUVER:
The Salmon Shop
123 Carrie Cates Court, Lonsdale Quay • 987-3474
Salmon is the specialty here (surprised?), especially spring fillets.

Screaming Mimi's
Lonsdale Quay Public Market • 987-3466
Live Dungeness crabs, mussels, clams to take home or have steamed and eat outside in the sun.

RICHMOND:
Super Seafoods
6020E Blundell Rd. • 271-1424
"The quality of their fish exceeds any fish store I

All About Oysters
Oysters should be tightly closed and have a fresh, sweet ocean smell to them, says Frances Ruvalcaba of the Amorous Oyster. The restaurant's West Coast oysters include Malaspina, Fanny Bays, Golden Mantle, Silver Mantle and Nootka. Staff rely on a special oyster-shucking knife to open its bivalves. "The shell is rounded at the front and tapers towards the back. Find a little indent in the muscle at the back, wiggle the knife in, give it a good twist and snap the oyster open," instructs Ruvalcaba. Open oysters just before serving. The restaurant serves them with a raspberry-shallot vinegar and lemon wedges, or tabasco, or for those who really like a chili fix, a bottle of Fear Itself (see page 235).

know," says local food lover John Levine. Live crabs, shellfish, "the most exquisitely fresh fish," plus unusual seafood such as flying fish roe.

T & T Supermarket
8181 Cambie Rd. • 279-1818
(see also: Burnaby; Vancouver)

STEVESTON:
Steveston Fish Shoppe
3420 Moncton St. • 277-3135
Known for salmon, halibut and crabs caught from the shop's own boats.

Steveston Docks
Adjacent to Bayview St.
It used to be more "authentic" — i.e. less commercial — but even dressed up, this boat-lined wharf still offers exceptional deals on unquestionably fresh seafood.

VANCOUVER:
Albion Fisheries
1077 Great Northern Way • 875-9411
Many top restaurants shop here. You can, too. Call and ask for prices over the phone, and then depending on what they have in stock, they'll have it ready for you. Some things they can't break into smaller orders: some smoked products come in 10-pound packages while shrimps are often sold by the five-pound bag. Prices change constantly. Product comes in every day. Shark, alligator meat, as well as salmon, caviar and shrimp. Open to the public Saturdays only 8 a.m. to 12 noon. One last thing: you must wear a hat when you go there to pick up your order.

Angel Seafoods
1345 Grant St. • 254-2824
Popular with sushi chefs for seafood direct from Japan. Pros buy wholesale — and whole sides of yellowfin tuna. Amateurs can pick up smaller amounts of fish, some of it pre-sliced. Rarities, such as sea urchin, abound.

Chef's Tip
"When I buy prosciutto or pancetta, I never buy slices. I buy ends from Santa Barbara Market. Some places will sell them to you at a discount. Save the rinds and put them in soups. You can do the same with Parmigiana rinds."
— Karen Barnaby, The Fish House in Stanley Park

Granville Island Smokery

1805 Mast Tower Rd., Granville Island • 684-4114
Recently moved from Granville Island (where the store
was called Angler Smokehouse), Heidi Reynolds has
specialized in hot- and cold-smoked salmon — she uses
an old Scottish recipe — since 1979. Her mild cure is
famous, as are her Indian candy, excellent salmon jerky
and fresh salmon cakes. Salmon is smoked and sliced
fresh every day.

Granville Island Fisherman's Wharf

Granville Island
Keep your eyes open as you bike or drive over to the
Island and you'll occasionally see roadside signs
directing you to fresh fish sold right off the boat.

The Lobster Man

1807 Mast Tower Rd., Granville Island • 687-4531
Up to a dozen kinds of oysters from Malpeque to
Golden Mantle. Live Dungeness and Alaska King
crabs, live Atlantic lobsters, mussels, manila, razor
clams, geoduck and butter clams, swimming pink and
Japanese scallops. Lobsters and crabs can be cooked
to order at no charge — just the thing for salads,
sandwiches and chowders. Culled lobsters and crabs
missing a claw, or, in the case of a crab, a leg or two
short of the usual number, are sold at discounted
prices.

Lox Royale

2115 Commissioner St. • 251-9844
Ask restaurateurs where they buy their smoked salmon
and this is the name that comes up most often. Their
cold-smoked salmon is very rich and delicate in
flavour, and good for salads and sandwiches. You can
buy it sliced and interleaved with paper in quantities
of half a pound and up, or treat yourself to an entire
side. Hot-smoked salmon comes in chunks of about
a pound — you can make a meal of it. You'll also find
cold-smoked black cod sold as whole fillets of about
three pounds each.

2-Minute Starter for 4

Buy a smoked mackerel fillet
— try Longliner Sea Foods
(Granville Island Public Market,
685-9016). Set on a bed of
lettuce leaves. Garnish with
lemon wedges. Mix sour
cream and Dijon mustard to
taste, and serve on the side as
a sauce.

An "R" in the Month

"What makes one type of oysters different from another is where they grow," explains Kim Schultz of Pacific Northwest Shellfish. Nootka Sound oysters, for instance, are bigger, chunkier and have a thicker shell than some other varieties. "As for that `r' in the month thing — summer is spawning season when all the oyster's body meat goes into sperm or eggs. The oyster is mushier, not at its peak. After they spawn, it takes another month or two to recoup their energies."

Most of the oysters hereabouts are cultivated. Growers take baby oysters and grow them in cages where they're safe from predators and grow faster. Shells are thinner, so towards the end, they are put on the beach where they grow thicker shells.

Pacific Northwest Shellfish grows its own oysters. Most are shipped overseas but in Vancouver they can be found at Produce City on Cambie, Seafood City at Granville Island Public Market and in the company's own store, West End Seafood Market, at Robson Public Market.

Macfarlane's Selected Fish Market
2233 West 41st Ave. • 261-1226
John Macfarlane is the third generation to sell fish to Vancouverites. His grandfather started the business in 1921, selling door to door with a horse and buggy. In 1928, he opened up on the 2200 block (close to where today's store is) and the business has been in its present location since 1933. Locals come here for salmon and the other fresh fish varieties that show up daily. Macfarlane's also carries Chilean sea bass, orange roughy on occasion, and haddock now and again. What's their big draw? Quality. John and wife Maureen make whole stuffed salmon to order, decorated with cucumbers and flowers to order. Gefilte fish, too.

Salishan Seafood
3903 Ke-Kait Place • 264-0021
Denise Sparrow sells home-smoked salmon.

The Salmon Shop
1689 Johnston St., Granville Island • 669-3474
Salmon, and smoked salmon as well as tuna, swordfish, halibut, sole, cod, snapper, shrimp, you name it.

Seafood City
1689 Johnston St., Granville Island • 688-1818
3277 Cambie St. (inside Produce City) • 874-0088
Pick up a live and wriggly Dungeness crab, a couple of pounds of mussels, or some beautiful salmon steaks. Handy market locations let you do all your grocery shopping in one fell swoop.

Seven Seas Fish Company
2338 West 4th Ave. • 732-8608
They catch 'em, they sell 'em — which means direct-to-you prices. Salmon here is unfailingly succulent. Fillets and steaks, Spring or coho, depending on season. Cod, snapper, buttery smoked mackerel...this is one of my favourite fish stores. For prawns, shrimp and live lobster and crab, they'll quote "market price," which means on par or below what you'll pay elsewhere.

T & T Supermarket
179 Keefer Place • 899-8836
100-2800 East 1st Ave. • 254-9668

West End Seafood Market
(formerly The Salmon Shop)
1610 Robson St., Robson Public Market • 688-3474
Salmon, of course – and smoked salmon, too – but they're also a popular stop for imported tuna, marlin and swordfish. Oysters come from their own farm in Fanny Bay. Time-strapped West Enders go for the marinated halibut, catfish and snapper.

To achieve perfection fish should swim three times — in water, in butter and in wine.
— Polish proverb.

CHINATOWN FISH STORES
Tanks full of Dungeness crabs and tilapia, plastic containers out on the sidewalk packed with mussels, clams and shiny black periwinkles, whole red snapper, sea bass steaks, sea cucumber, geoduck – this is fish at its freshest. Shop early in the morning and you'll see the live fish being unloaded off trucks from Campbell River and other fishing ports.

New Chong Lung Seafoods & Meats
595 Gore St. •
(no phone)

Pender Seafoods
284 East Pender St. •
687-5946

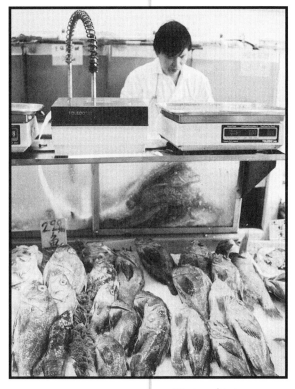

Chinatown fish store

Kam Tong Enterprises
276 East Pender St. • 683-0033

Hung Win Seafood
427 Gore St. • 683-7957

WEST VANCOUVER:

Village Fish and Oyster Market
1482 Marine Dr. • 922-4332

This market has ace-quality seafood. Check out the sandwich of the day — sometimes crab, sometimes shrimp — and the fish of the day. They also sell shrimp, tuna, black cod, sea bass, salmon. Crab, halibut and salmon cakes sell out every day (900 cakes a day!). Crab is the biggest seller. In the summer, there's teriyaki salmon, ready to be put on the grill. Thirty different kinds of fish, including monkfish or marlin. Also: Indian candy, smoked salmon. Everything to make sushi, too — even the rolling mats.

TIPS FOR BARBECUING WILD SALMON

B.C. Salmon Marketing Council

Every species of wild B.C. salmon works very well on the barbecue.

Pink salmon, because of its convenient average size (approximately 2 lbs/1 kg) and its attractive pricing, is a shrewd choice to barbecue whole or in fillets.

Sockeye is also an excellent choice to serve whole and its rich red flesh makes for outstanding fillets.

Coho and Spring yield especially handsome steaks and "roasts."

Chum is great value for money and particularly good on the barbecue with a teriyaki or smoky-flavoured basting sauce.

As far as great taste goes, all species may be used interchangeably.

Barbecue salmon over a medium-high heat. Fish is naturally tender and doesn't require much cooking time. An excellent rule of thumb when cooking fish is 10 minutes per inch of thickness, measured at the thickest point. When your fish is cooked to perfection, its juices will run clear and the flesh will separate into moist natural chevron-shaped sections when firmly poked with a fork. If it flakes without any encouragement, then you've overdone it. Always remember: salmon is best when it's cooked "medium rare"!

Because fish contains very little connective tissue it can fall apart if roughly handled, especially when you're barbecuing. Here are a couple of simple solutions to this problem:
- place portions in a hinged rack to hold over the coals;
- pack chunks of fish on skewers, "kabob-style";
- oil one side of a double thickness of heavy-duty aluminum foil. Punch numerous pencil holes through the foil and lay flat, oiled side up, directly on the barbecue grill. Place whole fish on foil slightly off centre. Halfway through cooking time, close foil over fish, flip package, reopen foil, lay flat and complete cooking.

CHEESE PLEASE

In France, go out to dinner, to someone's home, to a restaurant — anywhere — and you'll be offered a selection of cheeses as a matter of course. Drippingly luscious Camembert or Brie, sharp, pungent goat cheeses, firm cheeses like Cantal or Mimolette, all of them so concentrated in taste that even the smallest morsel floods your mouth with flavour.

Here in Vancouver we're starting to get hooked on cheese like our European cousins. Grating real Parmigiana over our linguine, serving ripe berries with a wedge of Brie on the side — it's a vast, fragrant world and the passport to all its pleasures is your local specialty cheese store. But don't stop there; check the International and European listings in this book too.

Cheese Whizzes

BURNABY:

National Cheese Company
7278 Curragh   •   437-8561
Over 200 kinds of cheese from 19 different countries are sold here. Among them is the company's Tre Stelle brand of cheeses made in Ontario and including havarti, provolone, bocconcini, mascarpone, mozzarella and feta, as well as sliced, shredded and grated cheeses.

DELTA:

Cheese Please
102-6345 120th St.   •   596-8982
Parmigiana, Romano, Swiss, Edam — this deli normally stocks around 50 varieties of cheese. Around Christmas they increase the number to some 120 different types from around the world.

NEW WESTMINSTER:

Cheese Please Plus
110-810 Quayside Dr.   •   520-5092
About 140 varieties, give or take a couple: English, Dutch, French, Italian, you name it, as well as fresh bocconcini.

Devonshire Cream

Thick and calorific, the kind that's served at the Empress Hotel in Victoria is made by Golden Valley Foods in Clearbrook. Devonshire cream is distributed widely — you'll probably find Jersey Farms Devon Cream in your local supermarket.

NORTH VANCOUVER:

Duso's Pasta and Cheese

Lonsdale Quay Market • 987-0511

(see also: Vancouver)

An extensive selection of cheeses includes Parmigiana Reggiano, buffalo milk mozzarella, gorgonzola, unutterably creamy mascarpone, Asiago and French cheeses, as well as myzithra, a Greek cheese like a Parmesan that can be grated over hot pasta.

B-N-Sales

991 West 3rd Ave. • 985-4527

Originally from Denmark, Benny Nordhoj has been selling cheese in this "secret" location near Capilano Mall since 1977. French, Italian, Danish, German, Swiss, British, Canadian – you name it, you'll find it, always at a bargain price.

VANCOUVER:

The Cheese Place

4255 Arbutus St. • 734-4255

Shiraz Nathoo's involvement with cheese dates back to when Robson St. was a food street. For 14 years, his Cheese Place was one of the highlights of "Robsonstrasse." In 1990, he moved to the Arbutus Shopping Centre. Nathoo stresses quality – "It must have flavour to it," he emphasizes (then you'll eat less, he says, and lose weight). Europeans come here for soft ripened cheeses from France, Brits for his assertively flavoured, aged Cheddars. Among his collection of other English classics are Cheshire, Double Goucester, Wensleydale and Stilton. If you've been there and done those, try some less traditional varieties such as Huntsman cheese – a "sandwich" of blue Stilton and Double Gloucester – or Five Counties, a layered combination of Derbyshire, English Cheddar, Cheshire, Double Gloucester and Leicester.

Dussa's Ham and Cheese

Granville Island Public Market • 688-8881

Arthur Dussa started selling cheese (at 25th and Main) in 1956 – he introduced Emmenthaler and cambozola to the city. Today, cheese-ophiles make a beeline for

Creme Cheeses

Skip the hard wedges for once and focus in on those sloppy blonde triple crèmes with the truly frightening butterfat content. Among the 250+ fromages at Forster's Fine Cheeses (2104 W 41st Ave., 261-5813) are Costello Blue from Denmark (think of blue whipped cream) and mascarpone torta, which layers mascarpone — itself no slouch in the cream department — with dolce latte gorgonzola.

his store at Granville Island. Over 250 types from 28 countries are on display. Among the names you may not recognize are a hard cheese called sardo from Argentina, edam from Czechoslovakia, an emmenthaler-type cheese from Hungary, not to mention sprinz, a hard Swiss cheese that some people grate over their pasta in lieu of more expensive parmesan. You'll find Mr. Dussa's favourite here, too: a 10-year-old Canadian cheddar — "a nice crisp cheese that's good with beer," he says.

Duso's Pasta and Cheese
Granville Island Public Market • 685-5921
(see also: North Vancouver)
Though you will find mozzarella and other staple cheeses here, pasta is the lure at this location.

Forsters Fine Cheese
2104 West 41st Ave. • 261-5813
See story page 60.

La Fromagerie at Lesley Stowe Fine Foods
1780 West 3rd Ave. • 731-3663
This store within a store puts the emphasis on French cheeses — unpasteurized whenever possible. A big hit with the elegant crowd who comes here is torta mascarpone, an illegally rich layering of gorgonzola and mascarpone. Sales of Montbriac and Bleu des Causses reflect Vancouver's enthusiasm for blue cheeses. Other big sellers are Shropshire cheese from England and classic Stilton.

La Grotta del Formaggio
1791 Commercial Dr. • 255-3911
See page 90.

Healthy Gourmet
Granville Island Public Market • 685-6639
Jim Wort, co-owner of the Healthy Gourmet, is famed for his goat's gouda cheese from Salmon Arm, as well as goat cheddar and goat feta. He focuses mostly on Canadian cheeses and carries goat's milk cheese from Quebec, Ontario and B.C. Those who can't or don't want to eat regular cheese will find a variety of non-

---

Peak Experience in Whistler
Cheek-by-jowl to his former home, the Chateau Whistler, Chef Bernard's Café (604-932-7051) is chock-a-block with Bernard Casavant's Ciao-Thyme line of chutneys, dressings and infused oils. Try the Cranberry Basil Vinaigrette or — a fresh switch on cranberry sauce — his Sundried Apricot and Cranberry Chutney. Planning a post-slope do? Casavant caters and whips up takeout, too. Far easier than lugging food up the highway. Call ahead and order foccacia sandwiches with grilled vegetables, vegetable canneloni in a tomato-herb sauce and cinnamon raisin-bread pudding with Kahlua spice sauce.

dairy cheeses — even grated parmesan — and cheeses made with vegetarian rennet.

The Menu Setters Fine Food & Catering
3655 West 10th Ave. • 732-4218

Hidden away in a mini-mall, this excellent store was a closely kept secret for years. Now every foodie knows that "Alice and Allison" means mother-and-daughter team Alice and Allison Spurrell, cheese maniacs who stock about 230 varieties of cheese at any given time. The updated list, issued weekly, includes four different Roqueforts (among them what's considered to be the best, the Carles brand), cheeses from Saltspring Island, Boursault and Boursin. There's even a cheese called Irish Blarney. Regulars include foodies who want to match a specific cheese to a particular wine, French-born Vancouverites eager for a taste of home (who get misty-eyed over the Larzac, a spreadable "blue" flavoured cream cheese in a pottery jar from the Roquefort area) and the growing number of people who simply want to learn more about cheese.

Chef's Tip

"I don't make sauces anymore. I just deglaze the pan with white or red wine."
— Robert LeCrom, Executive Chef, Hotel Vancouver

WHAT A FRIEND WE HAVE IN CHEESES

The aroma that greets you at the door of Forster's Cheeses in Kerrisdale could be bottled, given an "Essence of Forster's" label and sold as a gourmet treat to spread on bread or crackers. It's that intense. Instead of a counter, a cooler runs the length of the store. End to end, front to back, it's filled with rounds and wedges and blocks and squares in white and deep orange and every shade of cream and yellow in between.

Cheese. If you were a farmer a hundred years ago, you probably made your own. These days few people do — and while wine knowledge is growing by leaps and bounds, most people still can't tell their Asiago from their Danbo. The good news in B.C.? More and more people are making cheese. These are artisan cheeses created with love and skill: Chevre in Salmon Arm, sheep's milk cheese in Chase, and, on Saltspring Island, little goat cheeses, each with a tiny flower pressed into its base. All of it is delicious but it's also highly intimidating if your only previous experience with cheese has been from the top of a pizza or what's in the supermarket cooler.

"If you've only had mild cheese like Havarti, I'd start you on mild cheese that was a little different," says Stephen Forster, who has been selling from the store he runs with his wife, Elizabeth, since 1981 (and before that spent almost as many years working with cheese at Woodward's). He might suggest Lou Palou, a cheese from the French Pyrenees that's similar in strength and texture to Havarti; Redder cheese from Norway might be another possibility.

For many Vancouverites, the world begins and ends with cheddar. Fair enough, says Forster. "I'd give them a taste of Black River cheddar from Ontario," to demonstrate what an artisanal cheese is like. "That's what it used to be like and that's what it still should be like," he reminds me as the thin wafer of cheese, nutty, tangy, sweet and smooth, melts on my tongue. "That'll linger for quite a while," he adds. And it does.

"When you get into mass production of anything, quality goes down substantially," says Forster. "Economics are forcing small producers out. That

Preparing for Parmesan
"For grating, get aged cheese, at least two years old. If you want to eat it in chunks, buy fresh."
— Julio Gonzalez Perini, Villa Del Lupo

"Parmesan is easier to cut if you chill it in the fridge overnight."
— Fortunato Bruzzese, La Grotta del Formaggio

cheddar you tasted was two and a half years old. A good piece of cheddar you can work into your hand and it'll disappear [he demonstrates] like that," because it's made of little else but pure sweet milk.

What Forster likes to do is slowly extend the boundaries of his customers' cheese knowledge — and try not to let them have the same cheese twice in a row. If Bries and Camemberts are cause for salivation, he encourages them to push the envelope. "I'd suggest something with a washed rind such as a French Chaumes," he says of a cheese whose powdery bloom has been removed so that it can breathe as it ripens and develop more flavour at a younger age. Oka from Quebec has a "brushed" rind which causes something similar to happen. Eventually these customers will graduate to more complex flavours, says Forster, such as a Munster from Alsace.

Work your way through cows' milk, sheeps' milk, and goats' milk cheeses — and by that time you'd be ready to scale the pinnacles of pungency, the blue cheeses that occupy a whole corner of Forster's cooler. "Some people are deathly afraid of the blue because it's mould," he says. "But so is the white on the top of a Brie. So are mushrooms."

"I Love You, Little Mouse"
Valentine's Day (or whenever else they're in stock) skip the cliché long-stemmed red roses and give a heart-shaped cheese from France instead. Ask for "Coeur Selle de Chevre" at Lesley Stowe Fine Foods (1780 West 3rd Ave., 731-3663).

BREADS

Forty years ago, most Vancouverites thought "bread" was something white, soft, sliced and sold in a plastic wrapper. Today bread can mean a wholewheat loaf from the Safeway in-store bakery, a nut-studded bread from a specialty baker, flat lavash, pita bread, focaccia or ciabatta, bagels, Portuguese buns, corn bread or hundreds of other varieties.

And then there are the treats — the adds-an-inch-to-the-hips-but-who-cares stuff. Pastries, little and large. Wonderfully decadent cakes. If you've just signed up with Weight Watchers or Jenny Craig, skip this section.

Bakers and Makers of Pastry

COQUITLAM:

Van Den Bosch Patisserie Belge & Bakery
230-3025 Lougheed Hwy • 464-1077
(see also: Surrey, Vancouver, West Vancouver)
Being a chocoholic in Vancouver means you can get a Van Den Bosch fix almost anywhere. Try the zebra cake which marries white and dark chocolate and soaks it in cocoa liqueur, and the Triple Decadence with its three different kinds of chocolate mousse. Other indulgences are the hazelnut or chocolate caprices, St. Honoré cakes and chocolate merveilleuse which sates your chocolate urge with chocolate meringue, chocolate whipping cream, chocolate sprinkles and a piece of Belgian chocolate.

LANGLEY:

Ernie's Austria Bakery
1210 200th St. • 533-5565
For 36 years his bakery was a neighbourhood mainstay on Alma St. Before that, he was on Kingsway, and now he's in Langley. Ernie has been baking bread for well over 55 years. His rye breads — plain rye, sour rye, heavy rye and caraway — are famous. His French bread and cinnamon buns are almost as popular.

European Cheesecake Factory
101-20530 Langley Bypass • 533-1481
The factory is actually in Edmonton. Never mind, the

And Just How Many Calories Is That?
In one year, Purdy's Chocolates goes through nine tons of butter.

cakes and cheesecakes — all 40 different varieties — are here at very good prices. Blackout torte is the best seller, a two-layer with chocolate fudge icing, chocolate truffle in the middle. Just as deadly is the Belgian chocolate cake filled and topped with chocolate truffle creme. The 10-inch cheesecakes pre-cut into 14 slices include New York style, white chocolate-blueberry and strawberry.

NORTH VANCOUVER:

The Danish Pastry Shop
3105 Edgemont Blvd. • 987-1323
Famous for their addictive Copenhagens, evil little squares filled with custard, raisins and almond paste. Apricot, almond or apple kringles are another tasty way to add inches to your hips. On a less caloric note, try the tasty cheese and herb bread, or the heavy Danish rye.

SURREY:

Van Den Bosch Patisserie Belge & Bakery
Semiahmoo Centre • 531-8847
(see also: Coquitlam, Vancouver, West Vancouver)

VANCOUVER:

Angus Bakery & Café
3636 West Broadway • 733-9955
The name suggests a Scottish bun shop, but this West Side bakery looks more like a Parisian patisserie. Classic baguettes, four kinds of rye, terrific Danishes, a luscious apricot and walnut bread and loaves made with sunflower, flax, caraway or sesame seeds. Try the feather-light scones.

Benny's Bagels
2505 West Broadway • 731-9730
3365 Cambie St. • 872-1111
1780 Davie St. • 685-7600
5728 University Blvd. • 222-7815
This popular chain was started in Victoria in 1982 by Colin Gareau. The dozen or so varieties of bagel baked on-site at each store are Toronto/New York style, which means they're not boiled in honey water as they are in Montreal.

Crunch!
Highly recommended: the Manoucher frozen baguettes from Lesley Stowe Fine Foods (1780 West 3rd Ave., 731-3663). Five minutes at 400° makes them ultra crispy

Bon Ton Pastry & Confectionery
874 Granville St. • 681-3058
The window of this Vancouver landmark — it dates from the early 1930s — looks like a picture from a child's storybook. The Notte family make about 40 different confections. You can order a couple of them with a cuppa or take home a selection. Try a Prince of Wales — almond sponge filled with buttercream and jam — a chocolate éclair, a mocha filbert meringue or a fresh cream puff.

La Boulangerie
845 Burrard St. • 682-4568
Owned and run by the Sutton Place Hotel, La Boulangerie sells many of the cakes served at the hotel's evil Chocoholic Buffet, as well as individual pastries. Birthday and wedding cakes are made to order by hotel pastry chef Wolfgang Dauke. Butter, cheese and chocolate croissants, cinnamon buns, banana bread, brownies and muffins. Monday through Saturday, you can also find Ecco il Pane breads here.

Broadway Bakery
3273 West Broadway • 733-1422
Check out this longtime Greek fave where Jerry Zerbinos has been busy baking the recipes of his homeland for the past 20+ years. His big round loaf (karvele) and hefty flax bread are under $1.50 a loaf. Equally good prices on sweet bread (tsoureki), baklava and sesame seed buns.

Calabria Bakery
5036 Victoria Dr. • 324-1337
Concetta Armeni and her four kids plus a son-in-law keep the loaves baking in this busy establishment. It started in 1970 at Commercial and Broadway and has been in its present location for over 20 years. Customers come for the Italian bread (white or 60 percent wholewheat) and the focaccia. With ondi — Italian shortbread — and 10 kinds of biscotti, you'll find plenty of goodies to take home. Try the cannoli Siciliani, filled with sweetened ricotta. Other specialties are frisini (like rusks flavoured with fennel seed) and amaretti morbati (chewy almond cookies).

Carmelo's Pastry Shop

1399 Commercial Dr. • 254-7024
555 West Hastings St. • 681-7055

Italian St. Honoré cake, tiramisu, gianduja cake made with hazelnuts and chocolate, and classic cannolis are just some of the insanely good pastries Charlene Spadaro makes in her store.

Ecco il Pane

238 West 5th Ave. • 873-6888
2563 West Broadway • 739-1314

Crusty, crusty bread with good chewy insides that really give your jaws a workout. Casa, pugliese — made with 10 percent semolina — ficelle (an Italian baguette baked from the same dough as the casa). Made with wholewheat flour and millet, the integrale is especially good. Those who live in either of Ecco il Pane's neighbourhoods become addicted to rusticas — little sticks of sweet dough studded with Monukka raisins — and the chocolate-sour cherry buns and loaves, made in a heart shape for Valentine's Day. The desserts are terrific, especially the fresh-tasting torta con limone — lemon tart — and the crostata, a rustic pie brimming with fruits. At the West Broadway location, breads are baked in a wood-burning oven from Spain.

Not Just Desserts

1638 East Broadway • 877-1313

Notorious for Sin City — a chocolate frangelico mousse cake — and the gorgeous lemon meringue pie. Double chocolate fudge cake, a towering four layers high, is the cake you always wished your mother would make. Pies and cheesecakes, too. "Not just" desserts means pastas, salads and sandwiches as well.

Pacific Institute of Culinary Arts

1505 West 2nd Ave. • 734-4488

Fifth generation French pastry chef Paul Massincaud instructs aspiring patissiers in the arts of authentic crust and crumb. Results go on sale daily. You'll find pains au chocolat, croissants, muffins and Danishes, as well as tarts, including chocolate ganache and pecan versions, sold whole or by the slice. Special order birthday cakes too.

Panne Rizo
1939 Cornwall Ave. • 736-0885
Good news for people with food allergies. Panne Rizo only sells wheat- and gluten-free baked goods. As well as sesame and butter crust loaves, there are "artisan" breads, hamburger and hot dog buns, even croutons and savoury bread crumbs, all rice-based. On the pastry side, you can indulge in cookies, muffins, cinnamon buns, pies and cakes. You can also order birthday and special occasion cakes.

Pâtisserie Bordeaux
3675 West 10th Ave. • 731-6551
See page 82.

Stuart's Bakery
Granville Island Public Market • 685-8816
Customers line up for the plain and chocolate croissants, big raisin scones, cranberry and orange loaf, the cinnamon-raisin bread structurally based on a classic cinnamon bun and the pane sostanzioso speckled with flax and sunflower seeds.

Terra Breads
2380 West 4th Ave. • 736-1838
Granville Island Public Market • 685-3102
The black or green olive loaves and fougasse (a bread shaped like a ladder) are a staple at many dinner parties. The fig and anise bread is magnificent toasted and spread with a little cream cheese. Terra Breads also sells Italian cheese bread, baguettes both French and sourdough, potato and chive loaves, walnut bread, and current and millet bread. All are baked in a stone-hearth oven. Fridays, they put out loaves dense with

Terra Breads

pecans and dried fruit. Fridays and Saturdays are the days to find challah. For a quick snack, grab a slab of pane all'uva (grape bread), thyme-flavoured apple focaccia or a piece of their superb biscotti.

Tinkers Hatch Bakery
4894 MacKenzie St. • 261-4484

This is a real, old-fashioned bakery where everything (barring doughnuts) is made on the premises. John Gurney is a fifth generation baker with ancestors from Belgium. Gurney himself is from England and he makes about 40 varieties of bread, including plain white, multigrain, wholewheat and Hovis, as well as pies, pastries, cakes, and cheese, current and blueberry scones. Prices are very reasonable, especially for the decorated cookies — kids love 'em. Gurney also bakes coloured breads: green for St. Patrick's Day, orange for Halloween and pink for Valentine's Day.

Uprising Breads Bakery
1697 Venables St. • 254-5635

This East Side fave has been around since the 1970s, long before biscotti and foccacia became part of our culture. Known for its substantial breads, carob squares and chocolate chip cookies. Wholesome and delicious are key words here.

Van Den Bosch Patisserie Belge & Bakery
Arbutus Shopping Centre • 731-0055
Oakridge Centre • 267-1321
(see also: Coquitlam, Surrey, West Vancouver)

Trafalgar's at Sweet Obsession
2603 West 16th Ave. • 739-0555

The former Sweet Obsession grew into an entire bistro, but relax — they still make the same stupendously good cakes and desserts. Stephen Greenham and Lorne Williams' gateaux are by no means the cheapest around but they're good enough to be served at some of the city's top eateries. Twenty or so varieties include the lethal Triple Chocolate Mousse Cake in 6-, 8- and 10-inch sizes (the smallest feeds 8 to 10). Just as delicious are the lime raspberry tart with macadamia nuts and the chocolate-lined

French Bread (and Croissants)
For the "best breakfast," Hervé Martin of the The Hermitage buys a ficelle from Patisserie Bordeaux (3675 West 10th Ave., 731-6551). "You take the entire ficelle, cut it from one end to the other, and spread it with butter and apricot or strawberry jam." For "excellent" baguettes (although, to be genuinely French, "they should be a little more crunchy") Martin goes to Patisserie Lebeau (1660 Cypress, 731-3258). In his view, the most authentic croissants in the city are at La Boulangerie (845 Burrard St., 682-4568).

pastry shell filled with chocolate mousse and custard and topped with fresh fruit. The lemon dacquoise is superb. Individual portions easily stretch to feed two.

True Confections
866 Denman St. • 682-1292
3701 West Broadway • 222-8489
Stratospheric layer cakes and exceptional cheesecakes. A bestseller is the milk chocolate hazelnut cake, closely followed by the dark chocolate cake with hazelnut mousse coated with milk chocolate. If it says "chocolate" in the name it means real Belgian chocolate. Real butter cream and real liqueurs are among the other ingredients, and everything is made in-house. Sold whole or by the slice.

WEST VANCOUVER:

Milieu Patisserie Bakery
1471 Bellevue • 926-4555
Multigrain, sourdough, Russian and Danish ryes, baguettes and epis all baked on the premises. Locals also drop in for the muffins — especially the pumpkin-spice ones — and specialty cakes.

Van Den Bosch Patisserie Belge & Bakery
Park Royal South • 926-4401
(see also: Coquitlam, Surrey, Vancouver)

Nibble My Ear, and I'll Follow You Anywhere.
Around Christmas time, Tinkers Hatch Bakery (4894 MacKenzie St., 261-4484) makes gingerbread earrings — tiny decorated cookies attached to earring hooks. And, yes, says baker John Gurney, "We make single earrings for guys."

SWEET TREATS: Chocolate and More

Thought for the day: According to champion chocolatier Daniel Poncelet of Daniel Le Chocolat Belge, "The melting point of cocoa butter is close to body temperature. Nature made chocolate that way for a reason."

BURNABY:

Charlie's Chocolate Factory

3746 Canada Way • 437-8221

Strictly speaking, this is more a resource for home chocolate makers. But if you do get a sudden craving for giant amounts of Belgian chocolate, here's where you'll find dark, milk and white, sold by the pound, 11-pound slab, or 55-pound case.

LANGLEY:

Daniel Le Chocolat Belge

450-19705 Fraser Hwy. • 530-7786

(see also: Vancouver; West Vancouver)

Daniel Poncelet has been making chocolates since 1981 – and he knows a thing or two. For instance: dark solid chocolate left to melt in your mouth with a chaser of strong, black coffee is an irresistible combination. Try his hazelnut filling, or treat yourself to a dog, tennis player or the signs of the zodiac in chocolate. How good are Poncelet's chocolates? In 1998, he was the first North American to receive the top honour of "Grand Prix International Artisan Chocolatier" at the International Chocolate Festival.

RICHMOND:

Chocolaterie Bernard Callebaut

188-8120 No. 2 Rd. • 275-1244

(see also: Vancouver, White Rock)

Bernard Callebaut makes superb Belgian chocolates, hazelnut pralines, truffles, creme fraiche chocolates made from fresh whipping cream in different flavours. You can buy a small nut-studded chocolate bar for snacking or a big one-pounder in bittersweet, semisweet, milk or white chocolate. Technically, it's called a "baking bar." Ha! Worth picking up as well is Callebaut's Dutch process cocoa powder.

Like Water for Chocolate

Water or milk? Mexican hot chocolate — chocolate caliente — uses either, says Maria Zallen, manager at Que Pasa (1647 West 5th Ave., 730-5449), which stocks two brands: Abuelita, and the slightly-less-sweet Ibarro. Each hexagonal box contains a stack of six large individually wrapped tablets, which are a mix of chocolate, cinnamon and sugar. Snap off a chunk, melt it carefully in a pan, add your hot liquid of choice, then mix. An ordinary whisk will do but true aficionados whip their drink to a froth with an authentic Mexican molinillo, $7.12. Cinnamon sprinkled on top and a cinnamon stick for stirring are added refinements. Mocha fans can also try blending chocolate caliente half and half with fresh-brewed coffee.

How Purdy's Gets the Chocolate Around the Cream in its Chocolate Creams

It's Vancouver's version of the Caramilk secret. Here's how it's done. Once it's been mixed and left to cool, the cream mixture — orange, lemon or coffee, the flavour doesn't matter — becomes stiff like cookie dough. It's stiff enough to be stamped into rounds or squares, and stiff enough to hold its shape when the melted chocolate is poured over it. But... mixed into the filling is an enzyme called invertase which, over a 10-day period, slowly breaks down the filling and makes it creamy.

Display at Chocolate Arts

VANCOUVER:

Chocolaterie Bernard Callebaut
2698 Granville St. • 736-5890

Chocolate Arts
2037 West 4th Ave. • 739-0475
Owner Greg Hook uses organic fruits in his chocolates, which must make them good for you. Chocolate Arts is known for its chocolate moulds designed by Haida artist Robert Davidson. Hook's ground- and diet-breaking Grand Cru, "a straightforward chocolate truffle," is made with Valrhona guanaja chocolate — 70 percent cocoa solids. Creations for Valentine's Day include the Romeo, a sleek dark pyramid that hides a blackberry creme and truffle filling. The Juliet pairs light chocolate with organic peach purée and dried peaches macerated in peach schnapps. During October, Hook transforms pumpkin as magically as did Cinderella's fairy godmother. This isn't ordinary run-of-the-patch pumpkin, you understand, but organic Sugar pumpkin from Hazelmere Farms in the Fraser Valley. First, Hook bakes it in its skin till soft. Then he blends it with milk chocolate and his own secret mix of pumpkin pie spices. The penultimate touch is a bath in milk or dark chocolate before the truffles are rolled in almond praline for a bit of crunch.

Daniel Le Chocolat Belge
124 West 3rd Ave. • 879-7782
1105 Robson St. • 688-9624
2820 Granville St. • 733-1994
4447 West 10th Ave. • 224-3361
(see also: Langley; West Vancouver)

House of Brussels Chocolates
Outlets throughout the lower mainland
Factory Outlet: 208-750 Terminal • 687-1524
The factory outlet sells mostly first-quality chocolates

(some seconds) but usually has more specials than the company's other stores around town. The delectable hazelnut hedgehog, which was first invented by Brussels, moves fastest.

Lee's Candies
4361 West 10th Ave. • 224-5450

In the summer, chocolate-lovers go for the lemon chiffon truffle. Peanut brittle, chocolate mint truffles and nut barks are the big sellers year-round at Lee's, a mecca for the sweet-toothed for close to half a century. Chocolate novelties from the store's terrific selection of vintage moulds — a bunny on a motorcycle for instance — make great gifts. Lee's also produces chocolate chess pieces (see sidebar).

Over the Moon Chocolate Co. Ltd.
2868 West Broadway • 737-0880

Chocolate pianos, houses, motorcycles, cows and other objects add up to chocolate heaven. Only the strongest will could resist the chocolate-dipped cherries marinated in Kirsch, the miniature buddah filled with orange cream and Triple Sec, or the Kitsilano Delight made with roasted almonds, pistachios, hazelnuts, caramel and nougat.

Purdy's
2777 Kingsway • 454-2700
(Plus branches in virtually every shopping centre in the G.V.R.D.)

Everyone has their favourite Purdy's chocolate or bar. The Kingsway store carries "seconds" at proportionally lower prices. The more upscale Bonté line is patterned after European chocolates.

WEST VANCOUVER:
Daniel Le Chocolat Belge
Park Royal North • 925-2213
(see also: Langley; Vancouver)

WHITE ROCK:
Chocolaterie Bernard Callebaut
240-15355 24th Ave. • 531-6777
(see also: Richmond, Vancouver)

Brownie Hunt

If you like your brownies dense, rich, nutty, fudgy, marshmallowy and sufficiently large to satisfy two chocolate cravings, hunt down the Rocky Road brownie made by Sweet Things Pastries (105-3100 Production Way, Burnaby, 420-3511) and sold at various coffee shops and cafés around town. Cheerfully admitting, "There's very little flour in these — but there's lots of chocolate," the company also lists a hazelnut toffee bar among its temptations. At Gutenberg's (104-345 Robson St., 669-4452), it's known as the "library square." In your quest for the ultimate experience for your sweet tooth, you may uncover Sweet Things' caramel fudge brownie or the white chocolate and wild cherry version. Buying in bulk from the factory (call a day ahead) will save a few pennies.

I SCREAM, YOU SCREAM...

More evidence of Vancouver's place on the world food scene is our amazing array of ice-cream flavours. Here are some of my favourites.

VANCOUVER:

Amato Gelato
88 East 1st Ave. • 879-9411
Fans of ice-cream maestro Mario Loscerbo have a hard time choosing: Amaretto, chocolate hazlenut, licorice, strawberry, banana-fudge, caramel crunch, double chocolate fudge, rum and raisin, spumoni — I've had them all, and they're all worth recommending. His sorbets are pure essence of fruit: apple-cranberry, blackcurrant, lychee, melon and a headily wonderful passionfruit. Don't worry if you're miles away from the source. Chances are high your local specialty store or supermarket carries some of the line.

BC Gelati
1102 West Broadway • 733-2979
Clay Heinz and Mike Molinari used to run a gelati shop in Verona, Italy. Now they are making their gelati

Chocolate Chess
"Checkmate" takes on new meaning at Lee's Candies (4361 West 10th Avenue, 224-5450). The West Side store moulds chess pieces in white, dark or milk chocolate.

and sorbets on West Broadway. Among the former, hazelnut, tira misu, the very strong coffee and "kiss" — a mixture of chocolate and hazelnut — are strong sellers. Rather than imported purées or jams, they use fresh fruit only in their gelati and sorbets. Depending on the season, you'll find strawberry, blueberry, peach, pear and other lip-smacking flavours. Spiked with shavings of zest, the lemon sorbet is like a blast of fresh air on your palate.

La Casa Gelato
1033 Venables • 251-3211
See page 249.

Mum's Italian Gelato
855 Denman St. • 681-1500
2028 Vine St. • 738-6867
You've done mocha, done chocolate, done vanilla. So you're ready for Mum's moka, which, thanks to its mix of espresso beans, coffee, cocoa and Belgian chocolate chunks, has a real caffeine kick to it. Flavours change often, depending on the time of year. Try to drop by on a hot night when they're selling candied ginger and fresh lemon cones. Bliss.

Tia Ana (Venezia Ice Cream)
5752 Victoria Dr. • 327-8614
It's now a Portuguese restaurant, but Daniel Alexander still makes the same great ice-creams and sorbets. He's hot on authentic ingredients, hence the little black specks of real vanilla and the zing of lemon juice. Flavours change with the seasons. The Nocciola — hazelnut — and the torrone, made from real nougat, are terrific. The mango is out of this world.

The Life Story of Death by Chocolate

Restaurateur John Bishop gives full credit to caterer Lesley Stowe for dreaming up the death-defying chocolate terrine. But it was he and his staff who created the suicidal presentation, splattered with raspberry coulis. For a long while, staff would just fling the raspberry coulis at the terrine. Messy, very messy. Then along came a very bright culinary student who suggested that cornering the chocolate terrine on a plate in a cardboard carton might contain the splatters. It did — and to this day, that is how Death by Chocolate is made at Bishop's.

ETHNIC AND IMPORTED INGREDIENTS

This evening we ate pasta topped with some crisped pancetta and real Parmigiana. Last night was an Asian feast — Singapore noodles, and a stir-fry of baby bok choy. In the fridge is leftover lentil salad — a French dish — roasted red peppers and olives for a Mediterranean platter, and a jar of fiery Korean kimchee. In the cupboard are Mexican hot sauces, Indian chutneys and Thai rice noodles. We in Vancouver live in a world-class city for food — and what we put on our tables reflects this.

In the early eighties, only two places in town sold fresh ravioli. Now, fresh ravioli is as close as your local Safeway. Around the same time as the ravioli appeared, Vancouver opened its first Thai restaurant. Lemongrass was once thought very exotic; now the corner store carries it. But while the whole Vancouver area has been showered with new ingredients, it's out of the question for every single store to carry every spice and seasoning. That's when we turn to the hundreds of ethnic specialty stores: Commercial Drive or East Hastings for Italian cheeses; Powell St. for Japanese pickles; West Broadway for baklava and tsatsiki.

If you're passionate about food and travel, the cheapest route into another country or culture is by way of the grocery store. Spend a morning in Main Street's Punjabi Market section, sniffing the cumin and cardamom, and blissing out on the saffron and peacock and hot pink silks of the saree stores. It's an instant trip to India. Watch a Chinese woman carefully hook up fish after fish by the gills in search of the best one. You can tell that freshness is valued highly in Cantonese cuisine.

Even if it's just for an hour or two, exploring Vancouver's ethnic areas with an empty basket is a huge adventure — that is, if you're ready to take a few chances. Unidentifiable greens, peculiar sauces, strange-looking meats — how do you know what they taste like or how to use them? The trick is to ask. Ask the person beside you. Ask whoever's behind the cash register. Ask the granny behind you in the lineup. If you're shy, you'll never find out.

Experimenting with new foods is like getting off a plane and finding yourself in a new country. You can stick with the tried and true...or you can step off the beaten track with gusto and courage.

Asian Ingredients

Immigrants from around the Pacific Rim have brought a dazzling array of their native dishes to Vancouver: Malaysian curries; Singapore noodles; incendiary Korean dishes. We love 'em all. When your menu is pan-Asian, here are some stores that reliably come up with the goods.

NORTH VANCOUVER:

Pepperpot Food & Spice Company
Lonsdale Quay Market • 986-1877
Fish straight from the ocean, good butchers, great produce. One swing through Lonsdale Quay Market can set you up with pretty well everything you need for an Asian supper. Pepperpot is the place for fresh screwpine leaves, galangal, tamarind and lemongrass, as well as an impressive selection of hot sauces both Asian and non-Asian.

VANCOUVER:

Bonanza Market
265 East Hastings St. • 688-6824
Aptly named, the Bonanza Market bursts at the seams with hard-to-find ingredients. It's a favourite haunt of many chefs around town for Thai basil, kaffir lime leaves, turmeric and galangal, all sparklingly fresh. In the cooler you may also come across candle nuts and laksa leaves (otherwise known as Vietnamese mint, but not, in fact, part of the mint family). Laksa leaves are essential to Malaysian laksa but often used in Vietnamese salads or with spring rolls. On the shelves are legions of curry pastes, Knorr tamarind soup base, Hawaiian-made Korean kim chee mix, shrimp sauce from Singapore and a huge variety of spring roll skins, round and square, in different sizes. Feel peckish? Check out the freshly made Vietnamese sandwiches at the back of the store.

Kimchee

What dill pickles are to deli cuisine, kimchee is to Korean food. In Vancouver we mainly know this ubiquitous pickle — often made from daikon or cucumbers, usually from Chinese cabbage — as a mind-blowing melange heady with garlic and cayenne. In Korea, versions differ by region. Near the ocean, picklers add fish and tiny fermented shrimp. In the north where it's colder, they ladle on the chilis. Addictive and a cinch to make, kimchee is basically chopped vegetables left to mature at room temperature in salt water with ginger, garlic and cayenne. When it tastes sour enough, store in the fridge. Find ready-made versions at Korean grocery stores (particularly the Kimchee Oriental Deli at 1022 Kingsway) or, on the West Side, try the brutally fiery version sold at On Broadway Specialty Foods.

On Broadway Specialty Foods
2696 West Broadway • 738-0326
This ultimate corner store is packed with bulk foods and a huge selection of Chinese, Japanese, Korean, Indian and other ingredients. The best source of ethnic ingredients and bulk foods west of Main, period. A bewildering choice of rice spans black Thai, sweet gluten and a wild rice mix. Scads of grains as well as black bean powder, house-made kimchee, Hon's potstickers, Thai curry pastes and Knorr Tom Yam stock cubes, indispensable for hot and sour soups. They also carry non-Asian foods such as Callebaut chocolate in bulk, as well as bargain cheeses and cold cuts.

South China Seas Trading Company
Granville Island Public Market • 681-5402
If you don't want to trek to Chinatown, this store carries a terrific selection of condiments (especially hot sauces) and fresh Asian herbs and vegetables. Usually you'll find tiny Thai eggplants, Thai basil, kaffir limes and galangal, not to mention spices, different rices, fresh noodles, Indian and Thai curry pastes and cookbooks. Free recipe cards, too.

Sunrise Market
300 Powell St. • 685-8019
Japanese pickles, noodles galore (both fresh and dried), Malaysian curry mixes, Singapore curry sauce. Meats and soy products at the back. An enormous selection of vegetables and fruits out front.

World of Rice
126 Gore St. • 683-7833
Chinese rice, Japanese rice and rice from Thailand — about two dozen kinds, from 8.8 kg bags of Double Happiness Sweet Rice to 20 kg sacks of Golden Medal Fragrant Rice. Line up at the wicket, say what you want, pay for it, then take the receipt to the warehouse to pick up your order. But that's only part of what you'll find at Rice World, which, judging by the Rice Noodle Price Index, has some of the lowest prices in Chinatown. Cakes of brown sugar, soy sauces, canned basil-seed drink — root through the cartons and shelves

and you'll find all manner of basic goodies including addictive sweet-sticky-hot Chili Sauce for Chicken.

Australian

Those from the Land of Oz speak wistfully of the foods of their homeland: tart and tangy red quandongs (or desert peaches), the barramundi fish and the witchetty grub. Sorry, you won't find any of those in Vancouver — but you can track down a few tastes of home at the following stores.

NEW WESTMINSTER:
Galloway's Specialty Foods
702B 6th Ave. • 526-7525
(see also: Richmond; Vancouver)
Vegemite!

RICHMOND:
Galloway's Cash and Carry
9851 Van Horne Way • 270-6363
(see also: New Westminster; Vancouver)

VANCOUVER:
Galloway's Specialty Foods
904 Davie St. • 685-7927
Pacific Centre • 669-3036
(see also: New Westminster; Richmond)

Meinhardt Fine Foods
3002 Granville St. • 732-4405
Vegemite and Tasmanian Leatherwood Honey.

British

Given the number of Brits who now call Vancouver "home" (or "'ome" if they're from certain parts of London), it's not surprising that British groceries are fairly easy to find.

ABBOTSFORD:
Clayburn Village Store
34810 Clayburn Rd. • 853-4020
Someone once wrote, "Behind the British stiff upper

Kitchen Capers

Caperberries, which look like large capers, are the fruit of the caper shrub. (Regular capers are its flower buds). Serve in salads or as a garnish.

lip hang some of the most rotten teeth in the world." Perhaps this is because all true Brits love their sweeties. Worth a drive is the Clayburn Village Store, built in 1912 and restored and run by the Haber family. Here's what you'll find: bonbons, aniseed balls, pear drops, Mintos, sherbet lemons, coconut mushrooms, wine gums, licorice allsorts, Murray Mints ("the too-good-to-hurry mints") as well as Pontefract cakes and chocolate eclairs. How about a nice spot of tea? Scones with jam and cream, pies and desserts made from local berries are on the menu. Ploughman's lunches, too, with (usually) English cheeses.

COQUITLAM:
Marks & Spencer
Coquitlam Centre • 464-1832
(see also: Richmond, Surrey, Vancouver, West Vancouver)
A popular haunt for biscuits, crisps and sweets (that's cookies, chips and candy to non-Brits), marvellous jams, marmalades and lemon curd, lots of packaged cakes for afternoon tea, and frozen pre-made dishes.

NORTH VANCOUVER:
The British Butcher Shoppe
711 Queensbury • 985-2444
Robert Goodrick makes about 50 different types of sausage, and some of his sausage recipes date back to the 1700s. Oxford, Cambridge, Birmingham, Manchester, Irish, Lincolnshire — his list of varieties sounds like a tour around the U.K. The English Breakfast is the most popular. All Goodrick's sausages are chemical-free and made with fresh pork from Chilliwack. Christmas time, he sells chipolatas. Goodrick is also famous for his hams. He's the only butcher in North America, he says, to make true English gammon: pork that is cured and dried but not smoked — a process that takes two to five weeks. Legs of pork can be turned into cold-smoked ham or "boiled ham" as it's known back home. Sliced, it's highly popular, or you can order a "green ham" to cook yourself. Other familiar treats include jellied tongue, Melton Mowbray pies from Vancouver Island, and Goodrick's own meat pies: steak and kidney, steak

and mushroom, chicken or steak, each about five inches across, weighing up to a pound and filled with nothing but meat (no vegetables). The shop also stocks British groceries such as Penguins (chocolate-covered biscuits), tinned mushy peas, Lucozade (a vivid yellow glucose drink), Chivers Jellies (jellos in Canada) and – a huge seller – Robertson's Lemon Barley Water.

RICHMOND:
Marks & Spencer
Lansdowne Park Shopping Centre • 278-7796
(see also: Coquitlam, Surrey, Vancouver, West Vancouver)

Ray and Mary's British Home
3986 Moncton St. • 274-2261
Despite the postal address, this corner of the old country is actually in Steveston. So you can lunch on fish and chips nearby, then go in and stock up on meat pies, sausage rolls, black pudding, Ayrshire bacon, British sweets (candies), dandelion and burdock pop, Tizer – another favourite British beverage – and Devonshire clotted cream.

SURREY:
Marks & Spencer
Guildford Town Centre • 584-1042
(see also: Coquitlam, Richmond, Vancouver, West Vancouver)

VANCOUVER:
Chinatown
Strange but true: a tour of the grocery stores on Pender, Gore and Keefer Streets will often uncover favourite British treats, such as Rowntree's Fruit Gums and Robertson's Jelly Powder, which have circumnavigated the world (almost), travelling from London to the ex-colony of Hong Kong and across the ocean to Vancouver.

The House of McLaren
125-131 Water St. • 681-5442
Ex-Brits pining for Polo Mints, Sherbet Fountains and Cadbury's Flake bars will find them here.

Marks & Spencer
Oakridge Centre • 266-3015
1056 Robson St. • 689-7535
(see also: Coquitlam, Richmond, Surrey, West Vancouver)

Marks & Spencer
Park Royal Shopping Centre • 925-1104
(see also: Coquitlam, Richmond, Surrey, Vancouver)

Chinese

Bok choy, fresh bean sprouts and black bean sauce are now staples in most supermarkets – Canadian Superstore carries an exceptionally broad range. For more obscure ingredients, Chinatown is the place to look. Chances are you'll discover what you're looking for on East Pender or Keefer Streets between Main and Gore. For a cornucopia of live fish, meats, vegetables and sauces under one roof, try:

BURNABY:
T & T Supermarket
147-4800 Kingsway • 436-4881

RICHMOND:
T & T Supermarket
8181 Cambie Rd. • 279-1818

VANCOUVER:
T & T Supermarket
179 Keefer Place • 899-8836
100-2800 East 1st Ave. • 254-9668

West Enders can find barbecue pork, plus duck, chicken, roast pork and other meats at:
Hon's Wun-Tun House
1339 Robson St. • 685-0871

West Siders can try:
Ihua Bakery
3522 West 41st Ave. • 261-0189
Taiwanese breads, BBQ buns and steamed buns.

Daikon

Apart from bok choy and sui chow, the Asian vegetable you'll see around most often is the Japanese radish — better known as daikon, which means "great root." Pickled (food colouring turns it yellow), it often shows up in sushi rolls. Raw and grated, it pleasantly complements sashimi. Shredded it's a crunchy addition to salads, especially in sunomono or, more Western-style, paired with crisp apples. In Korea, daikon is made into soup and eaten for breakfast. You can stew it, too. Either way, all you do is peel it, use what you need and store what's left in the crisper drawer.

Produce City Plus
3277 Cambie St. • 872-7771
BBQ meats and produce.

Southland Farm Market
3012 West 41st Ave. • 264-0112
A wide selection of Asian and Western produce.

Star Asian Food Centre
2053 West 41st Ave. • 263-2892
BBQ meats and produce (take-out food too).

Treasure World Market
2105 West 37th Ave • 266-6081/266-6093
Canned, dried foods, pickles, fresh produce – some of it locally grown. BBQ chicken and pork. Sushi ingredients.

French

For French pâtés, jams and nut oils, your best bets are Lesley Stowe Fine Foods (1780 West 3rd Ave., 731-3663) or Meinhardt Fine Foods (3002 Granville St., 732-4405). For a wistful reminder of that patisserie on the Left Bank or that boulangerie in Bordeaux, it's either a ticket to Paris or a bus-ride to one of the following:

NORTH VANCOUVER
La Baguette et L'Echalotte
Lonsdale Quay • 987-0227
(see also: Vancouver)
Famous for their baguettes, rustic "peasant-style" breads and half-cooked breads you can bake at home and pull fresh from the oven. Check out the magnificent pastries too. The Granville Island outlet also carries pâtés, cornichons and other French staples.

VANCOUVER:
La Baguette et L'Echalotte
1680 Johnston, Granville Island • 684-1351
(see also: North Vancouver)

Fortune Cookies
According to Judith Lane, a corporate concierge, the best fortune cookies come from the New Apple Farm Market (2856 West Broadway, 739-6882). Each package is different from the next.

Fresh bread at
La Baguette et L'Echalotte

81

La Boulangerie
845 Burrard St. · 682-4568
Croissants and French breads made in the kitchens of the Sutton Place Hotel next door.

Boulangerie La Parisienne
1076 Mainland St. · 684-2499
Baguettes, croissants, both plain and filled, black or green olive bread, plus classic French pastries.

Pacific Institute of Culinary Arts
1505 West 2nd Ave. · 734-4488
Students at this culinary school produce extremely good baguettes and croissants which are sold from a tiny bakeshop.

Patisserie Bordeaux
3675 West 10th Ave. · 731-6551
Baguettes, épis, croissants and French treats such as éclairs, gateau St. Honoré, croquembouche and millefeuilles.

Patisserie Lebeau
1660 Cypress St. · 731-3258
Olivier Lebeau trained for four years in his native Belgium. His belief? "We eat with the eye first," which explains why each of his pastries is a miniature work of art. His éclairs and pies look almost too beautiful to eat. Popular with regulars are the individual mousses made from authentic European ingredients: mango, dark chocolate, cassis-framboise. Sundays he makes ethereal Brussels which he serves with fresh fruit and whipping cream in the café section of his patisserie. Lebeau also bakes a small selection of breads.

German

Some big lusty sausages, a loaf of rye, a jar of pungent, lip-smacking mustard: German cooking is famous for its hearty rib-sticking flavours. If this kind of food is new to you, keep an open mind, grab an empty basket and plan a trip to some of these stores.

LANGLEY:

P & G Sausage

108-20551 Langley Bypass • 533-1990

Weisswurst, bratwurst, beer smokies, European wieners and schinken (a cured, air-dried and smoked meat similar to prosciutto).

VANCOUVER:

Bavarian Bakery & Delicatessen

6471 Victoria Dr. • 325-5200

Light rye, dark rye, sour rye, old country rye, Black Forest Cake and apple strudel.

Fraserview Sausage & Delicatessen

6579 Fraser St. • 325-1814

Sausages, obviously. Cheeses such as harzer, esrom, German butter cheese and tilsit, Tchibo coffee, Bahlsen cookies, sauerkraut, dumpling mixes – all from Germany. Health products, magazines and newspapers too.

Freybe Sausage

716 East Hastings St. • 255-6922

Weiners, bratwurst, landjaeger, liver sausage and more.

Polonia Sausage House

2434 East Hastings St. • 251-2239

Close to 50 varieties of fresh and dried sausages made on the spot. They're best known for their ham-garlic sausage, Ukranian sausage and European style ham. Fresh meat is sold here too.

WEST VANCOUVER:

Black Forest Delicatessen

Park Royal South • 926-3462

Jurgen Burkhardt is a master butcher, sausage maker and a chef by trade – a true artisan. Weisswurst, knackwurst, smoked meats, weiners, they're all exceptional. Try the schinkenspeck (pork that's been dry-cured and smoked) or slightly leaner baurnschinken. Customers come here especially for baurnbrot (farmer's bread) and steinofenbrot (stone oven bread). Home-baked German pretzels too.

Kohlrabi

White, purple or green, resembling a turnip with skin problems or — let's be kinder — a sputnik, the kohlrabi doesn't win any ribbons in the looks department. A byblow of the cabbage family, it's basically a swollen stem (and those curious nubs are where its leaves used to be). Firm and plump is better than wrinkled, small means tender, and anything larger than a golf ball needs to be peeled. Tasting turnip-like but sweeter, raw kohlrabi is pleasantly crisp, making it an oddball but flavourful coleslaw ingredient. Sliced or julienned, it can be steamed until tender-crisp as a side veggie, or added in chunks to cold-weather casseroles.

Greek

If your parents or grandparents originally came from the land of Homer, chances are high that they settled in Kitsilano. If you wander along the back laneways in summer you may occasionally catch a whiff of roast lamb — a whole roast lamb — from a barbecue.

BURNABY:

Zorba's Bakery & Foods
7173 Buller Ave. • 439-7731
Olives, feta, olive oil, dolmades, pita bread and spinach dip, plus tzatsiki, homous, spinach-and-cheese pies, all homemade. Alot of their goods go to supermarkets. You can buy direct (for much less).

VANCOUVER:

Kefalonia Mediterranean Fine Foods
Yorkville Market, 1855 West 1st Ave. • 739-4448
Terrific olives from Greece, Morocco and France as well as fetas, olive oil and Greek honey and jam.

Minerva Mediterranean Deli
3207 West Broadway • 733-3954
Olives, feta cheese and olive oil are only the start. The big draw here is the food made fresh every day by Dennis Notaris and Georgia Georgiopoulos. Tzatsiki, eggplant dip, taramasolata, wonderful homous, dolmades, spinach pies. Take it home and you have a party, especially if you pick up some tapes of Greek music. Minerva sells those too.

Parthenon Supermarket
3080 West Broadway • 733-4191
A not-just-Greek chorus of wailing broke over the West Side the night the Parthenon burnt down in January 1998. The community pleaded and six months later the store was back, just a block west of the original location. Olive aficionados can zero

Olives at Parthenon Supermarket

in on the Sicilian spiced kind, heady with lemon peel and chilies, or Moroccan dry, or jumbo green and more. Gazillions of cheeses and cold cuts include a head-spinning choice of fetas and feta crumbs at bargain prices. Among other stops on this cook's world tour are fig jam from Egypt, authentic Dijon mustard and canned beans, lentils and chickpeas. Check the freezer case for New Zealand lamb legs.

Indian

You'll swear off those expensive little jars forever once you've costed out cumin and coriander here in the heart of the Punjabi market where turnover is swift and freshness guaranteed. Scoop up some cinnamon bark (which doesn't look at all like the kind you see in Western stores), sweet-smelling cardamom, vivid yellow turmeric and mustard seeds and you'll have the basics. To get your tongue in training, fill a bag with spicy Indian snacks (they look like "Nuts 'n' Bolts") to eat as you go.

Check out the kitchen equipment, too. Rolling pins used for chapatis (unlike North American ones, where the pin moves, you have to do the hard work). You'll see tiffin carriers — tall stacked stainless steel containers, the equivalent of a lunch box. The *kadai* looks like a wok and is used for samosas and pakoras. The *thava* is a heavy cast iron griddle meant for chapatis, which then go on a wire grid called a roti fluffer which is placed over the burner.

Goldmines of eggplants, spices, chutneys, rice and everything else from the Indian sub-continent, these stores are all within a block of one another.

Chef's Secret
The basmati rice you'll find served at Vij's is a brand called Tilda.

VANCOUVER:
All India Foods
6517 Main St. • 324-1686

JB Foods
6607 Main St. • 321-0224

Singh Foods
6684 Main St. • 327-4911

International

DELTA:

Jentash Marketing
8188 River Way · 940-8586
Strictly wholesale, except for their annual Open House which is usually held in November and open to the public. Prices are less than retail. Thousands of products from all over the world, mostly imported. Sable & Rosenfeld antipasto, Evian water, the Asian Home Gourmet line.

LANGLEY:

Ingredients Etc.
302-20771 Langley Bypass · 533-0747
Parmigiana and other cheeses, curries, chutneys, Thai ingredients, flavoured and other oils, spices and different flours. Black olive pesto, artichoke dip, different garlic butters and salsas, all made in-house, as well as homemade salad dressing and pastas. Tons of teas and coffees.

NEW WESTMINSTER:

Galloway's Specialty Foods
702B 6th Ave. · 526-7525
(see also: Richmond; Vancouver)
Galloway's has been around since the 1930s and it's still the store many people think of first when it's time to do Christmas baking. Dried or crystallized fruits, mincemeat and almonds are only the start. When it's time to replenish your herb shelf or pantry, one stop here will do it. Spices, flours, beans, chutneys, European mustards, even rarities like candied violets — they carry around 8,000 different items. The cash and carry warehouse provides 15 percent discount.

RICHMOND:

Galloway's Cash and Carry
9851 Van Horne Way · 270-6363
(see also: New Westminster; Vancouver)

VANCOUVER:

Galloway's Specialty Foods

African Bread
For take-out injera, the tangy flat bread of Ethiopia, go to Nyala African Hotspot, 2930 West 4th Ave., 731-7899.

904 Davie St. • 685-7927
Pacific Centre • 669-3036
(see also: New Westminster; Richmond)

Gourmet Warehouse
1856 Pandora St. • 255-5119
Caren McSherry sells products from around the world at deep discounts. Unusual pastas, flavoured oils from California, sun-dried tomatoes, foie gras, real Russian caviar, Dijon mustards, dried fruits from the Okanagan, estate olive oils, preserved fruits from Italy, La Mancha saffron from Spain, and sea salt from France and Portugal. Some quantities are restaurant-sized so you may want to chip in with a friend.

Lesley Stowe Fine Foods
1780 West 3rd Ave. • 731-3663
Silver Palate condiments from the U.S., delicacies from France, pastas from Italy, preserves, jams, oils (it's possible to drop some serious money here). Regulars zero in on the house brand four-seed crisps (the

Lesley Stowe Fine Foods

ultimate form of melba toast), Parmesan crisps and honey-garlic croutons. Duck confit at Christmas. Exceptional cheeses in La Fromagerie. Magazines and cookbooks too.

Meinhardt Fine Foods
3002 Granville St. • 732-4405
A splendid array of products from North America and Europe. Cheeses from France, England and Italy. From France come cornichons, dried mushrooms and the Hediard line of rice, pickles, jams and chocolate. From Italy comes Lamborghini pasta. Also there for picking: caviar, specialty olives, specialty oils, including olive oils from Italy, California, France, Portugal and Greece. Local products include Mezza Luna pasta, Saltspring Island goat cheese and chocolates from Over the Moon and Rogers'. Meinhardt's carries truffles once in a while but they also stock milk and bread as well.

Italian

While Commercial Drive still remains Little Italy in the eyes of Vancouverites, many Italians have moved east and set up shop in North Burnaby. Still, a Saturday morning ramble down The Drive or along East Hastings will net you all kinds of wonderful edibles. Go around Easter and you'll find chocolate eggs wrapped in big puffs of shiny metallic paper. Come December you can pick up the perfect gift for everyone on your list — the fruit-studded bread called "panettone."

BURNABY:

Bianca-Maria Italian Foods
2469 East Hastings St. • 253-9626
Originally owned by a Bianca and a Maria, this store now belongs to Susan Renzullo (her husband is a cousin of Carmelo Renzullo, who owns Renzullo Food Market). Here you can pick up arugula paste — "add a little bit of paste to garlic and onions for a pasta sauce," says Susan Renzullo, "then garnish with fresh arugula" — as well as sun-dried tomato paste, pine nuts, dried fruits and the ingredients for tiramisu: the

---

Italian for Beginners

Porcini = "little piglets," which more or less describes the shape of these deeply-flavoured fungi.
Bocconcini = "little mouthfuls" of mozzarella.
Zucchini = "little squash" (which is when they're at their tastiest).
Panettone = "big bread."

ladyfinger biscuits called savoiardi, the mascarpone and the chocolate powder. Among the baking necessities sold here are vanilla powder; baking powder for gnocchi; lemon, almond and rum extracts from Germany for flavouring cakes; and anise flavouring to make the flat cookies called pizzelle — and the machine to make them too. Phew! Note: Try to go there when the store isn't busy. Susan Renzullo is a goldmine of recipes.

Cioffi's Meat Market and Deli
4156 East Hastings St. • 291-9373
Easily worth a trip across town for the fresh poultry and Italian sausages. Awesome veal shank for osso buco.

Pasticceria Italia
2828 East Hastings St. • 251-6800
Known as "the Italian pastry shop," and owned by Lena and Mario Toteza, this is the source of the best cannoli in the city according to one Italian chef (maybe because the Totezas make their own cannoli shells). No preservatives, no animals fats, real eggs. Irresistible sfogliatelle (flaky, ricotta-rich pastries). Regulars come for the baba au rhum, or "peaches" — pastries filled with vanilla or chocolate cream and a whole almond, and then drizzled with rum.

Ugo and Joe's Lucky Meats
2404 East Hastings St. • 253-6844
When in Rome, no problem. When not, Ugo and Joe's is a good bet for huge variety and magnifico home-made sausage.

VANCOUVER:
A Bosa and Company Ltd.
562 Victoria Dr. • 253-5578/253-5656
There are deals galore in this East Side favourite. Pastas, whole salamis, giant chunks of real Parmigiana, coffees, bottled water and attractive plates and platters from Italy.

European Meat Market
540 Victoria Dr. • 254-5923

Italian Source
Maria Tommasini Robertson of Vita e Vino, the Italian wine society, recommends the "really good sausage" at Zarah's on Granville Island.

Try the veal roast rolled with ham, prosciutto, cheeses and spices; also recommended: the coiled cheese sausage.

Ferrazzano Italian Deli
795 West 16th Ave. • 873-8604
Balsamic vinegar, De Cecco pasta, fresh bocconcini, pancetta, all in a non-Italian neighbourhood. Sandwiches too, such as salami and provolone or ham and caciocavallo.

La Grotta del Formaggio
1791 Commercial Dr. • 255-3911
Parmigiana, Friulano, Asiago, pecorino, provolone, caciocavallo, buffalo milk mozzarella, mascarpone — basically, if it's an Italian cheese it's here. Also here: pasta, including spelt varieties, olive oils, all kinds of balsamic vinegar — some 50 years old. You can also pick up extra virgin truffle oil, pesto and bottarga di tonno — tuna roe which is grated to add to pasta, chickpea flour, dried chestnuts and chestnut flour to make traditional cakes and pastries.

Italian Canadian Delicatessen
4355 Dunbar St. • 228-8615
Though leaning towards international foods these days, this West Side deli is still a reliable source for pasta, bocconcini, prosciutto, salamis, sausage, polenta and dried mushrooms.

J, N & Z Deli Smoked Meats
1729 Commercial Dr. • 251-4144
Smoked and cured sausages, pork loin, pepperoni, kolbasa and more are all made on the premises with no nitrates or preservatives. Spicy or mild, the sausage from central Serbia called sremske is a best seller. Fresh pork and veal is sold on Fridays and Saturdays.

Renzullo Food Market
1370 Nanaimo St. • 255-9655
Carmelo Renzullo has imported Italian specialty foods since 1964. Olive oils, balsamic vinegars, pastas, cheeses — one Vancouver chef comments, "Good prices on cheeses, and an excellent price on Parmesan"

Buffalo Milk Mozzarella
The kind served at Il Giardino and Villa del Lupo can be found at La Grotta del Formaggio (1791 Commercial Drive, 255-3911). It arrives from Italy every second week.

— Italian prosciutto, and chinotti, a soft drink made with mineral water and herbs. Sweet tooths can work their way through the Balocco line of cookies. A must at Christmas are the Motta or Alemagna brand panettone and the pantoro, which is like an Italian sponge-cake. At Easter, Renzullo's carries the dove-shaped colomba bread.

Santa Barbara Market
1322 Commercial Dr. • 253-1941
Terrific for cold cuts, fresh and dried sausages, cheeses and olive oil, all at great prices. More pasta varieties than you dreamed possible, including the Lifesaver-shaped anelli Siciliani. Sparkling mineral water from Italy, boneless baccala, fresh basil, bulk olives — you can race through your shopping list here and still have change for a cappuccino up the street. A zoo on Saturdays; shop mid-week if you can.

Santa Barbara Market

Scardillo Grocery
2580 East Hastings St. • 254-4611
Angela and Ben Scardillo are famous in the Italian community for their home-made cheeses. Bocconcini, ricotta, mozzarella and a mild variety called scamozza.

Tosi Italian Food Import Company
624 Main St. • 681-5740
Like an old-fashioned country store inside, and completely lost in the middle of Chinatown. Ring the bell to be let in. Extraordinary deals on amaretti cookies, real Parmigiana, dried porcini, pasta and the arborio rice you need to make authentic risotto. If you garden, pick up some seeds to grow a variety of real Italian greens. Home winemakers can buy California grape juice by the 23-litre bucket to make their own chenin blanc, zinfandel, cabernet and other varieties.

Vito's Pastry Shop
1748 Commercial Dr. • 251-6650
Here's the place to buy pizza dough, cream horns and cannoli. Feeding the gang? Pick up a big oval loaf with a hole in the middle — it's called "canat" in the Puglia region, which is where baker Vito Salterio comes from.

WEST VANCOUVER:
Scaldaferri's
2409 Marine Dr. • 922-8887
Here's where West Vancouverites head when they need a fix of fresh bocconcini or a package of amaretti. Superb selection of olive oils from Sicily, Israel and Greece, organic and unfiltered. Also: unusual cheeses such as aged provolone.

Japanese

Rice for making sushi, nori for wrapping rolls and wasabi for adding a touch of fire inside — all are much easier to find than they used to be. So are soba noodles and even frozen tuna for homemade sashimi. For these and other Japanese groceries, the following stores are your best bets.

COQUITLAM:
Fujiya Japanese Foods
203-403 North Rd. • 931-3713
(see also: Richmond; Vancouver)

RICHMOND:
Fujiya Japanese Foods
100-8211 Westminster Hwy. • 270-3715
(see also: Coquitlam; Vancouver)

VANCOUVER:
Fujiya Japanese Foods
912 Clark Dr. • 251-3711
(see also: Coquitlam; Richmond)

Kay's Seafood
338 Powell Street • 684-4012
Some fresh, but mostly frozen seafood for sushi.

Jewish

Vancouver has yet to equal the number of delis or bakeries you'll find in Montreal or New York – but it's getting there...

RICHMOND:
Siegel's Bagels
5671 No. 3 Rd. • 821-0151
As close to traditional Montreal-style bagels as you'll find this side of the Rockies. To my mind (as a former Montrealer) the best in the city.

VANCOUVER:
Kaplan's Deli Restaurant and Bakery
5775 Oak St. • 263-2625
Real deli food, real deli atmosphere. Booths, giant servings and a vast menu (over 250 items) of authentic dishes. Smoked meat comes from Montreal twice a week. Lox is tender as sashimi, and smoked to order. "Croissants" here are made of rich "cinnamon bun" dough and crunchy with bits of walnut. People come from far and wide for owner Serge Haber's karnatzlach (a Romanian dish of spicy ground beef) and the chopped liver sweet with onion. Marinated herring, pickled smoked tongue, dill pickles made the old-fashioned way, Winnipeg goldeye, a little of this, a little of that. Don't forget the poppy seed cookies or the kichles ("nothings") – little twists of sugar-sprinkled pastry.

Omnitsky Kosher
5866 Cambie St. • 321-1818
Known for kosher delicatessen foods: corned beef, smoked meat, pastrami, hot dogs, chicken hot dogs, beef hot dogs, turkey, beef and chicken salami, all made from scratch at their own commissary 20 minutes away. Omnitsy's other claim to fame is their coleslaw, which is made from an 80-year-old recipe.

Sabra's Kosher Bakery and Deli
3844 Oak St. • 733-4912
Everything is kosher: cabbage rolls, stuffed eggplant, potato latkes, falafel and a minimum of 13 different

Kosher Salt
This special salt can be found at Meinhardt Fine Foods.

salads. Also: breads, cakes, pastries and bagels. Popular for falafels. Everything is made by owner Simon Kahlon.

Solly's Bagelry
189 East 28th Ave. • 872-1821
2873 West Broadway • 738-2121
Authentic bagels and unquestionably and irrefutably the best cinnamon buns in the city: huge, buttery, sinful. Also superb knishes and blintzes, and other ways to add to your waistline. (See sidebar, page 250.)

Mexican

BURNABY:
La Salza Mexican Products
4140 East Hastings St. • 299-8983
Everything you need to make your own Mexican food, plus pozole, menudo and tamales to take out.

NORTH VANCOUVER:
Jalisco Mexican Foods
Lonsdale Quay Market • 986-6344
Mexican cinnamon and piloncillo (pure sugar-cane juice formed into a cone) as well as ancho, pasilla, guajillo and other peppers sold loose. Salsas, beans, Mexican chocolate and Mexican jelly desserts.

VANCOUVER:
Que Pasa Mexican Foods
1647 West 5th Ave. • 730-5449
A shelf of hot sauces includes the three-alarmer El Yucateco, which is made from habaneros and, according to staff, is the most volcanic of all sauces. Sampling allowed. Check out the blue cornmeal and the green sausages — chorizo verde seasoned with fresh chilis and cilantro. Mulato, pasilla, ancho and other chilis sold loose from wicker baskets. Masa harina for making your own tortillas.

Cool Middle Eastern starter
Super-thin radish slices, a chunk of feta and coarsely chopped parsley: eat with wedges of pita bread.

Middle Eastern

Like all ethnic cuisines, once you've stocked your cupboard with the basic ingredients, making authentic Middle Eastern treats is easy.

Couscous, the essential grain, is made from semolina and — if you don't own a couscousiere (few people do) — can be made in a steel colander or steamer over the simmering lamb or chicken stew (the tagine). ("Couscous" also refers to the dish itself.) Harissa is a lively chili-based relish. Indonesian sambal oelek is a reasonable stand-in. Preserved lemons add zing. Most of Vancouver's Iranian food stores are concentrated on the North Shore, an area popular with people from Iran because its setting reminds them of Teheran.

Persian Snack

An authentic way to enjoy Iranian lavash flatbread is to spread it with creamy feta cheese or wrap it around chunks of chicken cooked kebab style.

NORTH VANCOUVER:

Golestan Bakery
1554 Lonsdale Ave. • 990-7767
Persian breads, such as lavash and barbary, and pastries. Also known for wedding cakes.

Iransuper
987 Marine Dr. • 987-0987
Preserved lemons, olives from all around the Mediterranean, feta cheeses of all kinds (including a double cream version), spices galore, including pre-mixed kebab spice. All in all, this store has one of the best selections of Iranian foods around.

Meat Shop & Deli
1346 Lonsdale Ave. • 983-2020
3026 Edgemont Blvd. • 983-2227
Kabob kobideh mix (like Iranian hamburger) seasoned with salt, pepper, saffron and onion; yogurt sodas; packs of dried parsley; lavash; plus jams from Iran.

Nancy Bakery
1589 Garden Dr. • 987-5544
Excellent source of barbary, lavash and sweet breads.

Pars International Foods
1801 Lonsdale Ave. • 988-3515
This long-established store, in business since 1981, stocks Greek, Italian and East Indian foods as well as Iranian. Just some of the treats you'll find on the shelves are sour grape juice, mint syrup to dilute and make into summer drinks or a dip for romaine lettuce leaves, and Iranian nougat — great with cappuccino.

Rose Bakery
1537 Lonsdale Ave. • 980-2649
Traditional Iranian pastries, including tiny flower-shaped ones made from chickpea flour. Puff pastry twists called papuni; danmarki — Danish pastries Iranian style — rich with coconut and walnuts. Everything is made on the spot.

Yaas Bakery and Supermarket
1528 Lonsdale Ave. • 990-9006
Arrive at the right time and they'll just be pulling their lavash bread, with its join-the-dots lines, out of the oven. You can use it as a wrap, or for thin-crust pizza or burritos. Check out the French, Danish and goat feta, and Persian-style Lighvan cheese, which is the creamiest of the lot. You'll also find pomegranate juice, barberry juice, yogurt cheese and fresh yogurt. Don't miss their Persian ice-cream flavoured with rosewater, pistachios and saffron.

PORT MOODY:
Atlas Plus Food and Dairy
2605 St. John's St. • 936-0100
International foods with a strong Persian focus.

VANCOUVER:
Bulk Food Ring
865 Denman St. • 669-4050
A West End source for nuts, dried fruits, jams, teas, Persian garlic, rose water, pickles and other Persian cuisine necessities.

WEST VANCOUVER:
Mitra's Bulk Food
1451 Clyde Ave. • 913-0660
Pick up a bottle of mint, orange blossom or rose water to drizzle over desserts or mix with water for a refreshing soft drink. Pickles, vine leaves, Persian honey, lavash and cheese, too.

Newfoundland

NEW WESTMINSTER:
Pappy's Newfoundland & Caribbean Market
1003 Royal Ave. • 522-9480
For anyone from the Rock, it's like coming home. There's Chalker's salt beef, salt herring and salt cod steaks. Bidgood's tinned seal meat, partridgeberry jam, Beef Iron & Wine, bakeapple jam and cod tongues. Hardbread, sweetbread, jam jams, spearmint nobs and peanut butter kisses – and a ton more Newfie staples.

Philipino

Goldilocks Bake Shop
1606 West Broadway • 736-7744
Pandesal is a dinner roll, pandesiosa is sweet bread topped with butter and sugar, pandeleche a sweet dinner roll, and monay a milk and egg bread. Mamon is a soft sponge cake available plain or in different flavours – mocha, chocolate, ube (purple yam) – or with cheese, butter and sugar on top.

Portuguese

VANCOUVER:
Union Food Market
810 Union St. • 255-5025
Regulars come here for the corn bread, which is baked fresh every day. Other draws are the wonderful sausage made by the owner's brother in Toronto, bacalhau – salted cod – codfish balls, shrimp croquettes and Portuguese sausage buns. (See page 239.)

Chef's Tip
"If I'm doing something on the barbeque, such as grilling onions, I do two or three times as many. I can use the extra on pasta sauce or in a salad dressed with balsamic vinegar and olive oil. I do the same thing when I boil potatoes — I cook two or three times as much as I need. It's not leftovers, it's thinking like a chef."
— Andrew Skorzewski, Rainforest Café

Portugal Meats & Groceries
2145 Kingsway • 438-3022
Gill Santos brings in bacalhao — a staple on Portuguese menus — all kinds of cheeses, olive oils, olives, dried beans and more. You'll find pork to make pork and clams, spicy chourico and other sausages, fresh fish (or frozen sardines for the real flavour of Portugal) as well as cornbread, chourico buns and pastries.

Russian

BURNABY:
Perestroika Products
8626-A Joffre Ave. • 451-0606
Mark Tsemak makes bread the old-fashioned way, with flour, salt, water and yeast. No fats, no sugar. Try his dark sour rye, multigrain, or his "unbleached, untreated, double density white." All breads weigh a kilo. The Russian-born Tsemak makes strudels from bread batter with blueberries, cherries and ground, cooked poppy seeds. "Finally, dessert with fibre," he says. You can buy kolbassa made to his specifications: lean, stuffed one-bite perogies, vegetarian borscht and piroshki stuffed with broccoli, spinach and potato, or cheese and potato, or potato and onion, or pure lean beef. Hit the sampling counter.

VANCOUVER:
Slavic Delicatessen
2327 East Hastings • 253-1391
Smoked fish, sausages, Russian herring, Russian black and red caviar.

Scandinavian

Buy some Danish salami, a hunk of cheese, a loaf of rye and you have the makings of a picnic or an easy supper. Amongst them, these three stores provide an impressive introduction to the joys of Scandinavian food. What else can you call it but a real smorgasbord?

NORTH VANCOUVER:
Jolly Foods
111 Charles St. • 929-7937

"The Ukrainian and Russian restaurant (3124 Main St., 876-5810) sometimes sells home-made fruit leathers and preserves made from fruit grown in the Okanagan."
— Kerry Moore, *The Province*

Not easy to find but worth the trip if you're looking for rulle polse – pressed cured spiced meat – in pork, veal, lamb and Norwegian sylte fladsk versions, Danish salami or old-style salted beef. Cheeses include Norwegian goat cheese, Esrom and occasionally Norwegian Nokkel. Try the Swedish cured ham, or the roast pork with apples and prunes. Medister – a fresh Danish sausage – is a popular buy here, too. The shelves are crammed with jars of lingonberry sauce, salmon pâté, marinated herring and cucumber or red-cabbage-and-apple salad. The final essential, rye bread, is in the cooler.

RICHMOND:
Ikea
3200 Sweden Way • 273-2051
If you're there buying a sofa anyway, stock up on lingonberry jam, gingerbread cookies, Gammel Dansk bitters, Ramlösa bottled water, Kristall soft drinks, Siljans rye crisps, Norwegian bread and Swedish coffee.

SURREY:
La Charcuterie
8-19080 96th Ave. • 882-0881
(see also: Vancouver)
Six thousand square feet of imported foods.

VANCOUVER:
La Charcuterie
190-3665 Kingsway • 439-3354
About 2,000 items from northern Europe. Gevalia coffee, fish balls and fish cake from Norway, pickled cabbage and beets from Denmark, chocolate from all over. Fruit syrups; mayonnaise; gooseberry, cloudberry and lingonberry jam; dozens of mustards; and "any kind of pickled herring you want," says owner Salam Kahil. He ships goods as far afield as Utah and Oregon. Special mixes let you make your own rye bread or potato dumplings. Scandinavian meats range from salamis to spiced pork roll and homemade liver pâté – Kahil produces 300 pounds a week. Cheese? Danish Blue, Tilsit, Tybo, Danbo, Goudas, Edams and tons of others.

Lunch Scandinavian Style
For rullepulse sandwiches, check Pia's Take-A-Lunch, 605 West Pender St., 684-2737.

Scottish

BURNABY:
Auld Scottish Larder
4022 Hastings St. • 294-6616
Everything is made on the premises, including haggis (all year round), Scotch pies, bridies — pastry-wrapped potatoes, onions and beef — sausages with no additives or preservatives, sausage patties, baked ham. Also: Ayrshire bacon cured on the spot, smoked bacons, Scottish marmalades and black treacle.

VANCOUVER:
Laidlaw's Scottish Bakery
8269 Oak St. • 263-0563
Meat pies with water pastry, bridies — beef and onion with flaky pastry — turnovers, Cornish pasties with shortcrust pastry, shortbread-based apple charlotte, oat cakes, shortbread rounds, Scottish black-crust bread. Also: Aberdeen rowies, plain or with cheese; Scottish bread rolls; black pudding; Ayrshire bacon; potato scones; Eccles cakes.

WEST VANCOUVER:
Peter Black & Sons
Park Royal South • 922-5116
Saucissier Peter Black looks to his native Scotland for inspiration (with the exception of his South African boerewors sausages, in the authentic coil). His Ayrshire beef sausage comes classically shaped or as patties. Also available: sun-dried tomato and turkey, chicken and apple, lamb and mint in regular and spicy.

South African

VANCOUVER:
Marpole Quality Meats
8482 Granville St. • 261-4642
Known for the biltong (beef jerky), boerewors (beef sausage) and dry sausage made by Kenny and Noreen Lok, who come from South Africa. The Loks also stock South African cookies, tea, Pronutro cereal, Ouma rusks, Ceres fruit juices, and Top Deck and Dipped Flake chocolate bars.

Firm Foundations
Suavely smooth or rib-sticking chunky, soup recipes frequently call for stock. Nix those chemically nasty cubes. Making a batch of your own doesn't take time — only time on the stove and a massive pot to hold dem bones. Most supermarkets can ante up chicken necks and back. For heftier stuff, you need to visit a dedicated butcher such as Jackson's Meats for beef or veal bones. For down-to-earth advice on building a stock portfolio, check out *Home Bistro* by Toronto food writer David Kingsmill (Key Porter Books). Cheats head for The Stock Market on Granville Island where chicken, fish, turkey, beef and vegetarian stocks are all priced by the litre.

Demystifying Chinatown

It's 9:30 a.m. in Vancouver's historic Chinatown and the narrow sidewalks are already dense with shoppers. Glossy barbecued ducks hang in rows in shop windows. Stalls are piled high with neatly bundled vegetables, white, purple — and dozens of different shades of green. To a curious food lover, the stores hold hundreds of mysteries, and chef, cookbook writer and consultant Stephen Wong is the ideal person to unravel them.

THE VEGETABLES:

Wong pauses at a produce display piled high with yard-long green beans, choy sum (a yellow-flowered brassica) and fresh lotus root, which looks like a string of pale sausages. He points out pea sprouts: "You can use them in salads," he says. "Pea tops are more mature and better in stir-fries." He indicates a bundle of long stems, pale green at one end, dark green at the other. Tasting like garlic crossed with asparagus, and good in a stir-fry, they are the flowering stalk of the garlic plant. Soya beans resemble small pea pods with pointy ends. You steam them, toss them with salt and eat them as a snack, "shelling" them with your teeth. Purple and green amaranth can be fried with a little bit of garlic, oil and chicken stock.

Produce in Chinatown

THE COOKED MEATS:

A few doors down is the Chinese equivalent of a deli, its window filled with brown and glossy meats. What are they and what do you do with them? The big fat sausages, close to a foot long, can be sliced and eaten with Chinese mustard. "Dried Chinese sausages are called lap chung," explains Wong, "and Chinese bacon is called lap yuk. 'Lap' literally means 'waxed' — they look waxed, but aren't. Most commonly you'd steam these sausages whole over rice, scored so the oil comes out and flavours

BBQ duck

the rice. Add some greens on the side, and you've got a meal."

And that's the point with many Chinese foods. They're very easy to work with. You can also use sausages, says Wong, in a version of egg foo yung. Steam them, slice them, fry them a little. Beat some eggs, chop in some green onions and add that to the pan. Serve the omelette flat or folded. Sounds simple.

Lap yuk (bacon) is especially used in winter in a dish similar to risotto made with glutinous rice. "Fry the rice with the bacon," says Wong, "then add stock and keep frying until the liquid is absorbed. Add soy sauce and chopped green onions."

Butterflied BBQ duck (the flattened kind) is prepared using a northern Chinese method. A whole (i.e. unflattened) BBQ duck is Cantonese and is cured differently: it's a bit sweeter. In either case, you can buy the whole duck, or a half, or a quarter of it. Its most common use is chopped on rice, says Wong, or chopped in fried rice. The BBQ pork next to it can also flavour fried rice or Singapore noodles. Wong's recipe for these can be found in *Five Star Food* (The Vancouver Sun); *HeartSmart™ Chinese Cooking* (Douglas & McIntyre) contains instructions for a low-fat version.

The whole roast pigs that hang in some stores are sold by the piece. Put some roast or BBQ pork in a pan with ginger and onions, and fry it up quickly, Wong instructs. "Mix together some oyster sauce, sesame oil and a little stock and add this to the pan along with some soft or medium tofu cubes. Braise for 15 minutes and toss in some green onions."

THE SEAFOOD:

Next stop is a huge market with a giant freezer filled with fish. "Some of these can be scored, deep-fried and put in a savoury sauce," says Wong. A hot and sour sauce made from plum sauce and chilis is one suggestion. Grass fish is a Chinese freshwater fish, typically used in fish congee. Tilapia can be barbecued Singaporean- or Malaysian-style. Whatever fish you buy frozen, choosing it takes skill, says Wong. What you have to look for is a "glazing" of ice over the surface of the fish. What you don't want is "snow" in the package, a sure sign that some of the moisture in the fish has seeped out and frozen, leaving the texture of the fish more like cotton wool.

"Frozen shrimp are often good buys," he adds. "The quality is generally good. Again, look for sufficient glazing." Green-lipped mussels can be skewered, brushed with sauce and put on the barbecue.

Not far away is a store specializing in fresh fish. In tanks bubbling with

Shopping for seafood

aerated water are live rock cod and flounder. Clams squirt tiny fountains, ink-black mussels glimmer — and information comes thick and fast. "Little blue crabs are eaten for their roe," says Wong. "Local prawns are the way to go, and live prawns are worth the money. Once they're dead, the enzymes quickly cause deterioration. Periwinkles? Just fry them with black bean sauce."

ORGANIC FOODS: Eating Naturally

Reading in the supermarket has always been a popular hobby. Who hasn't indulged in a quick flip through *The National Enquirer* while standing in line? These days, when we read in the store we're often reading labels, looking for information. Specifically, what exactly is in that box of cereal or can of soup we're thinking of buying?

A problem occurs when we get to the meat and produce department. That peach may look luscious and ripe but we can't be sure how many pesticide baths it received. And meat? Who knows if the pig behind that roast or chop was hormonally enhanced. The solution is to choose organic foods.

Vegetables grown without pesticides used to get a bad rap. Derogatory terms like "lumpy" and "ugly" were thrown at them just because they didn't have the cookie-cutter perfection of supermarket tomatoes and apples. Increasingly, we've come to realize that physical perfection — in tomatoes at least — may not be such a good thing. A "Certified Organic" sticker means that produce has to be grown to exacting standards. An "Organic" sticker on meat means that the animal or bird was given only organic feed and no hormones or medications. Organic chickens have more space to run around, too.

Organic and Natural Food Stores

Jams, cheeses, pasta (not to mention dazzlingly fresh organic produce) — you can shop with a clear conscience at any of these places.

ALDERGROVE:
Richmond Specialty Mushrooms
26227 62nd Ave. • 857-8959
Peter Graystone is the source for pink, yellow, brown and white oyster mushrooms, all organic. Capers and Choices are two places to find them, also the East Vancouver Farmers' Market and the Granville Island Public Market on Sundays the rest of the year.

BURNABY:
Mandeville Garden Centre
4746 Southeast Marine Dr. • 434-4111
Organic fruits and vegetables grown on local farms, free-range eggs, natural grocery products.

MAPLE RIDGE:
Roots Natural Organic Foods
22254 Dewdney Trunk Rd. • 467-1822
Organic produce, meats and dairy; most beans, grains and flours are organic. Nothing with preservatives, or artificial colours or flavours, enters the store.

NORTH VANCOUVER:
Queensdale Market
3030 Lonsdale Ave. • 987-6644
Organic produce, meats and groceries.

PORT COQUITLAM:
Poco's Natural Foods
2329 Whyte Ave. • 942-5612
Opened in 1976 by Maaike Hartman and still run by Maaike and Boy, her husband. "People sometimes wonder how we do our inventory," he says, alluding to the huge variety of goods they carry. Among them, certified organic-only fruits and vegetables, and "all the grains we can lay our hands on."

RICHMOND:
Seacoast Produce
12235 No. 1 Rd. • 271-4386
Organic produce and dry goods.

SURREY:

The Organic Grocer

508-7380 King George Hwy. • 501-0116

The largest selection of organic produce outside Vancouver, organic and transitional meats and poultry, organic cheeses and fresh organic milk from Ontario, bulk foods, vitamins, also foods for special needs diets.

TSAWWASSEN:

Earth's Good Harvest

1077 56th St. • 943-3035

This long-time favourite — it's been there since 1979 — only carries produce from farms that are certified organic or "transitional," which means the farmer is actively working to acquire organic certification. Strawberries come from farms that practise integrated pest management (where bugs are used to kill other bugs). The philosophy here is to buy locally as much as possible during the season. Earth's Good Harvest also carries cereals, grains, vitamins and herbs.

VANCOUVER:

Capers

2285 West 4th Ave. • 739-6676

1675 Robson St. • 687-5288

(see also: West Vancouver)

Not cheap, but the produce quality is exceptionally high. Some vegetables, especially the brilliantly-coloured kales, are so beautiful you can hardly bring yourself to eat them. They carry meats, too, as well as a broad range of other organic products.

Choices Market

2627 West 16th Ave. • 736-0009

3493 Cambie St. • 875-0099

Brothers Wayne and Lloyd Lockhart opened the first Choices Market in 1990 and acquired their Cambie Street location in 1998. Produce, meats, gourmet groceries, natural foods — you can do all your shopping here.

Fresh flowers outside Capers

Circling Dawn Organic Foods
1045 Commercial Dr. • 255-2326
Chards, kale, hot peppers: the selection is great here, especially in the fruit department where – depending on the season – you can gather papaya, apple-bananas, red bananas, figs and cherimoyas. Bulk organic foods include Orca beans (yup, they look just like a whale) and blue-green "French" lentils from Saskatchewan.

Westpointe Organic Produce
2839 West Broadway • 736-2839
Locals come here for the great selection of organic greens and berries. Natural foods, too.

Pro Organics
3454 Lougheed Hwy. • 253-6549
Monday through Friday, Pro Organics is a wholesaler that supplies restaurants and home delivery companies. Saturdays from 8:15 a.m. to 2 p.m. you can pick up any produce that hasn't been sold.

Organic Chocolate and Coffee
Yoka's Coffee (3171 West Broadway, 738-0905) stocks at least one and sometimes as many as three organic coffees, as well as Belgian Callebaut organic bulk chocolate, both bittersweet and extra bitter.

Organic produce at
a farmers' market

WEST VANCOUVER:
Capers
2496 Marine Dr. • 925-3316
(see also: Vancouver)

Direct Delivery Companies

If you live near an organic food store, no problem. Making it simple for those who don't is the ever-increasing number of companies that bring bouncily crisp produce — and more — right to your door.

It's a simple system, usually. You leave a cheque in the mailbox (or give them your credit card number). You come home to a big box of salad greens, beets, peaches, basil and whatever else is in season. Most companies let you phone up and find out what you'll be getting. Not knowing what you'll find is part of the fun. There are always surprises under the lid. The majority of companies purchase from B.C. farms first, then, as the season wanes, cast their net wider. Costs vary. Bonuses often include recipes for what's in your box and a weekly newsletter which tells you exactly where that head of lettuce you're holding was grown.

Brian's Fantastic Organics
925-7557
Weekly deliveries to the North Shore and Bowen Island. Flat rate for veggie boxes. Huge choice of grocery products available.

Cascadia Organics
318-3002
Large and small boxes with an even balance of fruits and vegetables or weighted towards one or the other. Delivers to North and West Vancouver. Extensive catalogue of organic dry goods available.

Dancer Vegetarian Foods
942-2315
This company doesn't supply produce but they do offer a wide variety of vegan foods, frozen and non-frozen, from about 35 manufacturers in B.C. Check the list, phone or fax your order, and they'll inform you when they'll be in your neighbourhood (they deliver to most of the Lower Mainland). No minimum order but there is a $3 delivery charge for orders under $100.

Evergreen Organics
871-1132

Small or large boxes delivered Tuesday through Thursday at night to keep produce fresh. Service available in Vancouver, North Vancouver, Deep Cove, Burnaby and New Westminster. Evergreen also offers grocery products such as rice, organic coffee, organic eggs, honey, beans and grains. A weekly newsletter promotes issues regarding social and ecological justice. The company has held public forums and is currently working on an organic building project in Bella Coola.

Go Organic!
988-3332

There are a couple of options here. Buying organic produce and natural foods from the travelling store is one. The truck delivers to the North Shore (Lion's Bay to Deep Cove), Kitsilano and Kerrisdale by appointment. The other is ordering your pasta, nut butters and anything else you need from a list of over 200 items. Go Organic! also makes its own line of prepared foods such as spicy millet salad, pesto and salsa.

Local Organika
222-1977

This is close to buying from a regular store in that Local Organika faxes you a list of organic and natural dry goods, then sends you a weekly updated produce list. You order just what you need by phone, fax or e-mail. Delivery throughout the Lower Mainland.

Organics Delivery BC
985-4394

Weekly delivery of large, small or custom boxes. List of other groceries available – from coffee beans to eggs to cornflakes – included with delivery. There's a discount if you purchase five or more deliveries. Delivery all over the Lower Mainland.

Organics to You
473-5001

This was the city's first, and is now the largest, delivery service. Weekly or bi-weekly delivery; substitutions by request. Bulk veggies available. Contracts local growers directly. Weekly and monthly bulk specials. Delivers throughout the Lower Mainland.

Small Potatoes Urban Delivery
728-7783

If you're on the search for organic, natural and environmentally friendly products of all kinds, check out this Vancouver company. As well as fresh organic produce, they offer everything from soup to nuts — including dog food, cleaning products, bread, milk, even fresh flowers, beer and wine. You can order by phone or log on to www.small-potatoes.com and fill in the e-mail order form.

Urban Organics
255-2004

Small or regular food boxes; 24-hour information line; weekly or bi-weekly delivery. One dollar out of every box goes to Lifeline Outreach Society.

BEVERAGES

Funny word: beverage. Few people actually use it in conversation but how else do you gather all the coffees, teas and juices under one all-encompassing umbrella? "Would you like a cold drink?"; "How about a hot drink?" It just doesn't work in North America where "having a drink" only means the alcoholic kind.

Vancouver is especially rich in places where you can sink a beverage, hot or cold. The city's British roots hang on in the many places that still offer a nice restorative cup of tea. There's Earl Grey, English Breakfast, smoky Lapsang Souchong, not to mention the medicinal teas from Asia and all the fruity, leafy, flowery, herbal teas that first gentled their way into the city in the 1960s.

On the other hand, there's nothing medicinal about coffee except for that first galvanic jolt it gives your heart in the morning. If you're 25 or over, Commercial Drive is probably where you tasted your first real espresso or cappuccino, years before the caffeine tidal wave thundered up from Seattle, leaving behind a Starbucks on every street corner.

Increasingly, you're also likely to find a juice bar almost next door. Aware that what we put into our body affects how it works, we're now downing high-octane, freshly squeezed drinks in place of colas.

And then there are beverages whose flavours conjure up an entire culture: fragrant chai from India; cooling yogurt-based drinks like lassi or doogh, meant to be drunk in a hot climate; bubble teas from Taiwan.

Quenching your thirst has never been easier.

Beans and Scenes
Once upon a time, before
commuter cups existed and
cappuccinos rarely ventured
west of The Drive, coffee-
houses weren't just places you
scuttled into for a long latte
and a stare out the window.
They were Centres of the Arts.
Perhaps the term "coffee-
house poet" rings a bell? Myles
of Beans (7010 Kingsway,
Burnaby, 524-3700) brings
back those long-ago times by
attempting to blend a little
entertainment with your
frothy coffee. Owner David
Myles makes the coffee
house's open stage available to
community or charitable
organizations who want to
stage fundraising or public
awareness events. Musicians,
poets or small theatre groups
can also strut their stuff.

A SIMPLE CUP OF COFFEE...

...Except that a cup of coffee isn't so simple anymore. It's a cappuccino or espresso or double-decaf low-fat latte. Everywhere you look in Vancouver, there's a coffee shop. Some are just fuelling stops, places to screech to a halt for a morning hit of high-octane java, and that's fine. Others are one-of-a-kind.

VANCOUVER:

Blue Parrot Espresso Bar
Granville Island Public Market • 688-5127
Sailboats, water, seagulls, the Blue Parrot has the best view of any coffee bar in Vancouver. Count yourself lucky if you score a table on the weekend.

Calabria Bar
1745 Commercial Dr. • 253-7017
Great for people-watching on a Saturday morning. Famous for its rococo decor and ever-growing statue collection.

Continental Coffee
1806 Commercial Dr. • 255-0712
Settle in on a Saturday morning, outside with your dog or inside with the paper. Coffee is served in handled "drinking jars."

Expressohead Coffee House
1945 Cornwall Ave. • 739-1069
Hip Kits crowd. Happening place that frequently hosts art exhibits.

J J Bean The Coffee Roaster
1904 Powell St. • 254-0161
Granville Island • 685-0613
About 40 different types of beans and blends are roasted fresh every day. Prices are slightly cheaper at the Powell Street location (the "factory outlet").

Melriches Coffee House
1244 Davie St. • 689-5282
Comfy, funky, no attitude. Poetry readings and live music.

Starbucks
Many locations in the Lower Mainland. Bargain hunters will often find beans at Costco.

Torrefazione Coloiera
2206 Commercial Dr. • 254-3723
Twenty kinds of coffee, mostly from South America and roasted in Richmond. Best known for their espresso coloiera which they supply to many restaurants, bars and coffee shops around the city. Extra Bar is a strong but mellow blend that's good in cappuccino.

Torrefazione Italia
2154 West 41st Ave. • 267-1003
Arabica beans roasted the Italian way from a company that originated in Seattle. Perugia is the bestselling blend for espresso; Napoli, a medium to full-bodied dark roast, for drip coffee. Also known for decaf coffees.

Vancouver's Best Coffee
2959 West 4th Ave. • 739-2136
Sam Buonassisi from Italy roasts his Columbian, Ethiopian, Peruvian and Chilean coffee beans, then mixes up his own blends – a job he's been doing for around 25 years. His bestseller (and personal favourite) is the house blend made from five different beans. "Gourmet" is a lighter blend. He also sells French and decaf coffees. Not a huge choice but java addicts come from far and wide to buy them.

Yoka's Coffee
3171 West Broadway • 738-0905
Twenty-plus kinds of Arabica beans are roasted right on the spot (including an organic variety). Many types are available as both medium and dark roasts. Five varieties of green tea, herbs for making tea, including echinacea, and Dutch cocoa powder. The Turkish brass coffee grinders make superb peppermills (see page 250).

Espresso, Starbucks Style
Pulling an espresso looks easy. It's not. Once you've pressed the yellow "start" button, the inky dark coffee must take between 18 and 23 seconds — precisely — to drip into the shot glass. Any more and it's bitter; any less and it's thin. Either way, it goes down the drain and you have to start over.

EYE-OPENING JUICES

Circling Dawn Organic Foods
1045 Commercial Dr. • 255-2326

Right before your eyes, they'll whip up a combination of fruits and veggies, everything totally organic, in 8 oz, 16 oz and 32 oz sizes. Wherever possible, Circling Dawn uses locally grown produce to create what they call "bio-regional" juices such as the Farm Direct blend of carrot, kale, celery and beets. Wheatgrass features in several drinks including the Gingergrass, which separates prettily in the glass: green on top, orange underneath. Calcium booster, refreshers, a plain and simple carrot juice, or a smoothie made with frozen fruit, fresh fruit, or apple juice, or soy or rice milk — you'll leave here bouncing with health.

OTooz The Energie Bar
Royal Centre • 684-0200

Pacific Centre • 684-0202

Waterfront Centre • 683-0216

(see also: West Vancouver)

Orange, pineapple, apple, grapefruit, beet, carrot, celery, grapefruit, cabbage and "green juice" — parsley, cucumber, broccoli, spinach and celery, individually or mixed any way you like. Big hits are the Roadrunner, a blend of fruit and veggie juices, and the B.C. Trio of celery, carrots and beets. Bananas, frozen yogurt or buttermilk can be added to any juice to create the thinking person's milkshake: a smoothie.

WEST VANCOUVER:

OTooz The Energie Bar
1517 Bellevue Ave. • 926-0258

(see also: Vancouver)

Happy Planet Foods

Upbeat name for an upbeat company that knows excellent products and environmental responsibility are not mutually exclusive. Happy Planet specializes in natural fruit juices, many of them organic, which you'll find at natural food stores, cafés and some supermarkets. The certified organic line includes "straight" juices — "Happiest Orange" and "Happiest Apple" — as well as veggie juices, smoothies, "fortified" smoothies and soy-nut-grain shakes in vanilla, chocolate and java flavours. The original line includes coolers as well. This is a company that walks the talk. Juice approaching its expiration date is sent to local food banks and shelters. Delivery trucks are restored vintage dairy trucks converted to run on propane. Fruit and vegetable pressings go to local organic farms for composting — which in turn feeds the carrots and berries that go into Happy Planet juices.

MOO JUICE

ABBOTSFORD:
Birchwood Dairy
1154 Fadden Rd., RR #2 • 857-1315
Come around 3:00 or 3:30 p.m. and you can walk through the barns and watch the cows being milked – there's a petting zoo too – at this working dairy farm. In their little store you'll find all kinds of milk and cream, as well as feta cheese, single yogurt and ice-cream, all made on the farm.

DELTA:
Jersey Farms
4190 46A St. • 946-5311
Milk from four farms is processed here, most notably into spoonable Jersey cream to go on your scones, extra-thick because its double-processed and because it's made from milk from Jersey cows.

VANCOUVER:
Avalon Dairy
5805 Wales • 434-2434
"The cream off the top of the milk" that our grandmothers used to pour over fresh strawberries or peaches can still be found. Look for Avalon Dairy's "standard" milk which is pasteurized but not homogenized. Don't shake the bottle. Just carefully spoon out the cream and drizzle it over your cornflakes. Sold the old-fashioned way in glass bottles, Avalon milk is in the coolers of supermarkets and specialty stores around town. For real nostalgia, buy it direct from the dairy, which has been on the same spot since the early 1900s.

Homemade Lemonade
It looks cool—that pale acid yellow—it sounds cool (think: "chink, chink" of ice cubes). As an icon of summer, a pitcher of fresh lemonade is up there with porch swings and pink gingham. The official Sunkist® recipe calls for the squeezing of a half dozen lemons, sugar to taste, and 4 cups of cold water. Mix sugar and juice, add water and ice cubes. What could be simpler? Others swear by cutting a half dozen lemons in chunks, pouring boiling water over them, then sweetening the mixture to taste before chilling.

TEA

BURNABY:

Murchie's Tea & Coffee

5000 Kingsway • 432-6800

(see also: Surrey; Richmond; Vancouver; West Vancouver)

As Vancouver's grandaddy of beverage purveyors, Murchie's is the name most people think of when they think of tea. How many kinds do they blend? Thousands, says company president and tea blender Gwen Murchie. Quality is tops. The No. 10 (named for No. 10 Downing Street), a blend of green and black teas good for an afternoon cuppa, was recently awarded the title of No. 1 Canadian Beverage. Rare white and yellow teas from China; herb teas and flavoured teas — which include Earl Grey, a tea that is scented with real oil of bergamot; super-strong Assam teas and mild Chinese green teas — you can spend a lifetime experimenting with the various brews. For English folks who like their tea infused from fine, fine black leaves, there's Fanning Tips. For those who like to settle back with a cup and a classic novel, Murchie's developed the Library Blend. The company also sells pure, blended and flavoured coffees, as well as "over-roasted" Vienna, espresso and light French blends for stronger brews. Murchie's may date back to Victorian days but it definitely keeps up with the times. A few years back, the iced-tea mix was given more tea flavour and less sugar. "I felt I improved the blend," says Gwen Murchie. These days, you can also sip black currant, mango and orange spice iced-tea blends. The Burnaby store carries a smaller selection, the Marine Drive location is more beverage-oriented. Either outlet can bring in any blend you want.

RICHMOND:

Murchie's Tea & Coffee
Richmond Centre, 6551 No. 3 Rd. • 278-6024
(see also: Burnaby; Surrey; Vancouver; West Vancouver)

SURREY:

Murchie's Tea & Coffee
1959 152nd St. • 531-7275
(see also: Burnaby; Richmond; Vancouver; West Vancouver)

VANCOUVER:

Murchie's Tea & Coffee
City Square, 555 West 12th Ave. • 872-6930
970 Robson St. • 669-0783
(see also: Burnaby; Richmond; Surrey; West Vancouver)

Secret Garden Tea Co.
5559 West Boulevard • 261-3070
This enchanting little tea shop sells Republic of Tea, Harney & Son teas from the U.S. and their own line of Secret Garden teas — about 40 different kinds, including bestsellers Secret Garden "Secret" tea and "Buckingham Palace."

Tearoom T
2460 Heather St. • 874-8320
The place that redefined the cuppa! Carries over 200 top quality teas — all their own blends (some of them served at leading restaurants). Prices are deceptive. Loose teas go twice as far as tea-bags and 110 grams makes 40 to 50 cups. Try Blue Eyes, a haunting melange of cornflower petals, caramel, rose hips, hibiscus and fruits, or Nobo Whole Fruit which has raspberries, strawberries and blackberries in the mix. Green teas come in Earl Grey, Strawberry or Vanilla varieties. And don't forget to pick up a packet of T's addictive chai — licorice, mocha, herbal, vanilla or ginger flavoured. In-house information galore and a tea tasting every second Monday.

Five Places to Have
a Nice Cup of Tea:

British roots mean that Vancouver has more places for a cuppa than the Queen has hats.

1. Pacific Institute of Culinary Arts
1505 West 2nd Ave.
734-4488
Tea and French pastries.

2. Secret Garden Tea Co.
5559 West Blvd.
261-3070
A little spot of olde England with its tea cosies, fireplace and tiny teatime treats.

3. Bon Ton Pastry & Confectionery
874 Granville St.
681-3058
Delectable pastries, and a pleasant escape from downtown chaos.

4. Fleuri / Sutton Place Hotel
845 Burrard St.
682-5511
On request, staff will prepare a special Japanese tea.

5. Ray and Mary's British Home
3986 Moncton St., Richmond
274-2261
Scones just out of the oven. Knitted tea cosies.

Ten Ren Tea & Ginseng Company
550 Main St. • 684-1566
Carries a large variety of teas from Taiwan. Known for their green teas, oolong, jasmine and ginseng teas, as well as smoky fermented tea called ti kuan yin.

WEST VANCOUVER:

Murchie's Tea & Coffee
Park Royal North • 922-3136
1950 Marine Dr. • 925-4551
(see also: Burnaby; Richmond; Surrey; Vancouver)

TEATIME TALES

The Art of Brewing Tea

From "Everything You Ever Wanted to Know About Tea But Were Afraid to Ask" by Tearoom T

1. Fill the kettle with fresh, cold and purified water. For maximum aeration, which provides the most flavourful cup of tea, water should be flowing from the faucet for at least a minute.

2. Heat water to a rolling boil for black and oolong teas, and to almost boiling (80°C) for green teas. Do not overboil or oxygen will be lost, resulting in a stale-tasting cup of tea!

3. Measure out one teaspoon of tea leaves per cup and place into an infusing basket. Never fill an infuser more than halfway as the leaves will not be able to expand properly. It is still always best to brew tea loose in a pot, using an outside strainer. The devoted tea lover dispenses with both infuser and strainer, preferring instead the company of a few leaves in the bottom of the teacup!

4. Rinse pot with hot water. Pour water over leaves, cover and infuse according to taste and type of tea. Black tea should infuse three to five minutes. The smaller the cut of the leaf, the shorter the infusion time. Oversteeping will result in a bitter cup! Remove leaves and serve.

5. Add milk (never cream!), honey, sugar or lemon to taste. In order to fully appreciate the delicate overtones of the tea, it is best to drink unadorned. If you have oversteeped your brew, however, add milk, as the caseins it contains will render the tannins insoluble and kill the astringency of the taste.

A Nice Cup of Tea

by Duncan Holmes

It was not until my dear old mother died a while back that I remembered how important tea was in the years that our family was brewing.

I was rummaging through the things that were left when mom moved on, and among the crochet hooks, safety pins and other knickknacks collected in a long and good life was a Second World War ration book.

Anyone under the age of about 60 won't remember these things, but ration books were issued to help governments maintain a degree of control on goods that were required elsewhere to help us defeat whoever it was we were fighting. When you needed these goods at the local food store, you handed over the book with your money, and before taking delivery of whatever it was you wanted, a coupon was clipped with a pair of scissors. When you ran out of coupons, you made do with what was left until the next book was issued at a later date. Meat was rationed, and so was butter and gasoline, and, among other things, so was tea. There were ration books for grownups and there were ration books for kids and I remember clearly that even though my coupon book entitled me to a proportionate share of tea, my parents used my coupons to add to their share of tea. Eight years old and already I was being ripped off by a couple of tannin addicts!

In war-torn South Australia, it was Amgoorie tea — "the tea you love to drink!" — that was the beverage of choice for almost everyone, and as we waited for imminent conflagration it was the mystery of tea, the inaccessible coupons, the aura of immense satisfaction produced among those who sipped it that, in short order, also hooked me.

Just as I learned how to change light bulbs, make my own bed and tie my own shoelaces, I also learned how to dip a cone-shaped sea-shell—say that five times fast!—that we used as a measure into the black, forbidden leaves, to bring water to a rolling boil in an electric "jug," to pour the water with youthful dash over the leaves in a Brown Betty teapot and to cover it all nice and snuggly with a stained old crocheted cosy. I learned to turn the pot three times to the right, then once to the left, the seemingly magic combination that would open the leaves in their boiling bath to wring out a maximum infusion of flavour.

I would learn that when it came time to pour, the milk would come first and the tea, hopefully more robust than "gnat's piss," would follow. In our house, we didn't use a strainer, which meant that prophetic tea leaves — we called them "strangers" — would occasionally float to the surface. Then, all day long, we'd be very wary of strangers.

I remember a fading picture on the side of the tea "caddy" of a dusky maiden from Darjeeling – or some other misty mountain place – with a sack, somehow suspended by a strap covering her forehead, that hung down her back. She was a picker of tender leaves in a romantic land far, far away.

I soon learned to say "aaaaaaaaaahhhh" after the first sip, just as my father did; to say, "as long as it's wet, I'll have another cup while you're up." Just as my father did.

I would go on to sample Twining's in the Strand and Earl Grey on the sunlit promenande of an ocean liner; to sip tea with plump, raisin-filled scones, double Devon cream and apricot jam in deepest, pinkie-extended England. I would learn about Jackson's of Piccadilly and Murchie's of Vancouver, about oolong lapsan, rose hip and chai; about red zinger, gunpowder, jasmine and flavourful "green," sloshed onto Formica tabletops in the harsh light of suburban Chinese restaurants; of "elevenses," of Peter Rabbit and his soothing chamomile. I would discover that the ceremony of tea, be it in Tokyo or Toowoomba, can bring us down by infusing its calming magic into our very souls.

I begin my days with a cup or three of orange pekoe with milk, a dash of CNN and a long aaaaaaaaahh.

I'm really glad that there's no more rationing. And I don't mind at all that a mother's knickknacks can keep stirring the memories.

L.D.B. Specialty Liquor Stores:

Vancouver:

1120 Alberni St. • 660-4572

Wine & Specialty Shop: 660-4571

5555 Cambie St. • 266-1321

3453 Dunbar St. • 224-4412

West Vancouver:

Caulfeild Village

5335 Headland Dr. • 922-8201

Park Royal Shopping Centre

570 Park Royal North • 981-0011

Winemakers' Dinners

One of the best ways of trying new wines is at a winemaker's dinner. These usually feature a single label with a four-course or more dinner designed to complement each wine. Winemakers and chefs work closely together. The Sutton Place Hotel hosts them regularly in its Fleuri restaurant. So do Chartwell in the Four Seasons Hotel, and Piccolo Mondo which focuses (not surprisingly) on Italian wines. Expect to pay $75 and up per person. Not every night prices but exceptional value for money in terms of the learning. Often the winemaker him or herself is there, in from Australia, France or California just for the occasion. Watch the local media for news of upcoming events or ask to be put on mailing lists for upcoming ones.

WINE AND BEER

Chris and Jim are coming for dinner along with that nice couple you met at the pottery workshop. So on Saturday morning you're off to the market to fill your basket with frilly lettuce, ripe scarlet tomatoes, a half dozen cobs of corn, pearly new potatoes and fresh berries from a farm in the Fraser Valley. You make a quick stop at the butcher's for a free-range chicken. Another stop at the bakery. A swing by the Italian deli for olives. Dinner's done, apart from the cooking. Now, what are you going to drink?

Once upon a time, you would have gone to your L.D.B. and picked out one of maybe three or four names (probably with "Blue," "Black" or "Rosé" in them). These days, you're as likely to spend a leisurely 10 minutes mulling over the choices in your local private wine store. Chances are high you'll buy — and pour with pride — a label that's made in the Okanagan.

We've come a long way. The joke when we first moved to Vancouver 20 years ago was that B.C. wine came in two strengths — super-strength and unleaded (and often with a screw cap). Today, that's as old-fashioned as thinking breweries only make two kinds of beer — bottles and cans. Go out for a casual meal these days and you'll see a six-pack or more of locally brewed names listed on the menu — even beer with names that are familiar city sights. How much closer to home can you get? Let's sample:

Private wine stores

Owned and staffed by people who are just plain nuts about wine, these can be a terrific source of information if you're still getting your feet wet. Go with an open mind and throw yourself on their mercy. You'll come away not only with a decent bottle in your price range but with the story behind it. Many stores hold tastings for their customers, where, for a few dollars, you can sample wines from a specific region or the same variety from a number of winemakers.

BURNABY:

Stone's Throw Fine Wines & Beers

1601 Burnwood Dr. • 421-3114

Big Rock beer from Alberta, Keith's India Pale Ale from Nova Scotia, Coopers from Australia (a beer that actually improves with age) — this store stocks about 150 brands of beer and some 500 wines. Here's where to look for B.C. VQA (Vintners Quality Alliance) wines, especially from small wineries — Stone's Throw is the only Lower Mainland retail outlet for the Kettle Valley label. It's also the only Canadian outlet for Hanging Rock wines from Australia. Manager Tom Baxter lived there for 22 years so the store boasts an exceptional representation of wines from down under. California wines, too. Occasional newsletters and tastings.

COQUITLAM:

John B Wine and Beer Store

1000 Austin Ave. • 931-2337

The John B specializes in microbreweries and imported beers, and carries almost 250 different brews. It's also known for its B.C. VQA selection, with most wineries represented. Their niche, staff say, is older wines from California, France and Italy. You can also browse through a wide selection of everyday wines from around the world, as well as the largest selection of dessert wines in B.C. Almost everything is unique to the store. For more information on the John B Wine Club, see page 195.

LANGLEY:

Domaine de Chaberton Estate Winery

1064 216th St. • 530-1736
See page 130.

LINDELL BEACH:

Columbia Valley Classics Winery

1385 Frost Rd. • 858-5233

Western Canada's first fruit winery makes raspberry, blueberry, blackberry, red currant, black currant, white currant and gooseberry wines from the berries it grows on its hillside farm overlooking Cultus Lake. All are available in the licensed gift shop.

Free Stuff from the L.D.B.
Wondering whether this year's vintage of Chateau Amazing is as good as last year's? Call up the L.D.B. and ask them. Heard about a new wine from Portugal but can't seem to track it down? Again, they can tell you where to find it — whether it's in their own stores or a private wine store. Similarly, if you only managed to scribble down part of the name, they'll do what they can to help you identify a wine.

Another service they offer brings wines closer to home — your home. Many wines are only available at the L.D.B.'s specialty stores (see below) but they will happily transfer any wine from there to your nearest outlet.

Matching wine with food is a real skill. If you're stuck, call them and one of their consultants will walk you through the menu (you'll usually find a product consultant right there at the specialty stores). They can also provide advice if you want to start building a wine cellar. Customer service line: toll-free 1-800-667-9463, or 660-9463. Hours: 9 a.m. to 9 p.m., Monday through Saturday.

Liquor Licenses

If you're hosting a public event — or a private event outside your home — where booze is involved, you need a liquor license. Application forms at your nearest L.D.B. outlet. They will fax it through to your local police department for approval. Allow a week to 10 days for the whole process.

Three's a Flight

Curious wine lovers can sample "flights" at 900 West in the Hotel Vancouver. Each selection lets you taste and compare three small glasses of wine (or spirits) with complementary or contrasting characteristics.

Sylvia Drimoussis at Broadway International Specialty Wine Shop

NEW WESTMINSTER:

Divino's Quayside Wine Cellar

101-810 Quayside Dr. • 522-4245

Wines that the L.D.B. doesn't carry is the criteria here. Monthly tastings showcase new products. Prices average about $15.

NORTH VANCOUVER:

Liberty Wine Merchants

Lonsdale Quay Market • 984-2583
Park & Tilford Centre • 988-2424
(see also: Vancouver; West Vancouver)

The Liberty folks try not to carry anything the L.D.B. does, and 90 percent of what they stock isn't sold anywhere else. As well as a huge variety of wines, you'll find printed information on tastings and new releases. Staff are friendly and, if you're new to wine, will cheerfully steer you in the right direction or help you find the right Merlot or Gewurtztraminer to pair with tonight's roast or stir fry. The Lonsdale Quay location carries B.C. wines only; other stores are international in scope and stock everything from simple country wines from southwest France to first-growth Bordeaux. Tastings are on an ad hoc basis.

VANCOUVER:

Broadway International Specialty Wine Shop

2752 West Broadway • 734-8543

A store that knows its neighbourhood, which explains why you can walk away from here with a first-growth Bordeaux or a big bottle of party wine. Spanning the globe, Stephen Li's selection is particularly strong on B.C. and California labels. Check out the dessert wine and half-bottle selection, too. Undecideds can pick the brains of the friendly staff.

Divino Wine Shop
36-1610 Robson St. • 683-8466
This store only carries wines from the Divino Estate in Oliver.

Liberty Wine Merchants
4583 West 10th Ave. • 224-8050
This branch is especially friendly towards students.

Marquis Wine Cellar
1034 Davie St. • 684-0445
"I want people to come in and discover something," says owner John Clerides, who sets his sights on small boutique wineries that don't have the marketing power to sell their wines but enjoy a cult or local following. "My job is to bring those wines to my customer," says Clerides. Every year, he heads off to France (and other wine-growing countries) to scout for wines. What he finds is eventually on the shelves in his store. Add your name to the mailing list and you'll receive newsletters full of information on labels and upcoming tastings.

WEST VANCOUVER:
Liberty Wine Merchants
Park Royal South • 925-3663
(see also: North Vancouver; Vancouver)

BREW PUBS:

A big trend these days is places where you can go out for a meal, and wash it down with a beer brewed right on the spot.

NORTH VANCOUVER:
Sailor Hagar's
221 West 1st St. • 984-2567
Around since 1986. No real "Hagar," but lotsa real ales. #1 seller is the Honey Pilsener: "an easy transitional beer to exploring the others," says brewer James Breuer. "Others" include Scandinavian Amber Lager, Belgian Style Wit, Narwhal Pale Ale, Grizzly Nut Brown Ale and — named after brewmaster Gary Lohin — the Lohin's Extra Special Bitter. Seasonal

Import your own wine
Fallen for that country wine while in Provence? Or read about a California wine in a U.S. magazine, and can't find it locally. One solution is to bring it in yourself. According to the L.D.B., "Alcoholic spirits, wine and beer (except draft beer) which are not listed or sold in B.C. Liquor Stores may be obtained by placing a Special Order. An order form may be obtained at B.C. Liquor Stores, or see store staff for more information. Special Orders are available to the general public and the licensees. They are normally subject to a deposit of 50 percent of the estimated retail selling price as determined in advance. Minimum order quantity is one case (the size of a case varies by product), unless otherwise specified by the supplier. Restricted bottle sizes and selling prices are also set for Special Orders." What the L.D.B. does is figure out how much it will cost to transport the wine, plus taxes, then tell you the price you'll have to pay.

brews? Try Raspberry Wheat Beer, Erik the Red, which gets its colour from crystal malts and, come Christmas, Thor's Hammer Barley Wine. Available at the Brew Pub (86 Semisch Ave., 984-3087) or Beer & Wine Shop (235 West lst Ave., 984-7669).

VANCOUVER:

The Creek Restaurant, Brewery and Bar
1253 Johnston St., Granville Island • 685-7070

Beer maker Don Harms brews enough varieties to keep Vancouver's growing number of beer enthusiasts on the hop. Lagers include Donny's Dortmunder and the Vienna-style Saltzburger. More in the mood for a German-style beer? Try the crisp, clean UpYourHeiny Pils, True Creek Alt based on the classic altbiers of Dusseldorf, Hellava Hefeweizen — a classically cloudy wheat beer — or Koolsch, a fruity, malty blonde. Master Bitter and Broadway Porter are more along the lines of British beers. Brews are only half the story here: winner of countless culinary competitions, Chef Robert Sulatycky's cuisine is exceptional.

Steamworks Brewing Co.
375 Water St. • 689-2739

The city's first brew pub, Steamworks has been a popular Gastown focus since it opened its doors in 1995. Brewmaster Conrad Gmoser covers the whole spectrum from Ipanema Summer White to Heroica, an heroic oatmeal stout. (Owner Eli Gershkovitch comes up with the names!) You can usually choose from seven on tap — Lion's Gate Lager is the most popular. Order a Coal Porter — a dark porter named after Coal Harbour — and they'll draw you what's known in the trade as a "nitrogen" beer, which is pumped with nitrogen instead of carbon dioxide. The difference? Smaller, finer bubbles and a rich creamy head. "We're in the best place in the world to make fruit beers," says Gershkovitch. Four weeks after raspberries come to market they show up in Steamworks' Framboise. Come Halloween, you can celebrate with Great Pumpkin Ale or Witch's Brew.

Yaletown Brewing Co.
1111 Mainland St. • 681-2379

Brewmaster Iain Hill usually has a half dozen varieties on tap. Some are served British style, i.e. at 10 degrees and with less carbonation than you may be used to. Try the Indian Arm Pale Ale, Frank's Nut Brown Ale, Red Brick Bitter and Double Dome Stout. Mainland Lager is a Munich-style brew. Hill also makes a light lager. There are seasonal products, too, such as Hill's Special Wheat — the yeast comes from a German brewery, which gives it a spicy character and a slightly fruity flavour.

MICROBREWERIES:
Beer Brewed in your Own Backyard

The last few years have seen the establishment of a host of microbreweries. All concentrate on producing beers the old-fashioned way with simple, honest ingredients. What else can we say but "cheers!"

DELTA:
Shaftebury Brewing Company
7989 82nd St. • 940-2887
www.shaftebury.com
Talk about dedication: Owners Paul Beaton and Tim Wittig lived for four months in a VW van while getting their brewery up and running. Launched in 1987, it now produces a half dozen types, among them Cream Ale and Honey Pale Ale, which contains B.C. honey in every batch. Wittig shot the label photo for Rainforest Amber Ale while hiking through old-growth forest. Making up the rest of the portfolio are Paul & Tim's Original Ale (a classic Brit ale), Wet Coast Winter Ale (brewed only during the winter months) and Hefeweizen Wheat Ale, which is unfiltered and therefore naturally cloudy. Available as draft, bottles and cans.

NORTH VANCOUVER
Horseshoe Bay Brewery
1481 Dominion St. • 984-2537
The story behind this microbrewery goes back to 1981 when John Mitchell launched The Troller, the first brew pub in North America and the first cottage brewery in Canada. New owner Cameron Allen took

Sangriaville
What's red and mellow as a July sunset — and goes down just as gently? Forget cran-tinis. Instead, that 1970s favourite, Spanish sangria, is back for its turn in the limelight. No, you can't toss in just anything alcoholic, you do need a recipe, and the one from El Patio (891 Cambie St., 681-9149) is among the easiest. Basically, it's a one-two-three system. Start with one litre of full-bodied red wine in a large jug. Next, add two ounces each of brandy and Triple Sec. Finish off with three ounces apiece of lemonade, orange crush and 7-Up. Add orange and lemon slices to garnish, and ice cubes just prior to pouring. Gypsy Kings optional.

over the brewery in 1996. Lightest to darkest, the ales made here are Pale, Indian Pale, Horseshoe Bay and Nut Brown. There's also Frambozen, a raspberry ale. You can sample them all at The Troller (6422 Bay St., West Vancouver, 922-7616) and at pubs from Surrey to Whistler.

VANCOUVER:

The Bowen Island Brewing Co. Ltd./Coquihalla Brewery
330 Bridgeway St. • 293-2282
www.bowenbrewing.com
Known for English style ales including a Blonde Ale, Bowen Ale, a traditional Special Bitter and Winter Ale, which is dark red in colour and includes dark sweet cherries. The most recent addition is Hemp Cream Ale — hemp has been used to make beer since the Middle Ages. Bowen Island Brewing merged with Coquihalla Brewery in 1997 and added Premium and Tattoo lagers to the line.

Granville Island Brewing Co.
Granville Island • 687-2739
Canada's first microbrewery opened its doors in 1984 in a 1920s building on Granville Island. The Island Lager was an immediate hit. Since then, the company has introduced a raft of other beers, all named after local landmarks which are featured on the label. Beers are brewed according to the Bavarian Purity Law of 1516 and are made only from malts, hops, yeast and water. Most of the beer is now produced in Kelowna. At the Granville Island location, brewing facilities are used strictly for new recipe development. Tours are offered three times a day; the admission fee includes samples and a souvenir tasting glass. This is the only brewery in Canada to offer experimental brews for sale. A limited supply is put out each Friday at noon under the "Prototap" label.

R&B Brewing Co.
54 East 4th Ave. • 874-2537
www.r-and-b.com
Partners (R)ick Dellow and Barry (B)enson have a traditional English Brewery in the False Creek area

Don't Throw Out That Beer Can
Most of us simply take our bottles and cans back to the liquor store for a refund. Members of the B.C. Breweriana Collectors put them on the display shelf. Cans, bottles, anything connected with breweries is a candidate for collection. Locally there are 60 people in the club. Worldwide, there are over 4,000. Annual dues ($10) include three newsletters and the chance to mingle with fellow collectors at trade sessions, brewery tours and get togethers. For more information, contact Larry Sampson, 430-1765 or visit the club's website at www.geocities.com/CollegePark/3203/

where they brew all their beers by hand. Red Devil Ale uses imported and local hops which are married with distinctive and traditional bittering and aroma hops from England. R & B's Raven Ale is a dark ale made with northwestern hops and North American malts. Seasonal beers include Sun God Wheat Ale in the summer, and Old Nick Strong Ale in the winter. Draft only (but party kits are available).

Storm Brewing
310 Commercial Dr. • 255-9119
It thundered on to the scene in 1995 with the dark, copper-coloured Red Sky Alt Bier. Since then it has produced others in the European tradition and in a fashion "reminiscent of the great beers of the Eighteenth Century." All beers are unfiltered, natural and unpasteurized. Hurricane India Pale Ale is rich, golden, intense and has a distinctive floral character. Twister Wheat Ale (available summertime only) is traditionally served with a twist of lemon. Highland Scottish Ale is malty and smooth. Continental Coffee Ale actually includes coffee from the Continental Coffee Co. Black Plague Stout is a dry oatmeal stout. Fruit Lambics are disinctively sour, with a strong fruit flavour from raspberry, blackberry and other fruits. Check your favourite café along Commercial Drive (and other spots around town). Chances are good you'll find a Storm Brewing.

Tips From the Pros:
How do you figure out how much to spend at the liquor store? According to Nicky Major of Major the Gourmet: "Figure three-quarters to a whole bottle of wine per person — and remember people are drinking more red wine these days. You can always take wine back if you don't use it." Beer drinkers average four brews each over the course of an evening. And, of course, keep a good supply of non-alcoholic drinks on hand.

WINE ON OUR DOORSTEP

British Columbia Wine Trails
P.O. Box 1319, Summerland,
B.C. V0H 1Z0
1-250-494-7733
www.bcwine.com/trails/
This quarterly, published in
B.C.'s wine-growing country,
offers comprehensive and
readable news about local
wines and winemakers. $10
annually.

Vancouver wine lovers needn't drive far to visit a vineyard. Domaine de Chaberton in the Fraser Valley is less than an hour from the city. Owner Claude Violet is a ninth generation winemaker from southwest France whose family has been in the business since 1644.

A visit to B.C. in the 1970s convinced Claude that this was where he wanted to live. By 1981, he and wife Inge were growing grapes for other wineries. In 1991, they opened their own. The list of international medals they have won since then fills a page, evidence of the knowledge and care that the Violets have brought to their south-facing 33 acres.

Depending on when you visit, you can see the grapes hanging full and heavy on the vine, tour the winery and bottling area, and sniff appreciatively where the smell of cedar walls mingles with that of oak barrels from France and acacia barrels from Hungary. The harvest is usually from late September to mid-October, not the best time to visit the winery, say Inge and Claude: "People are tired and there are a lot of bees, too," but any other time, visitors are welcome, and the wine store and tasting room is open year-round.

Here you can sample the Madeline Angevine, an elegant Loire varietal with a floral nose and flavours of apricot and apple, or Bacchus Dry with its muscat aroma and citrus flavours, or their famous Bacchus which, Inge points out, goes well with Asian food.

DINING IN

When your cupboard is stocked with spices from India and sauces from China, and a bowl on the table is piled with shiny red peppers; when your trip to the farmer's market filled your basket with arugula, blueberries and corn, and three kinds of cheese are ripening on the counter, you only need one more ingredient: know-how.

It's easy to find in Vancouver. Classes and courses teach us the basics — or the skills to become a near-professional. Local newspapers and magazines fill our kitchen drawers with clippings, ideas that help us make the most of seasonal peaches or pumpkins or plums. Season after season, Vancouver chefs generously publish their favourite ideas for local gourmets.

And when we want to eat well but are strapped for time, there's wonderful take-out — supper to eat in front of the TV, a "homemade" stock to add depth to a soup, a luscious dessert to crown a homecooked dinner. Eating at home has never been better.

LEARNING TO COOK

So, You Want To Be a Chef...

Creating wonderful cuisine that knocks your customers' – and the critics' – socks off may sound glamorous but being a professional chef is hard work. Eight hour days? Forget it, and remember you're working almost every night too. But if you do want to work with food, getting a good training is essential. Here are some places to start.

VANCOUVER:

Dubrulle International Culinary and Hotel Institute of Canada
1522 West 8th Ave. • 738-3155
Founded in 1982, this is the largest private cooking school in Canada. The 17-week Professional Culinary program begins with a grounding in the basics of classical French cooking. After that, it's on to pastry, Italian cooking, Chinese cuisine and more – enough to qualify graduates for a good entry-level position. Also offered is a 17-week program in pastry and desserts – everything from sweet doughs to soufflés. The teaching staff is led by French-trained chef Adam Busby, who worked at Bishop's for several years and has run his own restaurant.

Pacific Institute of Culinary Arts
1505 West 2nd Ave. • 734-4488
This private institute's six-month program in Culinary Arts begins with the fundamentals – nutrition, knife skills, stocks – and ends with three months of feeding real customers. P.I.C.A. is the only private culinary training institute in Canada with a student-operated white linen restaurant on the premises. (It even presents monthly "wine and dine" evenings.) The two 12-week Baking and Pastry Arts courses explore the entire field of bread making and patisserie. Both courses require an additional one-week industry practicum. All chef instructors are from Europe. Executive chef Walter Messiah comes from Monaco (yes, he did cook for Prince Rainier) and has taught French cuisine in the South Pacific.

How to Get a Job Cooking at the Hotel Vancouver
"We interview four or five times and we don't even talk about food. We assume you can cook if you apply. We want to see a good attitude. We look for someone who wants to come to work with a smile every day and is willing to learn. I don't want to hear 'I'm a good cook.' For a sous-chef position, we do a black box competition (applicants have to invent a number of dishes from a box of supplied ingredients). It's to see their style. Some of the dishes are more European, some are heavier...They'll be cooking for the people. It shouldn't be cooking done by the chef for the chef."
— Robert LeCrom, Executive Chef, Hotel Vancouver

Vancouver Community College

250 West Pender St. • 443-8443

The extensive 12-month Culinary Arts program begins with the basics of salads, sandwiches, vegetables, deep-fried foods, breakfasts and simple desserts. Next come classes in everything from grills to soups and stocks, as well as butchery, baking and basic kitchen management. Students prepare gourmet meals for JJ's — the college's own restaurant — as well as for cafeteria service. Also offered is a 10-month Baking and Pastry Arts (the results are sold in the college bake shop) a 6-month Asian Culinary Arts course, a 6-month Retail Meat Processing course — the college has a butcher's shop, too — and a 10-month Food and Beverage Management course that trains students for supervisory positions.

Professional Associations

Les Dames d'Escoffier

A group of professional women involved in gastronomy, hospitality and related fields, "Les Dames" raise funds to provide assistance to B.C. women who want to further a career in the beverage, culinary and hospitality arts. Awards are given annually and scholarships are open to all age ranges and career levels. Applications are accepted on an ongoing basis. For information and an application form, write to: Les Dames d'Escoffier Scholarship Committee, P.O. Box 60570, Granville Park Post Office, Vancouver, B.C. V6H 4B9.

Xclusively BC

Some of the best chefs in the province are among the members of Xclusively BC. All share a passion for promoting homegrown excellence in food and wine. Net proceeds raised by this non-profit organization stay in the province and provide bursary funds to B.C. residents interested in starting or furthering their education in food or beverage. For bursary information call: 641-1448.

How to Get a Job at Rainforest Café

"When hiring staff, you want some experience but the number one qualification is personality. This also involves the staff's general attitude to life. If they're energetic and interested in learning, they'll be good chefs."

— Andrew Skorzewski, Rainforest Café

DON'T QUIT YOUR DAY JOB:
Amateur Cooking Classes

There's always something new coming down the pipe in the world of cuisine. It could be a style of cooking, a focus on freshness or new ethnic dishes. Professional chefs stay on top of trends — and we home chefs can, too, through the wealth of cooking classes available in Vancouver.

MAPLE RIDGE:
Eileen Dwillies
20770 123B Ave. • 467-2249
Not surprisingly — since she spends half the year in France (see Provençal Getaways, page 137) — Eileen Dwillies showcases the big, bold flavours of the Mediterranean region in the popular cooking classes she teaches with her daughter Diane Formosa. Dwillies also offers classes at her home in Richmond.

NORTH VANCOUVER:
Ann Kirsebom/The Toast of the Town Cuisine Ltd.
987-9187
Ann Kirsebom teaches at local night schools and at Tools and Techniques. She will also help you brush up your skills at a private class in your home.

VANCOUVER:
Bishop's
2183 West 4th Ave. • 738-2025
Yes, they do hold classes here but competition is stiff to get into them. For information, call the restaurant.

Caren's Cooking School
1856 Pandora St. • 255-5119
Trained at the Culinary Institute of America and the Thai Cooking School at the Oriental Hotel in Bangkok, Caren McSherry-Valagao has been teaching since 1978. Instructor Trudy Douglas is Cordon Bleu trained. You'll find chefs from local restaurants on the roster — big names, too, like Jacques Pepin. Classes cover subjects like "The Tuscany Countryside" or "Along the Beaujolais Wine Trail." McSherry-Valagao teaches private cooking classes as well.

Love in the Kitchen
Sauté your way into his or her heart. That's the premise behind the "singles only" cooking class held periodically by Ambrosia Adventures in Cooking (922-6694). Participants learn how to whip up a romantic gourmet dinner for two before sitting down to wine and dine with other singles.

Cookshop at City Square

12th and Cambie St. • 873-5683

Get on the mailing list and you'll receive the Cookshop's bi-monthly calendar. Classes are held every day except Sunday, mostly in the evenings. In a typical week you could learn Irish cuisine on Monday, easy Thai on Tuesday and round off the week with Italian Country cooking, wok cooking, sushi and Indian breads and snacks, all taught by experts. The school usually offers three courses for the price of two.

Dubrulle International Culinary and Hotel Institute of Canada

1522 West 8th Ave. • 738-3155

Billing their courses as "cooking classes for the serious amateur," this professional cooking school shares its secrets with those who love to spend time in the kitchen — but not necessarily all their time. Held over a number of weeks, courses in basic and advanced techniques cover everything from knife handling to how to shape a perfect baguette. A "beginner's weekend" shows students the secrets of two workable menus with dishes in each that teach essential skills. Ardent amateurs with less time on their hands can sign up for individual classes that focus on stocks, shellfish, poultry and other delicious topics. The Dubrulle school also offers custom-designed cooking classes and wine seminars through the Vancouver Wine Academy.

Pacific Institute of Culinary Arts

1505 West 2nd Ave. • 734-4488

Want to learn how to make nothing but sauces? Seeking to brush up your Thai vegetarian skills? This school's Customized Casual Gourmet Classes let you call the shots as to what you learn and who else is there (you can go one-on-one or include your friends). Scheduled for evenings and weekends, these hands-on classes are popular for private birthday parties or get-togethers. One family of four from Alberta checked in for a full weekend for their vacation. Designed in consultation with executive chef Walter Messiah, topics may range from desserts, breads or sauces to a

Brush Up on Your Herbs
Growing ingredients on your own doorstep cuts the distance beween soil and table to zilch. Herbs don't come any fresher than that, as Daryle Ryo Nagata, Executive Chef at Waterfront Centre Hotel, knows. The Hotel presents a series of events that revolve around what flourishes in Nagata's third floor 1200-square-foot garden. As well as starring herbs on his menu, Nagata also links up with local gardeners, a herbalist and food celebrities for regular evenings that include a seminar, garden tour and multi-course dinner.

Classes Chez Vous
Hire chef and caterer Markus Wieland (Wieland's Home Cooking, 320-8486) and he can include a cooking class in your home as part of the dinner he cooks. Clients can also go shopping with him.

Soup 101
A well-known source of bargain breads and cookies, the V.C.C. bake shop (250 West Pender St.) also sells other products from its cooking classes such as take-out soup and Asian and western main dishes. Weekdays only — and it's first come, first served.

full menu built around salmon. For groups, prices are comparable to other cooking classes.

Lesley Stowe Fine Foods
1780 West 3rd Ave. • 731-3663
Get on her mailing list and you'll have advance news of Stowe's evening classes. Her sessions on how to make gift baskets — and foods for gift-giving — are especially popular, as are the Cookie Exchange class and her class for couples, which she conducts with husband Doug Hume.

Sylvia's Cooking Classes
4215 West 13th Ave. • 224-5444
February through May, twice monthly in her home, Sylvia Molnar demonstrates a number of recipes that add up to a splendiferous dinner. Themes range far and wide: Spanish, Italian, Turkish, "love food" and Ukranian soul food are typical.

Vancouver School Board
713-4500
Bargains in cooking courses can often be found at your local high school. Indian delicacies, sushi, Indonesian food — the options are far more exciting than "home ec" used to be. Call the Vancouver School Board for information or watch for flyers.

Vancouver Wine Academy
990-7640
Delve into the world of wine with two of the city's leading oenophiles, Liberty Wines' Park Heffelfinger and Beach Side Café sommelier Mark Davidson, who share their knowledge through the Dubrulle International Culinary and Hotel Institute of Canada (see pages 132 and 135). Courses taught are the Certificate and Higher Certificate Programs for the London Wine and Spirit Trust as well as wine appreciation classes.

WEST VANCOUVER:
Ambrosia Adventures in Cooking
4956 Marine Dr. • 922-6694
Taught by herself or well-known guest chefs, Maureen

Goulet's classes take place in various locations, including different hotels and her home. She's famous for her "singles only" sessions.

Tools and Techniques
250 16th St. • 925-1835
Watch for this lively Spring and Fall series of classes — there are usually one or two a week conducted by local chefs and cookbook authors.

Overseas Cooking Schools

Sample osso buco in Italy, taste the satiny miracle of real French foie gras, roam around colourful Asian markets. In your dreams? No, in your future if you sign up for a cooking holiday abroad.

Provençal Getaways
11373 Kingcome Ave., Vancouver • 277-0664
A former food editor for *Western Living Magazine*, Eileen Dwillies and her husband Paul own a charmingly restored house in a delightful village in Provence. Dwillies' cooking classes make the most of the abundance of local meats, cheeses and produce. The couple also lead excursions to northern Italy.

Chateau Drouilles
714-3131
www.meinhardt.com
Owned and run by Linda Meinhardt of Meinhardt Fine Foods, this twin-towered chateau set deep in the enchanting French countryside is straight from a storybook. Meinhardt teaches a regional approach based on what the markets and her two-acre garden produce (the other 78 acres comprise lawns, woods and meadows). Sample dishes are confit de canard with red cabbage, an evil chocolate mousse and a house hors d'oeuvres of goat cheese, fresh tomatoes and olives.

Money from Les Dames
Recipients have included a cheesemaker eager to study her craft in England and a pastry chef. Every year, the culinary organization Les Dames d'Escoffier awards thousands of dollars in scholarships to B.C. women. Funds are available to anyone at any career level (or any age) who wants to start or pursue a career in the culinary and related arts. Those interested should request an application by writing to: Les Dames d'Escoffier Scholarship Committee, Box 60570, Granville Park Post Office, Vancouver, B.C., V6H 4B9.

The Cookshop at City Square's Exotic Getaways
555 West 12th Ave., Vancouver • 873-5683
The Cookshop at City Square school director, Nathan Hyam, leads annual cooking tours to southeast Asia (where he lived for a while). Join the group and you'll get an insider's view of Asia with trips around the markets, dinners with local families, visits to lemongrass and other farms, and explanations of the roots of the cuisine. Hyam also conducts tours of the Pacific Northwest.

Ann Kirsebom/The Toast of the Town Cuisine Ltd.
987-9187
Every couple of years, local caterer Ann Kirsebom leads cooking cruises through the Mediterranean, the Panama Canal and other exotic parts of the world. It's called "The Ultimate Dinner Party" – and with good reason.

Villa Delia Cooking School
669-3732
www.umberto.com
If you've eaten in any of Umberto Menghi's restaurants, here's the chance to learn from the maestro himself at his charming 16th-century villa in the heart of the Tuscan countryside, 30 km from Pisa. The 10-day courses occasionally feature other Vancouver chefs. The course focuses on pasta, Tuscan bread making, and Tuscan cuisine. Classes occupy the mornings, leaving afternoons free for excursions to Florence, Siena and local markets. If you have to ask how much it costs, you can't afford it.

LEARNING TO POUR:
Making the Perfect Martini and More

Maybe you can whip up a terrific Manhattan, but doing it professionally takes training. Here are a couple of places to refine your skills.

BURNABY:
Westec School of Bartending
5679 Imperial St. • 435-8848

"A bartender," says the brochure, "has to be part diplomat, psychologist, businessperson, confidant and social director." The four-week, 80-hour course is taught both days and evenings. Founded in 1982.

VANCOUVER:
Fine-Art Bartending School
6L-601 West Broadway • 873-2811

A lot of martinis have flowed under the bridge since this company set up shop in 1973. Today's bartenders are expected to know not just about cocktails but about wines, shooters and special coffees, too. Day and evening classes. Two day seminars in Performance Bartending.

RECIPES FROM TIMES PAST

Leafing through the cookbooks hidden in the depths of the Vancouver Museum is like putting the city's everyday life under a microscope.

Its pages freckled, its ink faded to pale brown shadows, I come across a little hand-written book from about 1901 — somebody's cherished collection. It is filled with recipes that breathe the kind of comfort that must have met with a warm response after a hard day's work. There are treats, too. For cinnamon toast, one recipe reads, "Cut slices of bread 1/4 inch thick, remove all the crusts, cut the large slices into small squares and toast carefully. Spread with butter and sugar, cinnamon sprinkled plentifully. Return to oven until butter and sugar are melted into the toast." This wasn't an era when leftovers went to waste. "Crusts after making cinnamon toast can be made into bread pudding," the author reminded the user.

Soon printed books replaced recipes passed from neighbour to neighbour. Published around 1910 by the Vancouver Gas Co. Ltd., *The Modern Household Cookery Book* promised readers that if they phoned the number 5000 (there were fewer phones in Vancouver's early days) they would receive "full instructions given in your own home by our lady instructor" on how to get the best from their new purchase.

But, oh my, Vancouver was ahead of its time. Close to 90 years ago, trendy hostesses had already discovered edible flowers. One recipe entitled "A Sardine Suggestion" called for sardines, lettuce leaves and "should you be caught with short rations on a Sunday evening by friends who evidently expect to stay for tea, fall back on your nasturtium bed for aid." For those keen to duplicate this curious dish, the sardines were rolled in nasturtium leaves and the ends garnished with flowers.

Vancouver already had its Chinatown, and a Chinese cookery section included instructions for making pork with lily buds and recipes for Chinese dumplings. Anticipating the coffee shops that, by the 1990s, would be on every street corner, the book also included a recipe for Choca — a beverage made from

---

Really Fresh Chicken a No-No in Vancouver

Forget the idea of legally keeping a half dozen hens in the back yard and having fresh eggs on your doorstep. The Vancouver/Richmond Health Board says it's strictly verboten. "No person," reads the bylaw, "shall keep or permit to be harboured any horses, donkeys, cattle, swine, sheep or goats, or any live poultry or fowl, including ducks, geese, turkeys, chickens, pheasants or quail, or operate any apiary or otherwise keep bees for any purpose in the City."

one third freshly made coffee, one third chocolate, and one third hot milk.

Published in about 1920, and supported by advertisers, *The Brides Book of Household Management* was approved by the Board of Trade. "Please ask for B.C. goods and remember the slogan 'Let British Columbia flourish by her industries,'" it admonished the newly wed. Choices were gloomy. A bride could either stay home and cook string beans for a recommended 45 minutes — carrots needed an hour! — or go out for supper at The Duchess Tea Rooms at the corner of Hastings and Seymour, an establishment whose primary boast was that it had been "opened by a returned nursing sister."

Mind you, there were a few sparks of culinary light. Under the chapter headed "Special Dishes from Overseas" appeared mention of occhi di lupo — "this form of pasta you can buy at any Italian store" it reminded the reader, and a salad dressing included the information that "chervil may be procured from the vegetable stands the year round."

Some food ideas from the past sound just plain weird. In the roaring 1920s, *Reliable Recipes* by the Triple Entente Chapter of the Imperial Order of the Daughters of the Empire saw the light of day. Among its suggestions was a Tea Dish from Miss Leonie C. Lalonde. "On a very fine wire gridiron (or one made of wire net used for screens)," she wrote, "place some slices of salt pork, cut as thin as possible; on each slice lay a good sized oyster, or two small ones; broil and serve hot. This with coffee, crisp toast and chopped cabbage, makes an ideal lunch or tea dish." Maybe in your book, Miss Lalonde, but not in ours.

From the early 1940s on, the bible of Vancouver homemakers was the Edith Adams cookbook published each year by *The Vancouver Sun*. The *Third Annual Collection* reminded readers that the newspaper offered a daily prize of a dollar for the best recipe. The cookbook also contained instructions for making Bridge Candy, and Spaghetti and Steak Spanish Style (which meant with onions and canned tomatoes). The *Fourth Annual Collection* led off with a recipe for raspberry vinegar. Nouvelle cuisine salad dressing? Uh-uh. This was a warm weather beverage

Weird Ingredients 101:
Dried Lemons

They look like little brown nuts, they're packed with flavour and you can find them in Iranian grocery stores. Soak a handful of lemons overnight and purée with an equal quantity of dates. Thin with water and spike with a dash or two of hot sauce for a dazzling grilled chicken.

meant to be diluted with ice water. Among the book's other temptations were a Ladies' Aid Ham Loaf and something called Shrimp and Olive Surprise.

The *Sixth Annual* extolled the virtues of the "average middle-class French housewife" who went to market daily and used every last scrap of the boiling beef. The *Eighth Annual Cook Book* promoted "Vitamins for Victory" on the front cover, whose graphics also included a Union Jack and a woman in the square-shouldered clothes typical of the time. By the time the next edition came out, culinary choices were narrowing. A recipe for Wartime Whipped Cream relied on gelatin for its stiffness. A coffee substitute added six cups of cooking bran and molasses — both roasted — to one cup of the real thing. "Bee-nut" butter was a concoction of white beans and Bovril. The *Twelfth Annual Prize Cook Book* of 1948 flirted with the idea of foreign food — but not too seriously. The four cloves of garlic and pinch of saffron in its recipe for bouillabaisse were strictly optional.

The years rolled on. More and more prepared foods appeared on the shelves. *An Autographed Album of Recipes* compiled by the Vancouver and District Home Economics Association in 1963 included instructions for jellied salads, pizzas made with brown 'n' serve rolls, lasagna pie, shrimp foo yung and Spanish paella.

Today's focus on fresh ingredients was still a long way down the road. A recipe for Seafood Bisque called for two cans of tomato soup, a half can of pea soup, a can of chicken consommé or bouillon, and a can of crab, shrimp or lobster. Only when she got to the cream (one cup) and the sherry bottle (3/4 cup) was the home cook allowed to put the can opener down.

Forget the history books. Rooting among old recipes tells you how people *really* lived.

Multi-Purpose Onion Gunk

Get out your biggest frypan. Heat enough oil to film the bottom. Add as many sliced onions as will fit in the pan — really pack them in. Turn the heat down and cook the onions slowly for as long as it takes them to reduce to a brown, sweet mixture. Use in sandwiches. Dollop on hamburgers. Serve with grilled chicken. Make lots and keep in the fridge.

RECIPE SOURCES: Publications and Websites

Saying there are too many cookbooks out there is a bit like saying there's too much chocolate. Those who are at their happiest wielding knives and stirring pots know that the perfect recipe lurks just around the corner – reason enough to buy one more book or clip one more recipe.

Local Newspapers and Magazines:

CityFood
Dedicated to food, food and nothing but food in and around Vancouver (with frequent excursions to Whistler). Informed, opinionated, frequently funny – and on top of that, free. Themed issues – Italian food, coffee and so on – include plenty of recipes.

The Province
Food coverage on Wednesdays, much of it concerned with local producers, restaurants and trends.

Vancouver Magazine
The food page in each issue includes a recipe from a local restaurateur or food professional.

Vancouver Sun
Wednesday is Food Day. Feature stories cover the whole spectrum of food, from local strawberry growers to what Vancouver's most cutting-edge restaurant chefs are up to. The *Sun*'s "Edith Adams Cottage" is a Vancouver institution. Though now a lady of considerable years, old Edith consistently keeps up with the times (see pages 152-3).

Western Living
Food stories and restaurant reviews invariably include recipes.

Food Mysteries Solved!
Ever leave a hot pot to cool and then find yourself unable to lift off the lid? Wonder why leaving out that one small ingredient results in a culinary disaster? What happens when a cake rises or a sauce thickens? These are the questions that fascinate Anne Gardiner and Sue Wilson, Vancouver's own Inquisitive Cooks. The two intrepid culinary scientists teach the Science of Cooking at UBC and write a weekly column that appears in numerous Canadian newspapers. For more information on the Inquisitive Cooks, you can visit their website at: www.inquisitivecook.com.

Websites That Cook

Out there in cyberspace are hundreds and thousands of recipes floating around. Read them through, print them out, see if they work — and if they do, print out a dozen more copies. That way, you'll never have to get stressed about getting stains on your cookbooks.

B.C. Salmon Marketing Council
www-bcsalmon.ca
Smoked salmon and fennel potato pizza; baked salmon steaks with ginger ratatouille. Yum. Preparation tips and fast facts, too.

B.C. Turkey Marketing Board
www.uniserve.com/bcturkey
December 26th, you'll gobble up the ideas in the "Christmas and leftovers" section. Today's turkeys are sold in pieces as well as whole so that you can whip up a turkey pizza or spicy orange turkey stir-fry. P.S. Did you know B.C. has the second highest per capita consumption of turkey in Canada?

CityFood
www.cityfood.com
New site under construction at time of publication. Given the content of the "parent" magazine, bookmark it right away.

Fraser Valley Farm Direct Marketing Association
www.bcfarmfresh.com
Want to know where to buy emu meat, or honey on the comb, or 50 varieties of apple? Steer your way around this information-packed site, print out a map of the farms you want to visit and head off for a day in the countryside. As well as 63 farms in the Fraser Valley, the site also includes North Arm Farm in the Pemberton Valley, which supplies produce and fruit to the Chateau Whistler Resort and other Whistler restaurants.

Pacific Palate
http://quadriga.com/pacificpalate/
You've heard them on radio and seen them on TV.

Now you can print out the recipes featured on Don Genova's Pacific Palate. Everything from shellfish to culinary feats from Seattle.

Sunrise Soya Foods

www.sunrise-soya.com

"You too can tofu," promises this bright and lively site. Recipes, buying, cooking and storage tips — you'll find everything here to convert you into a believer.

Radio and Television

The broadcast media are fickle about switching allegiances, but, at time of publication, spinning the dial or zapping the channel changer would bring you news at these places, days and times. Restaurants, growers, events, visiting food and wine personalities, trends — you'll find them all covered.

The Best of Food and Wine

CFUN 1410 AM • Saturdays, 11 a.m. to 1 p.m.
Food writer Kasey Wilson and wine expert Tony Gismondi provide a well-rounded view of the Vancouver — and beyond — culinary scene.

Food and Wine Show

CKNW 98 • Sundays, 6 to 7 p.m.
A lively, upbeat hour hosted by cooking school owner Caren McSherry.

Pacific Palate

CBC-AM • Tuesdays, 8:20 a.m.
CBC-TV • Wednesdays, 6:30 p.m.
Culinary adventures and investigations hosted by radio and TV food personality Don Genova.

Marketing Councils & Other Sources

These organizations are a huge mine of free recipes and food information.

ABBOTSFORD:

B.C. Blueberry Council

P.O. Box 8000-730, V2S 6H1

If your mind can't reach beyond putting blueberries on your cornflakes – and you just went mad and bought a whole flat of these glorious berries – these are the people to contact.

BURNABY:

B.C. Tree Fruits

439-0829 • www.bctreefruits.com

Apples, peaches, pears and plums. For facts and recipes, these are the people to call.

SURREY:

B.C. Turkey Association

534-5644

Don't know how long to roast that 14-pounder? Looking for recipes for different cuts of turkey? Like to know how to smoke a turkey? Here's your contact.

VANCOUVER:

The British Columbia Salmon Marketing Council

267-3030 • www.bcsalmon.ca

Useful information on how to choose and prepare different species of wild B.C. salmon. *BC's Best Salmon Recipes* and *BC's Best Salmon Recipes II* feature dishes created by fishers, gillnetters, fish-sellers and marine biologists as well as professional chefs.

Sunrise Soya Foods

253-2326 • www.sunrise-soya.com

Recipe Hotline at: 1-800-661-BEAN

This local company is doing what it can to raise the profile of one of the most misunderstood foods in the western world. Everything you ever wanted to know about tofu – and more.

The discovery of a new dish does more for human happiness than the discovery of a new star.

— Brillat-Savarin

COOKS and BOOKS

Take a gourmet into any bookstore and he or she will narrow their eyes, set their sights and be in the depths of the cookbook section before you can say "Wolfgang Puck." Most Vancouver bookstores have strong cookbook sections, but for the ultimate source, there's only one place to go: Barbara-Jo's Books to Cooks (1128 Mainland St., 688-6755).

Owner Barbara-jo McIntosh is an excellent chef and former restaurateur, which means she really knows what she's doing. This shop of culinary arts and letters is total bliss-out time for cookbook junkies. There are over 2500 titles to choose from (and more coming in every day), including professional titles for aspiring chefs. What McIntosh doesn't carry, she'll hunt down for you. Cooking demonstrations by authors and local chefs let you watch the technique, sample the dish and walk away with the cookbook.

For the record, you won't find a single cookbook by a Vancouver chef on my bookshelf. Not one. They're all in the kitchen. The reason? They work. I can't count the times I've leafed through Bill Jones and Stephen Wong's *New World Noodles* at 4 p.m. looking for supper ideas, or whipped up one of the sumptuous but essentially simple soups in *Bishop's: The Cookbook* for a special dinner party. Any one of the books on this list will make you a better cook.

Barbara-jo McIntosh, author of *The Tin Fish Gourmet* and owner of Barbara-Jo's Books to Cooks.

Asian Tapas and Wild Sushi
by **Trevor Hooper**
(Whitecap Books)
The former owner of Raku is known for his intelligent mixing of East and West. Here he shows you how to do it. Recipes are presented seasonally and combinations suggested — like Corn Cakes with Jalapeño Créma for summer and Tamarind Spiced Green Beans for winter. This book is worth the price for Hooper's easy-to-follow instructions on how to become an instant expert at making sushi rolls.

Bishop's: The Cookbook
by **John Bishop**
(Douglas & McIntyre)
The next best thing to eating there. Glorious soups and salads, simple bistro dishes like grilled flank steak with crisp summer greens, or roast halibut fillet with red onion and strawberry salsa. For dessert? What else but Bishop's notorious Death by Chocolate. Wine suggestions included. At the back are recipes for all the stocks required. Lazybones can buy them from The Stock Market on Granville Island.

Diane Clement at the Tomato
by **Diane Clement**
(Raincoast Books)
Habitués of the Tomato Fresh Food Café will recognize many of the recipes. Among them, the vitamin-packed Susi Q made with bananas, strawberries and orange juice, and the restaurant's comforting Indonesian Squash Soup. Hefty sandwiches include versions made with roast chicken and lime basil mayonnaise, and open-faced focaccia topped with roasted vegetables. Old-fashioned meat loaf, Santa Fe Corn Pie...Clement nicely straddles dining-out food and the food you go home for.

Five Star Food and *Six O'Clock Solutions*
by **Eve Johnson** and the ***Vancouver Sun* Test Kitchen**
(The Vancouver Sun)
Recipes drawn from readers and chefs, and developed by test kitchen staff, make this a luscious grab-bag of treats. My copy falls open automatically at the Lemon Apricot Scones and Salmon with Roasted Red Pepper Sauce. *Six O'Clock Solutions* is just that: quick, tasty ideas for the frazzled commuter who flies in the door at six and wants supper on the table in half an hour. Pizza from scratch that takes less time than take-out, luscious pastas, stir-fries, revisionist burgers and more.

The Flavours of Tuscany
by **Umberto Menghi**
(Douglas & McIntyre)
A sensual wallow. Two among the many winners are Menghi's Eggplant Terrine — great for summer entertaining – and his definitive, ridiculously easy and never-fail Braised Veal Shank — or, as the poshies call it, "Osso Buco." Suggested wines are listed.

The Girls Who Dish!
by **Karen Barnaby, Margaret Chisholm, Deb Connors, Tamara Kourchenko, Mary Mackay, Caren McSherry-Valagao, Glenys Morgan** and **Lesley Stowe**
(Whitecap Books)
Subtitled "Top women chefs cook their best!" this is a luscious compendium of full-bodied recipes. Recipes are the kind that make you want to run right out to the kitchen and get down to work. Starters range from Kourchenko's creamily wonderful roasted garlic and onion flan to Morgan's double tomato bruschetta, its flavour heightened with sun-dried tomatoes. Notable among the salads is Mackay's warm shredded bread version (which makes sense; she's the baker at Terra Breads). Barnaby contributes a formidable "chicken with forty cloves of garlic and a mickey of brandy," Chisholm an equally comforting dish of duck breasts with roasted peppers, honey and balsamic vinegar. Sophisticated pasta in the form of penne with grilled asparagus and preserved lemon comes from caterer Lesley Stowe. Desserts range from the wildly rich to homey cookies.

The Girls Who Dish: (back) Lesley Stowe, Deb Connors, Mary Mackay, Margaret Chisholm; (front) Tamara Kourchenko, Caren McSherry-Valago, Glenys Morgan, Karen Barnaby.

HeartSmart™ Chinese Cooking
by **Stephen Wong**
(Douglas & McIntyre)
Cuts the fat without losing a bit of the flavour. Oil is often replaced with thickened stock. Skim milk powder stands in for heavy cream. And a non-stick pan is the secret weapon. Recipes marry East and West ingredients to create dishes like Salmon with Szechuan Pepper, and Spinach Fettucine with Moo Shu Prawns.

HeartSmart™ Flavours of India
by **Krishna Jamal**
(Douglas & McIntyre)
Another in the popular series from the Heart and Stroke Foundation. Jamal, executive chef at Rubina Tandoori, takes a lighter approach to classic Indian favourites. Drastically cutting back the amount of oil and using ingredients like low-fat yogurt makes these dishes healthier with no loss of flavour.

New World Noodles and *New World Chinese Cooking*
by **Bill Jones** and **Stephen Wong**
(Robert Rose)
Easy-to-make, vibrantly-flavoured recipes that draw on all the Asian ingredients that have now found their way into most Vancouver supermarkets. Features all kinds of noodles — fresh and dried — along with lemon grass, five-spice mix, a whole panoply of seasonings. Some combinations are irresistible, such as the five-spice maple-cured salmon.

Pacific Passions Cookbook and *Screamingly Good Food*
by **Karen Barnaby**
(Whitecap Books)
As much fun to read as they are to cook from. Standouts in *Pacific Passions* are Barnaby's recipes for Dungeness Crab Cakes and her luscious Sour Dried Cherry and Chocolate Pound Cake. And who could resist her "small feasts" in *Screamingly Good Food* — celebrations that we all should add to our calendar along with suitable food. "A Feast for the Last Tomato" is celebrated with Roast Leg of Pork with Crackling and Rutabaga Purée with Balsamic Vinegar. "A Feast for the Longest Day" is a vegetable buffet of Whole Roasted Eggplant with Tomatoes and Capers, and Grilled Zucchini with Mint, Yogurt and Feta Cheese.

Peasant's Choice
by **James Barber**
(Urban Peasant Productions Ltd.)
The most recent volume by the chef who has probably done more than anyone else in the city to introduce its residents to good food. Not fancy food, but honest joyful food made with good, fresh ingredients. Chicken consommé in a silver teapot, cold tomato soup whizzed in a blender, Lebanese cumin carrots, salmon with rhubarb and rice stuffing — everything's simple to make and huge on flavour. P.S. If you come upon any of Barber's early books, grab 'em, they're collector's items.

Scrambled Brains: A Cooking Guide for the Reality Impaired
by **Robin Konstabaris** and **Pierre LeBlanc**
(Arsenal Pulp Press)
Probably the most irreverent cookbook you'll ever have on your shelf. The recipe titles — Subliminal Alphabet and Naked Dinner Party — give some idea of the contents.

Tin Fish Gourmet
by **Barbara-jo McIntosh**
(Raincoast)
Why didn't someone do this before? A brilliant cookbook that celebrates all those seafood staples we keep in our cupboards. Makeshift suppers these aren't. Canned salmon meets up with Brie and asparagus in an omelette. A tuna casserole includes yams, red pepper, fresh basil and Parmesan.

Vancouver Cooks With Caren McSherry
by **Caren McSherry**
(Great Culinary Adventures)
A Mediterranean emphasis leads to brightly flavoured dishes: tortellini and chorizo soup, classic focaccia, addictive herbed cheese appetizers zinged with sun-dried tomatoes and fresh basil — that kind of thing.

Chef's Tip
"I make sure everything's completely chopped, prepped, grated and juiced before I start cooking."
— Barbara-jo McIntosh, Barbara-Jo's Books to Cooks

EDITH ADAMS COTTAGE

To Vancouverites, the name of Edith Adams rings as many bells as that of Betty Crocker or Aunt Jemima. Edith Adams is an icon. Eternally smiling, invariably clad in an apron, she's the mom, aunt or grandmother who always has a pan of fresh-baked cookies on her kitchen table — and knows everything there is to know about cooking.

"Edith" — or as she was known back then, "Miss Adams" — first showed up in the *Vancouver Sun* in 1912. (It's nice to imagine her as a shy young thing making up dainty tea sandwiches prior to a game of croquet.) As the years went by, she took on more responsibility, and, by 1947, had moved into her own "Cottage."

A forerunner of Martha Stewart, Edith Adams was a fount of information on everything to do with the home. A trio of home economists answered the phones, fielding questions on everything from how to make a loaf of brown bread to knitting, etiquette and even, on one occasion, on how to remove ballpoint-pen ink from a Cabbage Patch doll.

These days, the staff is smaller and they spend their time developing and testing recipes. All requests have to come by mail and include a stamped, self-addressed envelope.

"The most requested recipes are for UBC cinnamon buns and UBC muffins," reveals "Edith Adams," a.k.a. *Vancouver Sun* Test Kitchen home economists Ruth Phelan and Brenda Thompson. Other faves are for homey comfort foods: shepherd's pie, meat loaf, Sex in a Pan and especially chocolate chip and other cookies. "People specify either 'crisp' or 'chewy'," reveals Phelan; recipes in the files are marked accordingly. Around Christmas, letters to these culinary Santas often ask for instructions on how to make rich, dark fruit cake, shortbread and King George's Pudding as well as "yule logs" — chemical-impregnated newspaper rolls that burn with different festive-coloured flames.

Questions change with the seasons, with lots of pickling and canning queries in the summer. "There are heaps of questions about salmon canning," says

Phelan. "People also want to know if they can preserve antipasto by canning" — Edith's advice is to make a freezer version instead. Demand for vegetarian and low fat baking recipes is high, and there are more and more requests for dishes that cater to specific dietary needs — dishes that are gluten-free or high-calcium, for example. Checking her filing cabinets filled with an estimated 80,000 recipes, Edith can always come up with the answer.

Edith Adams may be a sprightly centenarian, but she's kept up with the times.

DINING IN:

Take-Out Food and Meals on Wheels

When you can't stomach the thought of cooking, there's take-out or "order-in": systems whereby other people do the work and you eat what's put on the table. Almost all restaurants (not just Indian or Chinese ones) will do take-out if you ask them, so if you have a sudden hankering for flambéed goose breast from Café Posh, call them up and see if they'll oblige.

BURNABY:

Takeout Taxi
3261 Smith St. • 451-4491
Solves the problem of what to do when you want pizza, he wants BBQ chicken and the kids have their hearts set on Chinese. $10 food minimum per restaurant. Delivers far and wide. Close to three dozen eateries to choose from. Thai, Indian, Italian, Chinese vegetarian, Vietnamese, Japanese, Malaysian, plus deli favourites, fish and chips, bagels, chicken and ribs.

SURREY:

First City Gourmet

10-7795 128th St. • 543-9667

Home delivery since 1993. Individual homestyle meals are frozen and delivered to door. Think of it: no shopping, no cooking — okay a little nukeing — and no dishes. Choices range from homey roast beef dinners and stews to pastas, Szechuan chicken and Mexican lentil casserole. Soups, desserts, waffles and pies, too.

NORTH VANCOUVER:

The Casual Gourmet

Park & Tilford Centre • 987-4300

Lip-smacking choices from chef Peter Vieser include fresh crab or shrimp salad on French baguette, tomato and bocconcini salad, and calories-be-damned florentines for dessert.

VANCOUVER:

Alma Tandoori

2529 Alma St. • 222-9779

Indian food via London, England. Try the butter chicken or tandoori chicken, or anything else on the menu. Highly recommended.

Chefs Secret Service

4434 West 10th Ave. • 222-9800

Take out healthy, colourful food from this catering company (and restaurant). Typical menu items: black bean burritos, filo-wrapped vegetable frittata, a crunchy beggar's purse packed full of sea bass or salmon with a sweet and sour salsa. Also: Grandma-type desserts, a tangy fruit tart with whipped cream, cheesecake, créme caramel, chocolate zucchini cake. Live music on weekends.

The Epicurean Delicatessen

1898 West 1st Ave. • 731-5370

As well as Italian groceries and authentic deli ambience, this corner of Italy features sandwiches with muscle. Various felicitous combinations of European ham, cheeses, pickled eggplant with juices that soak into the bread, and sundried tomatoes, all on foccacia,

Take-Out De Luxe

Traditionally (because I like to stay home but I don't want to cook), my birthday dinner is take-out from Meinhardt Fine Foods (3002 Granville St., 732-4405). Once, when a family dinner included a mix of vegetarians, carnivores and someone who couldn't eat garlic — and time was short — we cheated and bought every single dish here. Dishes change with the seasons. In late summer you might find BBQ baby back ribs or meatballs, risotto, grilled chicken breast, inventive pasta and other salads, roasted garlic and shallots, and loads more. For dessert, pick up a tangy lemon curd tart, a banana-mango cake or "Chocolate Decadence." In the summertime, it's fun to pick up a picnic, stroll into the heart of Shaughnessy and spread your blanket in the park at the centre of The Crescent.

are bargain priced. A seat outside near the fig tree lets you savour the smells perking through the window.

The European Delicatessen
1220 Davie St. • 688-3442
Samosas, Jamaican patties, smoked meat, Middle Eastern foods and more. Around the world in a sandwich shop.

Graem Castell's Finest Foods to Your Door
102-1633 West 11th Ave. • 731-5456
Known as "The Good Food Man," Castell delivers flash-frozen gourmet foods to your door. Steaks by the dozen, large shrimp, swordfish and mahi mahi, smoked black cod, chicken spring rolls, salmon Wellington — a huge selection. As a customer, you'll receive Castell's whimsical and witty newsletters.

House of Foccacia
102-500 West Broadway • 876-8433
Grilled foccacia and chicken shwarmas at bargain prices.

Take-out at
Lesley Stowe Fine Foods

Lesley Stowe Fine Foods
1780 West 3rd Ave. • 731-3663
What's available changes every couple of months but stalwarts are grilled Tuscan vegetables and crab cakes. Always on the menu are salmon, chicken pizzas, soups and salad — not to mention Stowe's legendary lemon dacquoise.

The Menu Setters Fine Food & Catering
3655 West 10th Ave. • 732-4218
Single servings or supper for two. Dishes in the cooler may include beef stroganoff, beef bourgignon, chicken breasts in a white wine sauce with mushrooms, three cheese and artichoke canneloni, chicken chili con queso and — very popular — shepherd's pie in traditional and chicken versions.

Minerva Mediterranean Deli
3207 West Broadway • 733-3954
Eat outside on the sidewalk or take out homemade Greek favourites like pastitsio, spinach pie, stuffed tomatoes, giro sandwiches, souvlaki, Greek and Mediterranean-style spare ribs or charbroiled chicken. Plan 'B': buy a stack of pita bread and a bunch of houmus, tsatsiki and olives. A recent addition to the menu is the spiced feta cheese spread from Northern Greece called chtipiti.

Nazare BBQ Mexican Chicken
1859 Commercial Dr. • 251-1844
About 20 spices are rubbed into the chicken before it's barbecued. Delicious.

Nyala African Hotspot
2930 West 4th Ave. • 731-7899
Injera (flat, tangy Ethiopian bread) and curries to go. You can also buy mango chutney in three strengths (mild, medium and hot) and a spicy sauce called kulet made from red peppers, onion, garlic and ginger. For a swift supper, just add chicken, beef or fish.

Pita Plus
2967 West Broadway • 733-9900
340 West 2nd Ave. • 876-6663
Inside a variety of pitas — sesame, multi-grain, flax seed, onion, vegetable or spelt (a wheat alternative) — go your choice of three salads from the 20 freshly made. Cheerful Mediterranean flavours. Marinated carrot or eggplant, homous, a zippy Turkish melange or marinated onions, tomato, parsley and spices, even good old potato.

Stock Market
Granville Island Market • 687-2433
Georges and Joanne Lefebvre specialize in the deeply flavoured stocks that are the backbone of great cuisine. Chicken, beef, veal brown and clear, lamb, fish stock and vegetarian stock are all made from scratch. Sauces range from port and mushroom to a ginger demiglace. Tasty chutneys, salad dressings and soups, too. This is the cheat's way to haute cuisine.

Potluck Pretense
Tapping gourmet sources can imply you've been slaving away for hours. For starters, decant the Parthenon's homous or tzatsiki into pottery bowls, and tote some barbary bread to crisp at 350°. Stuck with the salad course? Give a toss to sold-by-the-gram mixed greens or, failing that, the crispest romaine you can find, with The Stock Market's raspberry and ginger dressing. If soup's on your list, try their bean or squash for casual suppers, cream of broccoli or oyster soup for posh events. Mains? Cheat with meat from Meinhardt's: simple roast chicken, boeuf bourgignon or lamb ragout. Volunteer dessert, then let Capers supply a bumbleberry pie in its own glass pie-plate or Ecco Il Pane, a busting-with-berries crostatta di frutta which looks like it came straight from the oven. Yours, of course.

Sushi Bang

500 West Broadway • 875-0131

Made-while-you-watch sushi and nori. Party platters are a good bet.

Terra Breads

2380 West 4th Ave. • 736-1838

Sorta like pizza without the mess, foccacia sandwiches come topped with prosciutto, Roma tomatoes, sage and mozzarella. Daily special might be a teaming of artichokes, roasted mushrooms, mozzarella, parmesan and herbs. Chewy bread with a commendable sourdough tang. Fastest food: Saran-wrapped, they're ready to go.

Thai Away Home

3315 Cambie St. • 873-8424

Fresh Thai herbs, curry sauces, spicy salads, pre-marinated satay sticks (and peanut sauce to go with them) are all available for take-out or to eat on the spot. If you feel like doing a little cooking, you'll find pre-measured ingredients for classic Thai dishes like pad phai, and chicken and cashew nuts. Don't forget the (sp)iced Thai tea.

Sandwiches on South Granville

Should that leisurely trawl through all those expensive designer stores on South Granville have left your wallet severely depleted, elbow your way up to the window at Gianni (2881 Granville St., 738-7922). Saturdays only, staff dish out inexpensive take-out sandwiches of the lusty Italian kind, various combinations of prosciutto, provolone and other deli favourites, as well as pizza squares.

EATING WHAT'S GOOD FOR YOU

Certain stretches of some Vancouver streets — 4th Avenue, Commercial Drive, West Broadway — seem to be nothing but restaurants. Any time of the night or day, you can pick up food. Demonic desserts, big hunky breakfast muffins. Suddenly you're five kilos heavier. So many chocolate croissants, so little time. How do you cope?

Food is an important part of a balanced diet.
— Fran Lebowitz

"It's really very easy to eat well [read healthily] in Vancouver," says professional nutritionist Ramona Josephson. "We have every opportunity to follow the guidelines," she adds, referring to Health Canada's recommendation that we favour grains and veggies over meat and dairy products. "Other cities don't have access to the variety we have," Josephson points out. "So many people say they get bored with carrots, celery and tomatoes. In Vancouver, we have a huge array of grains and vegetables to choose from, not just in produce stores and supermarkets but at farmers' markets and ethnic markets, too."

Eating healthily at home is no big deal. Going out presents a different set of problems. Ethnic restaurants are often good for lower-fat choices, says Josephson. "Chinese restaurants stress grains and vegetables, but you still have to be careful. A lot of dishes are deep-fried." Her recommendations? "Start with hot and sour soup instead of egg drop soup. Have steamed dumplings, fish or chicken instead of anything deep-fried or batter-coated. Avoid things like spare ribs and sweet-and-sour pork — they're loaded with fat."

Mexican food, she'll tell you, can also be nutritionally dangerous — and she's not referring to that bottle of hot sauce on the table. Salsa is a better choice than guacamole (the fat in avocados is unsaturated but the calorie count is still high.) "Be concerned about refried beans, and anything with cheese in it such as quesadillas. Order chicken fajitas; then you can decide how much you want to wrap in your tortilla. Use lots of salsa and hot sauce. Grilled fish or chicken are good."

Some cuisines are easier than others. Tempura apart, you can order almost anything in a Japanese restaurant. "Italian restaurants are stop-go places. Pasta loaded with a clam and tomato sauce is a far cry from fettucine alfredo. Choose Italian bread over garlic bread, chicken cacciatore rather than lasagne or cheese- or meat-filled ravioli. Italian ice instead of spumoni."

The word on eating between meals? We have an abundance of coffee shops but very little to pick from in the way of snacks, says Josephson. "It's usually baked goods, which often contain lots of fat. Biscotti is a better choice. Many places you can get fruit salad or yogurt with a bit of granola." Wraps are a good, quick meal, she says, because they're usually loaded with rice and shredded vegetables. Bagel places call for caution. "Large bagels can be high in calories. Look for the smaller-sized ones, and ask for light cream cheese and tons of vegetables as a topping."

And when you're off to the movies, sigh, there are only two "safe" choices: sugar-free gum and a diet pop.

DINING OUT

If you love to eat out, there are few better cities in which to hang your hat than Vancouver. From small, inexpensive Asian noodle houses to the finest of modern French cuisine, we've got the lot. For the curious diner, it's an endless adventure: so many places to put your feet under someone else's table, and so little time.

Culinary explorations — especially ethnic ones — cost peanuts here compared with most big cities. Vietnamese pho houses can serve you big bowls of hearty soup you can season with basil, chilis and lime. Little Chinese or Japanese places can bring you dishes of intensely flavoured Shanghai noodles or ramen. Indian restaurants let you discover the extraordinary symphony of flavours that spices like cumin and coriander add to a dish. None of them will break your budget.

But when you do want to settle in for the evening, and settle down to a dinner you'll remember with pleasure for months, what a choice you have: casual bistros; big glamorous eateries; small, neighbourhood secret places.

So few pages, so many restaurants. The ones listed here only skim the surface of dining out in this truly remarkable city.

Bon appétit.

Farmers and Growers in the Limelight

Following on the success of the winemakers' dinners, the Four Seasons Hotel now holds seasonal producers' dinners. Same idea, except that instead of a winemaker telling you all about his labels, a farmer or grower does the same, course by course. A typical dinner might showcase farm-raised salmon, new potato varieties, venison, B.C.-made sheep's milk cheese and locally grown cranberries. Before everyone sits down, there's an opportunity to sample the products and talk to those who produce them. Call 689-9333 for info.

DINING OUT

Restaurants and Cafés

Four thousand? Two thousand? Three-thousand-if-you-don't-count-Starbuck's-and-McDonald's? Nobody's sure precisely how many places there are in the Lower Mainland where you can sit down and let someone else do the cooking. Choices, choices. The following list could be twice, maybe even three times, as long as it is. It's simply a small sampling of the many Vancouver restaurants worth trying. We've rated the cost of a typical meal from $ (budget priced) to $$$$ (top-of-the-line food, service and prices).

Please note: for ease of browsing, the restaurants are listed alphabetically (by municipality) below, and then by ethnic and special categories towards the end of this chapter (pages 181-183).

NORTH VANCOUVER:
Kilby's
3108 Edgemont Blvd. • 990-4334
Upbeat chef Steve McKinley produces lusty flavours. Local favourites are the California lamb marinated for two days in honey, red wine and spices, and the rib-eye steak with a port and Stilton sauce. Pasta, salads and burgers, too. Garden patio is heated year-round. $$-$$$

The Village Bistro
3135 Edgemont Blvd. • 980-5535
Neighbourhood in feel, mostly Italian in direction. Classic (and not-so-classic) pastas, bocconcini salad, veal marsala or Parmigiana. Asian influences, too — such as the tuna carpaccio with wasabi, lime and sesame oil, or the butterfly prawns with mango salsa and pickled ginger. $$-$$$

RICHMOND:
Chinese Food in the "New" Chinatown
Some of the most exciting Chinese restaurants are in Richmond. Stephanie Yuen, Food and Style Writer for *Sing Tao*, and Food and Wine Show Host on AM1320, suggests the following:

Canton Wuntun Seafood House
6610 No. 3 Rd. • 270-2927
One hundred percent home cooking: simple, delicious and loaded with flavour. This restaurant has been around for many years and is still going strong. $

Chili House Restaurant
205-4231 Hazelbridge Way (Central Square) • 278-9700
Very authentic Taiwanese-style spicy cuisine. Lots of unusual but pleasing dishes (some of them quite "challenging," adds Yuen). $$-$$$

Eastern Fortune Restaurant
8071 Park Rd. • 278-7878
A small restaurant with some of the best dim sum in town. The owner/chef was a famous chef in Hong Kong and is still well known for his unique cooking style. $$-$$$

Fook Lam Moon Chiuchow Restaurant
6820 No. 3 Rd. • 278-3386
Serves the best Chiuchow style congee (rice soup). Their tiny steamed bun for dessert is a must-try. $$$

Imperial Court Beijing and Szechuan Restaurant
#6-6360 No. 3 Rd. • 270-6169
Serves a variety of Beijing and Szechuan cuisine. Don't miss their daily specials, which are usually under 10 dollars. $$

Lin's Taiwanese Kitchen
8080 Granville Ave. • 270-1565
A hidden treasure of good and cheap Taiwanese home cooking. A bowl of rice loaded with sautéed ground pork and mushrooms costs about three dollars. $

Locke Garden
8251 Alexander Rd. • 231-9339
The only restaurant of its kind open 24 hours. Serves both Hong Kong-style Western food and typical Chinese dishes. $

School Cafeteria Food Goes Gourmet…

…at Vancouver Community College (250 West Pender St.). On a typical day you may find pan-fried filet of cod provençale, or roast leg of lamb au jus, or veal piccata Milanaise with Italian tomato sauce, all for well under half what you'd pay in a restaurant. And if you do want classic restaurant service, check out J.J.'s Dining Room. Prices are a couple of dollars more but it's still one of the best deals in the city. For around $15 you get a choice of main course — duck breast with blueberry, cranberry and pear compote, duck jus, and rack of lamb are typical — an appetizer (maybe baked Brie and caramelized onions in filo, or tuna carpaccio), soup or salad and dessert. The Four Corners Restaurant is operated and managed by the students of the College's Hospitality Management Program.

Cheap Treats

The dish called Bombay Bel at Surat Sweet (1938 West 4th, 733-7363) is a true bargain. Puffed wheat, chickpea noodles, a vegetable curry, tamarind sauce, and two power-packed chili chutneys arrive separately on your plate. Mashed together, they're a gorgeous mixture of flavours and contrasts.

Lung Kee Seafood Restaurant
8111 Leslie Rd. • 278-6688

The first Hong Kong-style gourmet seafood restaurant that marked its territory in Richmond still serves a very good bowl of plain congee and deep-fried long bread, and simple, delicious, very fresh seafood. $$

Neptune Shark Fin and Seafood Restaurant
100-8171 Ackroyd Rd. • 207-9888

The chef/owner is famous for his abalone recipe. Here's where to experience what seafood restaurants in Hong Kong are like. $$-$$$

New Castle Seafood Restaurant
11700 Cambie Rd. • 278-8818

One of the early arrivals to Richmond's food and restaurant scene is still the best banquet restaurant in the area. They set up a pan-fried station during lunch hours to serve hot pan-fried goodies. $$

VANCOUVER:

Adega
1022 Main St. • 685-7818

Classic Portuguese dishes like grilled chourico (chorizo) and caldo verde (potato and kale soup). For mains, satisfying choices are the carne de porco com ameijos alentejana (pork and clams) or bacalhau — salt cod served steamed, grilled or casseroled. $$

Afro Canadian
324 Cambie St. • 682-2646

Tiny Gastown location covers most of Africa. Injera — traditional Ethiopian flat bread — accompanies different spicy meat and vegetable preparations. You'll also find Moroccan couscous, Egyptian molokheya (veggies and beef), West African dumplings called "fufu" and Jamaican jerk chicken. $

Allegro Café
888 Nelson St. • 683-8485

Lively West Coast cuisine in a bright and cheery room. A legal beagle haven at lunchtime. Wide-ranging menu spans osso buco, paella, angelhair pasta with black tiger prawns. Numerous dinner specials. $$ to $$$

All India Sweets
6507 Main St. • 327-0891
Brilliant pink, green and yellow "sweets" are the main draw locally, but this spot is also worth a stop for authentic, thoughtfully spiced dishes. Tandoori chicken, mini-samosas, panir pakoras, dahi bhalls (lentil balls in yogurt), butter chicken and goat curry. Lengthy vegetarian listings plus a 40-item buffet. $

The Amorous Oyster
3236 Oak St. • 732-5916
A neighbourhood favourite for years. Three guesses as to the specialty! As well as bivalves in several guises, this cozy spot serves up inventive seafood and pasta dishes. Food a bargain given the quality; service is consistently friendly. $$

Annapurna
1812 West 4th Ave. • 736-5959
Indian vegetarian food known for its astute and subtle, often mild, spicing. Among the entrées, best-sellers are curried spinach and navrattan korma – a mixed vegetable dish. Try the haunting, smoked puréed eggplant and the malai kofta (meatballs without the meat). $

Apollonia
1830 Fir St. • 736-9559
One visit will make you a regular at this warm family restaurant. Harry Prinianakis does the welcoming, his wife Thea does the cooking. Extraordinary roast lamb (their biggest seller), terrific homous and tsatziki – the traditional Greek repertoire, prepared with love and skill. $-$$

Bacchus/Wedgewood Hotel
845 Hornby St. • 689-7777
Lushly elegant European surroundings. Big-flavoured food from the open kitchen: pan-roasted muscovy duck breast served with duck confit and potato goat cheese canneloni, oven-baked sea bass with a shiitake mushroom crust, or orecchiette with tomatoes, baby leeks and double-smoked bacon. Five-course tasting menu on request, by reservation only. $$$$

Chocolate Epicentre
The buzz on dark and creamy anything spreads like Nutella but shameless cocoa-heads know that the epicentre of utter degradation is the Robson and Burrard crossroads. First, a chocolate martini fix at Planet Hollywood, then a stop at Death by Chocolate (818 Burrard). Drooling, leaf through their book of choco-porn and let staff cater to your fantasies. A "French Affair"? A "Between the Sheets" complete with whipping cream (lashings, we hope)? Hardened addicts stagger on to the Sutton Place Hotel, where on Thursdays, Fridays and Saturdays they lay out their notorious chocoholic's buffet.

Banana Leaf
1016 West Broadway • 731-6333
Malaysian specialties. Good bets are sweetish char kuey teow (noodles with shrimp, sausage, egg, sprouts) and seductive curries. Gastronomic adventurers can order the fish-head curry or kachang ikan belis — anchovies with peanuts. Tuesday is crab night, when scuttlers go at a bargain price. $-$$

Bellavista
1408 Commercial Dr. • 255-2307
Chilean cuisine for a change? Try wine-steamed clams or empanadas to start, then one of the variations of meat-on-a-Chilean bun. Other good bets are the fried cod with a zippy salad and the traditional take on bouillabaisse, brimming with clams, mussels and crab. Buckets of cilantro in everything. $-$$

Bishop's
2183 West 4th Ave. • 738-2025
The restaurant most people vote for when someone else is footing the bill. Warm, intimate room, art-lined walls. Imagination and freshness are the secrets behind the much-praised West Coast cuisine. Death by Chocolate is a must for dessert. Exceptional service from genial host John Bishop. $$$$

Brickhouse
730 Main St. • 689-6845
Wrong part of town. Right kind of food. Pan-Asian meets West Coast cuisine at bargain prices. Check the cozy bar downstairs. $

C
1600 Howe St. • 681-1164
You've never tasted fish like this before — or seen such imaginative presentation. One starter is served on what looks like a miniature bookcase. Lobster, tuna, crab, caviar — take your pick. A must-try is the Saskatoon berry tea-smoked salmon gravlax. All this, plus a show-stopping view of False Creek. $$$$

Why Restaurant Food Costs What it Does

The textbook breakdown of a restaurant dish allocates a third each to food, overhead and profit.

Chef Dennis Green at Bishop's

Café de Paris
751 Denman St. • 687-1418
The romantic ambience comes straight from the Left Bank and the frites are the best in town. Traditional French dishes — bouillabaisse, confit of duck — are carefully prepared. Menu also incorporates West Coast influences. Periodic festivals focus on game or lobster. $$$

Chartwell/Four Seasons Hotel
791 West Georgia St. • 689-9333
Huge comfy chairs, fireplace and elegant decor are the setting for fresh and imaginative cooking. Seasonal menu features dishes like crab cakes with sweet-and-sour green tomatoes and gingered peach aioli, salmon with shrimp ratatouille, and veal chop with a fennel-cucumber ragout. Spectacular desserts. $$$$

CinCin
1154 Robson St. • 688-7338
The place to pretend you're in Tuscany. Wood-fired oven turns out mind-blowing grills and pizzas. Shared antipasti or three-course dinner, the food here never disappoints. On warm evenings try for a seat outdoors and eyeball the Robson Street scene. $$$

Cinco Estrelas
2268 Kingsway • 439-1124
Simple, authentic Portuguese tapas and mains such as pork with clams. Grilled sardinhas, bacalhau (salt cod) and bifé (steak topped with fried eggs). $-$$

Dawat
5076 Victoria Dr. • 322-3550
Beyond the little Indian sweet shop is a sophisticated dining room with complex and seductively flavoured dishes. Mussels swim in a copper pan (and a rich creamy sauce). Tandoori dishes come spitting and hissing: try the rack of lamb version or the cod tikka. $-$$

Del-hi Darbar
2120 Main St. • 877-7733
Famous for dosas — brown, crisp pancakes rolled

Chefs' Night Out
Richard Zeinoun and Lisa Gibson of Habibi's favour Star Anise (where Zeinoun used to work), Surat Sweet and, for take-out, Thai Away Home.

"Vij's is one favourite," says Andrew Skorzewski of Rainforest Café. "Also Surat Sweet — the food is so unlike other traditional Indian restaurants. Momiji's on Fraser is our inexpensive, go anytime Japanese restaurant. For a treat? I'm a bit of a gadfly. I go to Diva, Bishop's, La Toque Blanche."

"We have three children so we vote on where to go," says Assefe Kebede of Nyala African Hotspot. "Often it's Trafalgar's or York Pizza or Incendio. Small restaurants. We go out once a week. Sometimes to The Cannery, or Koko for Japanese."

Carol Chow of Beach Side Café likes Le Crocodile, Lumière and "Vij's for curries of any sort." She loves ribs in the summertime, hence her enthusiasm for Fatzo's. "I like to try different things."

around a spicy filling. Authentic southern Indian food. Try the chicken makhni in its sauce of nuts and butter, prawn masala, or tender skewer-cooked murg tikka. The nan bread is exceptional."Bombay snacks" on Saturday afternoons. Gracious service. $-$$

Diva at the Met/Metropolitan Hotel
645 Howe St. • 602-7788

Upbeat atmosphere, big glittery room and an open kitchen. What's on your plate is terrific too. Chef Michael Noble has a brilliant hand with fish — if smoked black cod is on the menu, go for it. Desserts are thoroughly glamorous, the Stilton cheesecake a new classic. Terrific wine list. $$$

Diva at the Met

El Patio
891 Cambie St. • 681-9149

On hot days, the airy rooftop patio is a find. On rainy days, inside always feels sunny. Core menu of tapas plus Mediterranean faves. Order the patatas bravas, albondigas (meat balls), swimming scallops or simply grilled chorizo. Sangria is the best accompaniment. $$

Fatzo's Barbecue and Smokehouse
2884 West Broadway • 733-3002

Long, slow-cooked barbecue is the focus in this funky, friendly eaterie. Ribs, brisket, chicken — all fall to pieces at the touch of a fork. Simple accompaniments like corn and potatoes place Fatzo's firmly in the deep south. $-$$

The Fish House in Stanley Park
8901 Stanley Park Dr. • 681-7275
Like a huge, rambling seaside cottage. Whacking great flavours reflect chef Karen Barnaby's generous touch. Crunchy-coated salmon cakes with commendable fries, pan roasted cod with pancetta and lemon pepper relish, or a bouillabaisse-like seafood hot pot. Spins on oysters, prawns; pastas, chicken and pork, too. Desserts are original sins. $$-$$$

Five Sails/Pan Pacific Hotel
300-999 Canada Place • 662-8111
A big, sumptuous room with a killer view of mountains and harbour makes this a favourite for special occasions. Fresh West Coast cuisine and exceptional lamb. Exciting approaches to duck and salmon. $$$$

Fleuri/Sutton Place Hotel
845 Burrard St. • 682-5511
Elegant, pretty room. Vibrantly flavoured dishes from chef Kai Lerman, who marries Eastern and Western ingredients with highly successful results. Lyrical soups, impeccable fish. Leave room, Thursdays through Saturdays, for the chocolate dessert buffet. $$$-$$$$

Le Gavroche
1616 Alberni St. • 685-3924
Gallic ambience and dishes that combine classical influences with West Coast verve. Examples? Fresh prawn cakes with corn fritters and cilantro aioli. Mussels steamed with lemongrass. Smoked Alaska black cod with burnt orange and anise coulis. If you're tired of making decisions, zero in on the table d'hote dinner, with or without matched wines. The wine list, by the way, is famous. $$$-$$$$

Grand Pattaya
656 Leg-in-Boot Square • 876-0676
Thai food plus a False Creek view. Prawn cakes bounce with fat, fresh seafood. The prawn pan cake — a different dish — includes ham and cashew nuts. Yum nua salad features charcoal-grilled beef marinated in lime juice and chilis. Yellow curry crab and steamed fresh tilapia fish also recommended. $$

Chef's Picks:
"All India Sweets has the best samosas, Hon's Wun Tun House is the best place for cheap Chinese, Shijo for sushi and Solly's for bagels."
— Anne Milne, Chef and Food Consultant

Grand King Seafood
705 West Broadway • 876-7855

Big traditional restaurant offers unforgettable dishes such as winter melon soup with seafood, and suckling pig. Unusual for a Chinese restaurant, Chef Lam Kam Shing's menu incorporates local ingredients such as salmon. Go with a group if you can. $$-$$$

Griffins/Hotel Vancouver
900 West Georgia St. • 662-1900

Taxicab-yellow, high energy room offers imaginative, bright-flavoured food throughout the day. Favourites are the buffets, hot or cold. $$-$$$

Gyoza King
1508 Robson St. • 669-8278

Atmospheric at night when it's crammed with homesick young Japanese locals. The gyoza (dumplings) are terrific. Order them by sixes or tens. They're all recommended — meat or seafood-based, and especially the vegetable with spinach variety — as are the noodle dishes. Try the rock-bottom priced specials, too. $

Hachibei
778 West 16th Ave. • 879-8821

Homey little Japanese restaurant. Try the gyoza and gomaae (spinach dressed with a sweetish soy sauce and sprinkled with sesame seeds). Order black cod if it's on the menu. Specials include homestyle accompaniments such as wilted cabbage cooked with smoky bacon. Chicken karaage is light and crisp and the tempura is better than average. $

Habibi's
1128 West Broadway • 732-7487

Lebanese food made with care and pride. Try foule (black beans liberally sauced with lemon and garlic) or warak anab, which are like spicier dolmades. Terrific baba ganoush and shinkleesh (a dried, herbed goat cheese). Pita bread, olives, pickles and peanuts included free. $

Havana
1212 Commercial Dr. • 253-9119
Gallery, theatre and restaurant serving real Cuban food. Sandwiches heap meats, cheese and grilled veggies on Cuban buns with sofrito, a mix of cooked peppers and tomatoes. Mains include jambalaya and red snapper with black beans. Tapas, too. Cuban breakfasts highly recommended. $-$$

The Hermitage
115-1025 Robson St. • 689-3237
Escargots, prune-stuffed rabbit ballotine and New York steak with Roquefort butter reveal chef/owner Hervé Martin's French heritage. Expect fresh variations on the classics, too. An endive salad is topped with goat cheese and Oriental noodles, sautéed chicken comes with ginger and raisin confit, salmon with a black currant cream sauce. Daily table d'hote lunch menu. $$$$

Herons/Waterfront Centre Hotel
900 Canada Place Way • 691-1818
West Coast cuisine features homegrown ingredients such as Fraser Valley rabbit or Campbell River salmon. Herbs are picked from the hotel's own rooftop garden. Typical choices are smoked chicken quiche, pan-seared bison, and curried crab layered Napoleon-style with poppadoms and served with mesclun greens. Super lunchtime buffet. $$$

Il Giardino
1382 Hornby St. • 669-2422
Dress up for this one and you'll be a match for the chic crowd. Attractive Tuscan-inspired interior but the place to go is the garden (if you can get in). Start with the antipasto then move on to veal. Conclude with the excellent tiramisu. $$$$

Irish Heather Bistro
217 Carrall St. • 688-9779
Cuisine from the Emerald Isle with West Coast influences. Samples? Rabbit in Three Guises — sausage, braised leg and roasted loin — with a dried cranberry jus, steak with whiskey sauce and garlic "champ"

The $3 Lunch

There are still a few places where a loonie and a toonie will buy you a meal. A big bowl of pho or noodles shared between the two of you is one possibility. Another is plain congee at a Chinese restaurant. It's rice porridge (much nicer than it sounds), usually with shreds of fresh ginger in its depths, and green onions and peanuts on top. The third possibility is banh mi — a Vietnamese sandwich made with a crispy bread roll, ham, shredded pork or meat ball, and marinated vegetables.

(mashed potatoes with scallions), and the lamb-based Kerry Pie. Guinness on tap. $$-$$$

Kalamata
478 West Broadway • 872-7050
A consistent award-winner. Stathi and Laura Rallis offer deep-flavoured, home Greek cooking. Paidakia, souvlaki with superb roasted potatoes, probably the best Greek salad in town — you're safe in ordering just about anything. Chicken liver lovers should zero in on the tender sikotakia. $$

Kirin Seafood Restaurant
555 West 12th Ave. • 879-8038
Definitive Chinese food. Slick decor, a mountain view and a leaning toward Cantonese cuisine. Menu runs from congee to $600 soup. Live lobsters and crab cooked a dozen ways. Try sesame prawns with lemon sauce or the dried tangerine and hot chili beef. Confused by the number of choices? Set meals are a wise idea. $-$$$$

La Bodega
1277 Howe St. • 684-8815
Dark, cosy and authenic. Traditional tapas — garlic prawns, chorizo, exceptional calamari, an arroz espanol that's a virtual paella. Intriguing, mostly meat specials include rabbit with tomatoes and peppers, anticuchos of veal heart and morcilla — blood sausage with scallops, or quail for the less adventurous. $$

Las Margaritas
1999 West 4th Ave. • 734-7117
It feels like Puerto Vallarta. All the gringo faves — enchiladas, tacos, burritos, fajitas — with combinaciones for the undecided. Surprises, too. Among them: tortillas filled with cilantro, pesto-marinated grilled salmon and red snapper in a snappy Veracruz sauce. Margaritas available by the glass (Regular, Large, Monster) or pitcher. $$

Lazy Gourmet Bistro
1605 West 5th Ave. • 734-1396
This big, open urban room is home to huge-flavoured

Soba Up
Recovering flu victims in search of comfort food could do worse than head into Shiro (3096 Cambie St., 874-0027), whose yaki soba would raise Lazarus from the dead. Topped with plenty of sinus-clearing shredded daikon, the noodles arrive on a cast iron platter, hissing and spitting — so sizzling hot that putting your head down to eat results in a facial sauna. Good value for a helping that only the starving will finish.

172

food. One of the best burgers in town (there's a nugget of cheese in its middle and a spicy sauce), soothing risottos, excellent pizzas — you won't be stuck for choice. Check out the special kids' menu, too. For dessert, no question: Nanaimo bars. $$

Le Crocodile
100-909 Burrard St. • 669-4298
A charming yellow-walled room is the setting for classic French cuisine from chef/owner Michel Jacob. Start with meltingly wonderful onion tarte then proceed to calf's liver or Dover sole (properly deboned at the table). The finest you'll taste anywhere. $$$

Lumière
2551 West Broadway • 739-8185
In a few short years, chef Rob Feenie has put Lumière on the international map with his daring but always thoughtful spins on contemporary French cuisine. Whatever he's working with — fish, fowl or foie gras — the flavours always shine through. Tasting menus include a vegetarian version. $$$$ (See page 186.)

Mirasol
181 East 16th Ave. • 874-3463
Discover the subtle and undeniably different flavours of Peruvian food. Everything from real anticuchos (made with beef heart) to papa a la huancaina, a mix of potatoes, cheese sauce and chilies. Mains are mostly meat, including aji de gallina, a gently fiery dish of chicken. Terrific roast chicken and fries. $-$$

Monterey Lounge & Grill/Pacific Palisades Hotel
1277 Robson St. • 684-1277
The big comfortable room plus a sidewalk patio makes this a favourite year-round. Chef Denis Blais combines fresh ingredients with global inspiration and the results are always vibrantly flavoured. You might start with a twice-baked Brie and roasted pepper soufflé with olive tapenade, then move on to sea bass with grilled asparagus and an orange sugar-cane reduction. Vegetarian dishes are exceptional. Herbs come from the hotel's own rooftop garden.

To Die For:
Death by Chocolate
135-8010 Saba, Richmond
276-2462;
818 Burrard St.
688-8234;
1001 Denman St.
899-2462.
Requesting "a French Affair" won't necessarily get the vice squad on your tail. It's one of the saucy dessert names at Death By Chocolate. "Between the Sheets" combines a cherub outlined in Ghiradelli cocoa powder, two crepes in a V-shape and a dollop of whipping cream. "Seduction" is a flourless chocolate cake with white chocolate curls, sliced strawberries and more of that whipping cream. Staff assemble all concoctions including "Forbidden Fruits" and "Crumble In My Arms" before your very eyes. Most desserts are big and rich enough to share.

Al Fresco Impromptu

"Spanish Banks? Six-ish? Monday?" Keeping basics on hand makes assembling a picnic, even on weeknights, a matter of minutes. Keep staples in the fridge: steamed new potatoes, hard-cooked eggs, roasted red peppers and pre-washed salad greens. Alongside — hence nicely pre-chilled — go Money's Marinated Mushrooms, bottled artichoke hearts, canned tuna, chickpeas or lentils (to toss with French dressing) plus drinks of your choice. By the door goes the basket of cutlery, plates and the roll of paper towel. En route, add the protein component: take-out BBQ chicken, deli ham and cheese. Throw in a fresh-baked baguette — and see you at sunset.

Montri

3629 West Broadway • 738-9888

Tops for Thai food. Montri Rattanaraj layers flavours with exceptional skill. Gorgeous tod mun (fish cakes) are a nice way to start. Salads — the green papaya one, especially — are terrific. The pad thai, the less-familiar pad see iew with broccoli and black pepper, the smooth curries and the chicken "swimming angels" are all worth ordering. $$

Musashi

780 Denman St. • 687-0634

Fun and always throbbing with action. Handy choice for cheap Japanese if you're down at the beach or have just done the Sea Wall. Sushi, maki rolls, teriyaki, tempura, gyoza — all the usual faves plus more interesting dishes such as barbecued oysters or sea urchin. $

900 West/Hotel Vancouver

900 West Georgia St. • 669-9378

A lofty glamorous room is the background to fresh-flavoured food that pulls in the bounty from local orchards, farms and pastures. Wine enthusiasts can sample "flights" of three different, but related, varieties. $$$

Nuff-Nice-Ness

1861 Commercial Dr. • 255-4211

So what if your budget won't spring for a trip to the real Caribbean? It will certainly fund Jamaican patties — vegetable, beef or chicken. Other popular dishes are the jerk chicken and curries of goat or chicken. Rotis, red snapper and ox-tail, too. Assertive spicing. $

Nyala African Hotspot

2930 West 4th Ave. • 731-7899

Injera — flat, spongy and tangy like sourdough — is both bread and plate. On it goes watt — gently simmered chicken, lamb or goat, or stews of peas or lentils, some gently spiced, some fiery. Homemade biltong and boerewors draw South African ex-pats. Tapas till late on weekends. $-$$

Ouisi Bistro

3014 Granville St.   •   732-7550

Louisiana cuisine plus the occasional West Coast favourite. Crab cakes, pepper shrimp, great gumbo (seafood or vegetarian) and a show-stopping jambalaya dense with sausage. Be warned, though: chili intensity can occasionally lift you out of your seat. Among brunch ideas are Po Boys built on baguettes and oyster loaf. $$

Ouzerie

3189 West Broadway   •   739-9378

Noisy, busy and lots of fun. Start with blisteringly hot saganaki zinged with lemon juice, or melitzano aromatic with mint and garlic. Souvlaki and lamb chops are sold by the piece. A side of potatoes and grill-browned loukaniko (spicy Greek sausages) are great together. $-$$

Phnom Penh

244 East Georgia St.   •   682-5777

955 West Broadway   •   734-8898

Award-winning Vietnamese cuisine. Order the garlic chili prawns, then order some more. Soups and noodle dishes are complex in flavour and delicious. $$

Piccolo Mondo

850 Thurlow St.   •   688-1633

Flawless Northern Italian cooking – dishes are elegant and robust. A smooth fish soup is heady with saffron, salt cod is baked with cream, pine nuts and raisins, and osso buco is given depth with green and black olives. Squid-ink risotto with scallops, and linguine with smoked Alaska cod, capers and red onion, are typical of the delectably different pastas. $$$

Planet Veg

1941 Cornwall Ave.   •   734-1001

Healthy Indian vegetarian food that leaves you feeling replete. Try the Katmandu spinach roti roll stuffed with vegetables, the house samosas or the Basmati rice pot, big both in size and popularity. Invariably packed. $

Vegetarian Alert

"The Buddhist Vegetarian Restaurant (137 East Pender Street, 683-8816) is a favourite of mine for unusual meals. Their incredible platters and soups feature mushrooms and fungi of all types, said to have different medicinal benefits (lacy Snow Fungus is good for smooth skin). My very favourite Chinatown meal is offered here — the Eight Treasures Won Ton Soup, a three-part soup in a huge bowl. It's a full meal for two if you add a side of spring rolls for starters. In the bowl are fresh vegetables of the day (maybe baby bok choi, broccoli, carrots) that have been stir-fried with about four or five types of mushrooms and fungi and mixed with golden deep-fried tofu. Gently placed on top is an abundance of crispy deep-fried won tons. The broth is served apart so you can assemble the ingredients in your own little bowl any way you wish. Lots of flavour and texture."

   — Victoria Pratt, public relations consultant to the food, beverage and hospitality industry

One cannot think well, love well, sleep well, if one has not dined well.
— Virginia Woolf

Provence
4473 West 10th Ave. • 222-1980
High voltage southern French flavours, a pretty room and terrific value. Every neighbourhood needs one of these. The antipasti — choose one, choose a dozen from the grilled veggies, pissaladière and salads on display — are deservedly popular. $$

Raincity Grill
1193 Denman St. • 685-7337
Wraparound view of the ocean competes with stylishly presented West Coast cuisine in this lively West End spot. Try chicken and baby vegetable terrine with peppered plum jam to start. Follow with local rockfish or halibut, or beef tenderloin with elephant garlic cream. Outstanding selection of wines by the glass. $$-$$$

Rasputin
457 West Broadway • 879-6675
Pirogies, sausages, insanely good cabbage rolls and the most impressive shashlik you'll ever see on a sword-length skewer. Starters cover smoked fish and marinated salads. Servings are giant. A blast on Saturday nights when the live music kicks in. $$

Roti Bistro
1958 West 4th Ave. • 730-9906
Bob Marley, Caribbean colours, friendly chef Harol Ramnarine — you could be in Trinidad. Rotis are flavour-packed pancakes rolled around beef, chicken, prawn, goat, conch or vegetables. Different heat levels, some incendiary. Chutneys on the side. Jerk chicken wings and jamaican patties, too. $

Sami's
986 West Broadway • 736-8330
Indian fusion food, i.e. West Coast ingredients married to cumin, coriander and chilis, from restaurateur Sami Lalji. A bargain. $-$$

Sawasdee Thai
4250 Main St. • 876-4030
Vancouver's first Thai restaurant. The pad thai is

recommended, as is the coconut milk-smoothed chicken soup. The stuffed deboned chicken wings are great. So are the "crying tiger" beef and a salad called larb made from minced and marinated beef, pork or chicken and horrendous amounts of chilis. Banana fritters for dessert. $$

Shiro
3096 Cambie St. • 874-0027
Hidden in a mini-mall just south of City Hall. Aim for seats at the central sushi bar where owner Shiro Okano cheerfully holds court as he whacks away with his cleaver. Friendly buzz, fresh sushi, good gyoza, amazing deep-fried squid and value-packed bento boxes at lunch. Lineups often. $

Sophie's Cosmic Café
2095 West 4th Ave. • 732-6810
Funky yard-sale decor plus homestyle food — especially breakfasts — means lineups are common at this longtime favourite. $-$$

Star Anise
1485 West 12th Ave. • 737-1485
Sophisticated at lunchtime, romantic at night. Dinner might start with chef Julian Bond's lobster and elephant garlic sausage with ginger relish, then go on to apricot chutney-filled lamb or venison Wellington. Star Anise has its own pastry chef — rare for a restaurant this size. $$$$

Stepho's
1124 Davie St. • 683-2555
Highly popular West End spot. Lineups are almost inevitable. Plates groan with humongous quantities of rice, roast potatoes, souvlaki or lamb and one of the better Greek salads around. Nice zippy tzatsiki, too. $

Surat Sweet
1938 West 4th Ave. • 733-7363
Peaceful room in glowing colours, amiable service and truly unusual food. Gujarati (i.e. Indian vegetarian) dishes. Curries, bhajia (chickpea-floured potato

Warming Ladles
The bite of November winds cues restaurateurs to put on the soup pot. At Café de Paris, it's French onion soup, naturellement. L'Hermitage's Hervé Martin dishes up a lusty cabbage soup redolent of onion and sautéed bacon. Behind this soup's profound flavour is essence of duck, but home cooks needn't bother with stock, Martin maintains. "Soup is a peasant dish. Good vegetables and fresh herbs are all you need, plus some potatoes to thicken it."

"chips"with tangy tamarind sauce). Whatever you order, leave room for shrikand, a yogurt dessert sparked with saffron and cardamom. $

Places to Try:
Pho Century Café
(14-4429 Kingsway, Burnaby, 439-9786);
Pho Dong
(2168 Kingsway, 443-0023);
Pho Hoang
(238 East Georgia St., 682-5666; 3388 Main St., 874-0832);
Pho No. 1 Vietnamese Restaurant
(160-4060 No. 3 Rd., Richmond, 278-8304);
Pho Thai Hoa
(1303 Kingsway, 873-3468)

Tak Sangka
3916 Main St. • 876-0121
Indonesian cuisine in one of Vancouver's oldest restaurants. The authentic Rijstaffel — "rice table" — includes sate, salad, veggies, fritters and more. From the à la carte side try lumpia — oversized egg rolls — noodle dishes and curries. Generous servings. $-$$

Tang's Noodle House
2805-2807 West Broadway • 737-1278
Authentic Chinese on the West Side. Decor includes Pepto-Bismol pink walls. This place is usually busy. Try the screamingly spicy wonton in spicy garlic and chili for starters, then gai lan in oyster sauce, seafood medley in black bean sauce and lemon chicken. The Singapore noodles are addictive. The set-price lunch is a bargain. $-$$

Tapas Tree
1829 Robson St. • 606-4680
Terrific contemporary (large) nibbles and mellow atmosphere make this a popular spot. Polenta with grilled veggies, grilled calamari, duck confit — it's hard to go wrong here. $$

The Templeton
1087 Granville St. • 685-4612
Authentic diner decor dates back to the 1930s — they still use a stove from the same era. The Portobello burger and devil burger with beets are the big sellers here. Tableside jukeboxes. $$

Tio Pepe
1134 Commercial Drive • 254-8999
Cuisine from the Yucatan. "Musts" include the flautas — corn "flutes" crammed with chicken, beef or veggies — and egg-battered nopales. Authentic dishes include banana-leaf-wrapped pork, barbecued pork steak or superb Yucatan-style fried prawns. More conventional Mexican dishes are also on the menu. $$

Tomato Fresh Food Café
3305 Cambie St. • 874-6020

Dishes and decor are both colourful. Yummy healthy food like Mom used to make, if Mom was an ace cook with a passion for fresh ingredients. Try the rib-sticking soups, classic vegetarian chili, real turkey sanwiches, Santa Fé corn pie, the West Coaster salad with Indian candy. For dessert? Five-fruit crisp or Fonzie's brownies. $-$$

Tojo's
777 West Broadway • 872-8050

Sushi restaurants proliferate but this one's still light years ahead of everyone else. Your best bet is to put yourself in the hands of chef Tojo Hadekizu and let him make the decisions. Inventive cuisine as well as popular standards like teriyaki and tempuras. $$$$

Vij's
1480 West 11th Ave. • 736-6664

The food and service both excel. Typical of Vikram Vij's Indian fusion style is zucchini with pomegranate sauce and chickpea salad, or savoury jackfruit on cornmeal chapati. Vegetable fritters are bathed with tomato-coconut curry, the Goan-style chicken curry is paired with saffron rice and the masala-marinated pork is served with garlic curry. $$

Villa del Lupo
869 Hamilton St. • 688-7436

A charming old house with delightfully intimate rooms is the setting for award-winning cuisine. Chef Julio Gonzalez Perini's approach melds Italian technique with West Coast ingredients to create dazzling results. Unusual pastas, duck and fish dishes are exceptional. Seasonal menu, but the highly popular lamb osso buco is a classic year-round. $$$

WEST VANCOUVER:
The Beach House at Dundarave Pier
150 35th St. • 922-1414

A seaside view and a jetty to stroll on after you've eaten. Beef tenderloin grilled with horseradish crust, salmon with mustard seeds, wilted baby bok choy,

Dinner on an Island
Bowen Island is a scant 20 minutes by ferry from Vancouver, but a world away in atmosphere. Plan it right and you can go there for dinner. A couple of nights a week — less in winter, more in summer — chef Brad Ovenell-Carter serves dinner at The Beggar's Purse (451 Bowen Island Trunk Rd., 947-0550). The three-course table d'hote menu changes weekly, building on whatever's fresh, local and in season. Starters might include a beet and beet-greens salad with walnut oil dressing, or a tomato, pepper and olive tart. Mains can include beef filet with merlot sauce, spearfish with vegetables Niçoise, or Japanese eggplant stuffed with mozzarella and garlic. For dessert, there are Granny Smith apple and blackberry sorbets. Ovenell-Carter suggests wines with each course and also offers a six-course tasting menu, with or without matched wines. The restaurant only seats a couple of dozen people so reservations are a must. Mainlanders should note that dinner can be timed to allow them to catch the last ferry back to Horseshoe Bay.

sea urchin and black caviar are typical of the fresh-flavoured menu. A popular spot for weekend brunch. $$-$$$

Beach Side Café
1362 Marine Dr. • 925-1945
The award-winning West Coast cuisine from Chef Carol Chow never fails to delight. A starter of duck confit with watercress and candied vinaigrette, and a main of Asian-noodle-crusted halibut with black bean ginger cream, give some idea of her range. Bonus here is the affable wine advice from sommelier Mark Davidson. $$$

Caspian
1495 Marine Dr. • 921-1311
A home away from home for the many Iranians who live on the North Shore. Start with sabzeh — fresh herbs, feta, radishes and Barbary bread, or kashk-badem-jan (an eggplant dip). Move on to kabobs — ground beef, chicken, fish and more — or long-simmered stews. Gargantuan servings. $$

The Salmon House on the Hill
2229 Folkestone Way • 926-3212
A stupendous view and Native Indian artifacts make this the place to take out-of-towners. Salmon grilled over alderwood is the draw here. $$$

Pho Basics

All over Vancouver you'll see restaurants with "pho" in their name. Pho is a Vietnamese soup with main ingredients that include a sturdy broth, rice noodles and various cuts of beef. Along with it you'll be served a bowl of icicle-crisp bean sprouts, sprigs of fresh basil, lime wedges and hot green chilis, which you add to your taste. Pho is one of the most sustaining and cheapest lunches/suppers/late-night snacks anywhere. A large bowl will usually appease two average appetites.

RESTAURANTS
by Category:

ETHNIC RESTAURANTS:

African
Afro Canadian
Nyala African Hotspot

Chilean
Bellavista

Chinese
Grand King Seafood
Kirin
Tang's Noodle House

Cuban
Havana

French
Café de Paris
The Hermitage
Le Crocodile
Lumière
Provence

Greek
Apollonia
Kalamata
Stepho's

Indian
All India Sweets
Annapurna
Dawat
Del-hi Darbar
Planet Veg
Sami's
Surat Sweet
Vij's

Indonesian
Tak Sangka

Iranian
Caspian

Irish
Irish Heather Bistro

Italian
CinCin
Il Giardino
Piccolo Mondo
Villa del Lupo

Jamaican
Nuff-Nice-Ness
Roti Bistro

Japanese
Gyoza King
Hachibei
Musashi
Shiro
Tojo's

Lebanese
Habibi's

Malaysian
Banana Leaf

Mexican
Las Margaritas
Tio Pepe

Peruvian
Mirasol

Portuguese
Adega
Cinco Estrelas

Just Add Vodka

If you have a hankering for the perogis and cabbage rolls that are made from scratch at Rasputin's (457 West Broadway, 879-6675), they do take-out.

French Celebrations
Since 1992, Café de Paris has held three food festivals a year. September is the month for the Couscous Festival, June marks the Lobster Festival and the chilly days of late October and early November are marked by a Game Festival. Special menus celebrate all three events.

Russian
Rasputin

Singaporean
Rasa Sayang Singapore

Spanish
La Bodega

Thai
Grand Pattaya
Montri
Sawasdee Thai

Vietnamese
Phnom Penh

West Coast Cuisine
Allegro Café
Beach Side Café
Chartwell
Diva at the Met
Herons
Monterey Lounge & Grill
Moustache Café
900 West
Raincity Grill
Raintree at the Landing
Star Anise

OTHER ATTRIBUTES:
Atmosphere Plus
Brickhouse
Havana
Sophie's Cosmic Café
The Templeton
Tomato Fresh Food Café

Bistro
Kilby's
Lazy Gourmet Bistro
Provence

Tapastree
The Village Bistro

Breakfast
Griffins
Havana
Sophie's Cosmic Café

Brunch
The Beach House at Dundarave Pier
The Fish House in Stanley Park

Buffets
All India Sweets
Fleuri
Griffins

Lunch
Allegro Café
Diva at the Met
Griffins
Le Crocodile
The Hermitage
Star Anise

Neighbourhood
The Amorous Oyster
Hachibei
Ouisi Bistro
Tomato Fresh Food Café
The Village Bistro

Romantic
Bacchus
Café de Paris
Le Gavroche
Piccolo Mondo
Star Anise
Villa del Lupo

Seafood
The Amorous Oyster
C
Diva at the Met
The Salmon House on
  the Hill
The Fish House in
  Stanley Park

Special Treat
Bacchus
Bishop's
C
Chartwell
Five Sails
Fleuri
Le Crocodile
Le Gavroche
Lumière
The Hermitage
Il Giardino
900 West
Piccolo Mondo
Villa del Lupo

Vegetarian
These restaurants are
dedicated vegetarian
restaurants. Bear in
mind that, these days,
almost all cafés and
restaurants have non-
meat dishes on their
menus.
Annapurna
Planet Veg
Surat Sweet

**If You're Looking for a
View:**
The Beach House at
  Dundarave Pier
The Fish House in
  Stanley Park
Five Sails
Raincity Grill
The Salmon House on
  the Hill

Take the Gang:
Fatzo's
Las Margaritas
Ouzerie
Rasputin

Where the Chefs Eat
"Nando's is my favourite for
chicken because it's so spicy
and done the real Portuguese
way."
— Caren McSherry, cooking-
school owner

DINING OUT ON THE WEB

Typing "Vancouver restaurants food" into your search engine will link you up with plenty of sites listing eateries in and around the Lower Mainland. Many, however, are short on hard-core information. The following are all particularly recommended:

BC Tel
bc.sympatico.ca
New restaurants, hot spots to eat, a calendar of upcoming food events — everything from classes to fundraisers, You can spend so much time wandering around this site, you'll end up phoning out for pizza.

Bishop's
www.settingsun.com/bishops
So what if it's only an occasional treat? Download the menu and the wine list and plan a dream dinner for when your ship comes in.

Commercial Drive
www.thedrive.net
North to south from Powell to 18th Avenue, east to west from Victoria to Clark, this neighbourhood website doesn't just list every restaurant, café and food store on The Drive. Can't remember the name of that bakery that sells pizza dough in bulk? This site lets you track it down as you "walk" through the neighbourhood.

Dining in Vancouver
www.cs.ubc.ca/spider/boritz/food/close.html
Vancouverite Jim Boritz specializes in brief but believable restaurant reviews for the UBC crowd.

District of North Vancouver
www.district.north-van.bc.ca
Click on Tourism, then on Dining Out, and discover a review of food-related sites, mostly stories from local writers on subjects like where to find food in the wee hours or all-you-can-eat buffets.

Best Place for Bargain Baklava

Never mind what's happening elsewhere in the city, even in the largely Greek areas of Kitsilano baklava prices have been slowly inching up. A dollar seems to be the going rate except at Broadway Bakery (3273 West Broadway, 733-1422), where you can still walk away with a lovely sticky chunk of it for under a buck: 80 cents to be precise. The same price will also get you rolled baklava, cataif or rolled cataif and various permutations of filo, nuts and honey. A couple of bucks gets you baker Jerry Zerbinos' lunch-sized spanakopita.

The Georgia Straight
www.straight.com
Restaurant listings and reviews.

The Vancouver Village Restaurant Guide
www.vanmag.com
Brief reviews adapted from *Vancouver Magazine*.

Webzines of Vancouver
www.webzines-vancouver.bc.ca
An eclectic and up-to-the-minute source of restaurant information. The reviews in "Adam's contrary list" are genuinely useful – he names dishes (and prices). Nor does he pull any punches if, in his view, a place doesn't match the hype or his expectations.

Choo-Choo Chew

Remember that scene with Cary Grant and Eva Marie Saint in the dining car in Hitchcock's *North by Northwest?* Resurrecting those long-lost days when relationships really were on the fast track is BC Rail's Pacific Starlight Dinner Train. Those who like their cuisine with a view can climb aboard, dine aboard and take in all the West Coast scenery and Howe Sound sunset they can handle. Wednesdays through Sundays through the summer, nine vintage cars from the 1940s make the return journey between North Vancouver and Porteau Cove. Purchased from the operator of a similar service near Seattle, the cars have been restored to their original splendour and given evocative names such as Moonglow, Indigo and Manhattan...And there's the three-course table d'hote dinner. Reservations necessary: 984-5500.

Where Chefs Eat

Says Michael Noble of Diva at the Met, "I really love Vij's. The food has great flavour and the mood is relaxed and casual. Lumière too."

Vikram Vij and wife Meeru eat at Provence on West 10th Avenue, or Beetnix — "really, really tasty pasta." For something special, they go to Lumière.

Kai Lerman of Fleuri in the Sutton Place Hotel eats mostly at home. "Otherwise it's Le Crocodile, Quattro or Lumière."

BEHIND THE SCENES AT LUMIÈRE

At 7 p.m. on a weeknight, Lumière is already a third full. Almost since it opened in 1995, the West Side restaurant and its modern French cuisine has received accolades. Critics far and wide have praised it to the skies. Regulars show up in droves. Back in the kitchen, chef Rob Feenie and Chef de Cuisine Frank Pabst are at the ready: "He's the technical wizard; I base it solely on taste," says Feenie.

It's tranquil for now, apart from the sizzle as a chunk of halibut hits the pan. Lined up on a stainless steel island are small saucepans containing the bases for the sauces that Feenie will build individually over the course of the evening. Lamb stock, dark and shimmering, will have shreds of preserved lemon and finely chopped Niçoise olives added to it at the last moment, just long enough for the flavours to become familiar but not overwhelmed by each other. A sauce to accompany seafood (the only one to which Feenie adds cream) is based on chicken, not fish stock: "That way you can taste the hijiki, soy and ginger," he explains. He spoons big, fat B.C. spot prawns onto a plate with the precision and concentration of a surgeon, then adds scallops so big that five weigh a pound. The result is luminous: the bass notes of the sauce stand back and allow the sweet freshness of the seafood to move to the foreground.

Though preferably local and seasonal, Feenie's ingredients come from many sources: Fraser Valley farms grow specific produce to order; suppliers will bring in a single case of an unusual California find; flowering chives and mint are picked from the staff's own gardens. This morning Frank Pabst raided Chinatown and cruised West Broadway produce stores. Six kitchen staff service the 50-seat restaurant — a far higher ratio than usual. On weekends it's even higher.

Cuisine of this standard is mind-bogglingly labour-intensive. To make just one salad garnish, Pabst must first hollow out a cherry tomato, add some pesto, then a mixture of couscous and vegetables, and finally a drizzle of vinaigrette. Sprinkled around the same salad are fresh fava beans that he has shelled, blanched, then skinned and split in half.

Sliced just before serving, house-made gravlax is arranged on crisped wonton skins and potato slices ringed with lemon crême fraiche dotted with jewel-like clusters of yellow and red flying-fish roe. The final touch: strips of preserved lemon and a sprig of lemon balm picked from a tray of living herbs. Nothing is overly ornate, but it's a dazzlingly effective dish because of the ingredients' own colours and the intelligent combination of tastes and textures.

Feenie designed the kitchen: it's not fashionably "open" but there is an opening large enough for him to know what's happening out there. On this fairly typical evening, candles frame each little couple or group in a pool of light. A customer requests

Chef Robert Feenie

vegetables "really, really cooked" emphasizes the server. Another diner asks for frites: not on the menu, but staff oblige.

It's all about making people feel happy, isn't it? Feenie smiles. He's working a 60-hour week, knows that this business is day-to-day work and that another customer just spotted those frites and wants some too. "I don't do it for the money. I do it for the passion," says Feenie. "When you're cooking, the most important ingredient is love."

TRANSLATING A CHINESE MENU

You know how it is: Up there on the wall of your local Chinese restaurant – or maybe on the table, or often both – are what seem to be food suggestions. But who knows? They're all in Chinese.

One morning I met with journalist Stephanie Yuen, who writes about restaurants for *Sing Tao* and talks about them on radio. Yuen is keen for her audience to understand Western cuisine and she's equally eager on breaking down the barrier between Caucasians and authentic Chinese food. For the purposes of the exercise, we met at Park May Guy Foods, a small place on Victoria Drive where Yuen and I shared a genuine Hong Kong breakfast.

It consists of congee plus a dish of your choice which is called, in Hong Kong, a "set." You can also tuck into Hong Kong style chow mein, which is a tangle of noodles, bean sprouts, onion, carrot and mushroom – familiar stuff, unlike the sausage-shaped Chinese doughnuts wrapped in a rice roll. Crunchy inside, slippery outside, with tiny pungent dried shrimp sprinkled on top and thick, sweet hoisin sauce for dipping, this is light years away from two eggs sunny-side up.

As Yuen and I ate, we discussed why so many Caucasians are nervous about ordering off the Chinese side of the menu. Once you do start to ask for a little help from the servers, you'll come upon all kinds of surprises – pleasant ones, usually. That $24.88 sign on the wall, for instance, may buy a meal for four of soup, hot pot, tofu with mixed greens, BBQ pork and chicken or duck, and vegetables. Get a group of 10 together, chip in 10 bucks each, and you can share a dinner of cold cuts, deep fried oysters, vegetables with two kinds of seafood, dry scallop soup, deep fried chicken, a "double grill" of steak and pork chop, gai lan, fried rice with beef, dessert, fruit plate and, to fill in the cracks, two live crabs, compliments of the house.

As Yuen translates, I try to find an entry point into the alphabet soup on the wall. Ah-hah! – a simple horizontal dash. It means "one" she tells me, just as two parallel dashes mean "two." What looks like a

Cheap Treat

Check out an Asian breakfast alternative next time you're in Chinatown. Try the Malaysian laksa at Kim Heng Noodles (617 Gore St., 681-3188). A great, flavour-packed slurp of noodles, cucumber, fish ball, chicken and one fat shrimp, all swimming in a chili-fired, lemony-coconut broth.

box stacked on top of two more boxes is the symbol for "grade" or "kind" says Yuen. "First grade," I read proudly. "Cold plate" she finishes, then throws me a curve: "It can also mean your character." We move on. A symbol that looks like an upside-down calligraphed "v" is "people" and what appears to be a miniature hydro pole equals "dried."A square-sided "M" is the symbol for "claw" and means chicken feet, which seems logical, although, somewhat confusingly, the symbol for duck feet means "palm" because duck feet are webbed. Five minutes in and I can already translate "10 first grade dried chicken feet." It's a beginning.

THE CITY'S SECRET GARDENS

High above the urban roar are several roof-top gardens, authentic *potagers* brimming with herbs and greens. Surrounded by glittering highrises, the south-facing 2,100-square-foot garden of the Waterfront Centre Hotel was first planted in 1993. Chef Daryle Ryo Nagata points out nine thyme varieties, sturdy rosemary bushes, stevia which he uses as a sugar substitute, and a bay tree. Quadrants of one bed are filled with arugula, teardrop tomatoes, onions and lettuce. Chives and garlic chives share another. Mint — notoriously invasive — has its own territory. "It's low maintenance," says Nagata. "It's all organic and it's automatically watered."

Executive Chef Daryle Ryo Nagata

Building a rooftop garden is no small task. In the case of the Waterfront Centre Hotel, enough soil to form a base three feet deep had to be raised from ground level. At Vij's, a popular Indian-fusion restaurant in the fashionable South Granville area, owner Vikram Vij and friends lugged sacks of soil down an alleyway and up a ladder to their final destination, a long, narrow space of 100 square feet. In this, Vancouver's newest restaurant garden, Vij plans to grow herbs for garnishes as well as experimenting with Indian varieties such as the curry leaf.

Vancouver's oldest rooftop kitchen garden is at the Pacific Palisades Hotel on Robson Street. Started in 1992, it has produced a cornucopia of produce over the years, from French flageolet beans and ruby Swiss chard to edible flowers. All are grown in a series of more than four dozen planters, each two feet square and automatically watered by a timer-operated sprinkler "drip" system.

"We make pestos, flavoured oils — and one summer we featured herbed mashed potatoes," says chef Denis Blais. Bay leaves, arugula, assorted parsleys — they all lead a healthy pesticide-free life. "We prefer to use biological controls," says Blais. "We bring in ladybugs to fight the aphids."

BREAKFASTS (AND BEDS)

It's what you eat on a trip that turns it from ho-hum into memorable. Snowy duvets, crisp sheets, downy pillows — the following places offer comfortable beds. More to the point, they also feature terrific breakfasts.

Bowen Island:
The Vineyard at Bowen Island
687 Cates Lane • 947-0028
www.vineyard.bc.ca
Just 40 minutes from the city puts you in a bedroom overlooking the pinot noir and pinot gris grapes that Lary and Elena Waldman grow in their vineyard. At breakfast, you might begin with broiled grapefruit, followed by smoked salmon eggs benedict or French toast and bacon. Homemade scones, muffins and croissants round out the menu (and your waistline).

Ladner:
The Duck Inn
4349 River Rd. W. • 946-7521
Alan and Jill York have a charming cottage right on the river with a view of Vancouver and the mountains. Watch the sunset from your own private dock, take the canoe out, or, if it's chilly, settle in by the wood-burning fireplace. After a sound night's sleep, help yourself to Alan's lox-style smoked salmon, bagels and cream cheese, or pop a half-baked baguette in the oven for fresh French bread to eat with Jill's homemade jams. A great place to stay if you want to do your own cooking.

River Run Cottages
4551 River Rd. West • 946-7778
Get away from it all close to the city. Guests stay in a floating cottage or a shore-bound one with waterfront deck. Breakfast is brought to your room and may start with homemade muffins or cinnamon buns and fresh-squeezed orange juice. Afterwards, there's an "infamous" eggs Benedict or a salsa-heated version of the classic eggs benny. Hot sauce also shows up in the special River Run eggs.

B&B 101
If you dream of hosting guests in your own home, Lyn Hainstock, who runs the Penny Farthing Inn in Kitsilano, teaches a one-day course on how to start a B&B. For information, contact the Vancouver School Board at 713-5000.

NORTH VANCOUVER:

Laburnum Cottage Bed and Breakfast

1388 Terrace Ave. • 988-4877

www.vancouver-b.c.com/LaburnumCottageBB

Delphine Masterton has been an innkeeper since 1985. Guests stay in the main house or in cottages in the beautiful park-like garden — the former is romantic enough for honeymooners, the other more suited to families. You can eat breakfast in the large country kitchen, complete with Aga stove, that overlooks the garden, or in the glassed-in breakfast room. Fresh juices pave the way for vanilla yogurt crowned with blueberry mousse, and crepes with vegetable cream pesto sauce topped with ham. Spread homemade jam on the fresh-baked scones and muffins.

Thistledown House

3910 Capilano Rd. • 986-7173

www.thistle-down.com

Ruth Crameri and Rex Davidson's craftsman-style house dates back to 1920. Breakfast might begin with Thistledown House blend coffee, and homemade granola with yogurt. Maybe some Russian black rye with wild cranberry jam to follow — or homemade challah? Limed papaya or mango compote cleanse the palate, then on to portabella mushrooms in a demiglace cream with a julienne of ham and a four-cheese polenta, or a Pacific salmon eggs benny garnished with flower petals. If you've got any room left, dig in to the fresh fruit platter.

Breakfast at Thistledown House

VANCOUVER:

English Country Garden

3466 West 15th Ave. • 737-2526

Carol Egan's gorgeous English perennial garden is a brilliant mass of shasta daisies, Japanese anemones, yellow loosestrife, day lilies and dozens of other varieties. Stay at her bed and breakfast and you can eat out on the deck. Typical treats? Smoked salmon and scrambled eggs with cream cheese and spring onions, or French toast with maple syrup and raspberry jam — homemade, as are all the jams and marmalades. Dessert is along the lines of blueberry buckle, apple slices or apricot strudel.

Heritage Harbour Bed and Breakfast
1838 Ogden Ave. • 736-0809

Stay in Richard and Debbie Horner's traditional-style house, and you can eat breakfast while you watch the morning boats set sail. Shake off the cobwebs with Italian coffee, then down a juice smoothie, homemade granola, a fruit plate of blueberries, cantaloupe, honeydew and watermelon, blueberry and oat-bran muffins before forking into "Scottie's nest eggs" — eggs and cream baked in a ham "cup" and served on an English muffin with Gouda cheese.

The Johnson House
2278 West 34th Ave. • 266-4175

Tins, coffee grinders, cash registers and much, much more. Sandy and Ron Johnson are avid antique collectors and it's all on display in their Craftsman-style B&B. Breakfast may kick off with a fruit platter followed by muffins, a specialty here: the blueberry-lemon and raspberry kind (the raspberries come from their garden) are famous. Next course? An apple pancake and ham, or cheese omelette with garden-grown herbs. The coffee comes from Bean Brothers in Kerrisdale, where it's roasted on the spot.

A Little Green House on the Park
1850 Grant St. • 255-0815

It may look Victorian but this charming house was only built a few years ago by Patty Verner and Peter Djwa. Breakfast begins with fresh fruit smoothies and homemade mini muffins in the design-award winning kitchen, then moves to the dining room or — in summer — to the clematis-covered arbour. Fresh and healthy are the keywords for dishes like fruit-stuffed French toast or scrambled eggs with porcini.

Great Escapes: Bowen Island Rockwood Adventures' Bowen Island day-trip focuses on a gourmet picnic lunch prepared by chef Manfred Scholermann. Forget the usual potato salad and coleslaw. Typical dishes in the hamper include shrimp, spinach and radicchio salad, breast of turkey with pecan chutney, cognac pâté with Cumberland sauce, fruit salad, Savary Island soda bread and orange spice cake. The full day tour also takes in a 2 1/2 hour nature walk around Killarney Lake and allows time for sauntering around the Island. The cost includes downtown pick-up and ferry fares (or a return journey by floatplane). Call 926-7705.

Penny Farthing Inn

2855 West 6th Ave. • 739-9002

Lyn Hainstock's 1912 house, with its secluded English country garden, sets the scene for breakfast on the patio. Sip freshly-squeezed juice as you nibble on fresh fruit and croissants, coffee cake or muffins. There are always four homemade jams on the table. To follow there might be strawberry crepes or an eggplant or salmon frittata, eggs benedict or mushrooms in a pastry shell. Dishes look beautiful, too – Hainstock often garnishes her dishes with edible flowers from her garden.

Ten Fifteen West Sixteenth Avenue

1015 West 16th Ave. • 730-0713

This graceful Arts and Crafts house was restored to its former elegance by owners Peter Eastwood and Philip Seth. The mood is elegance from a bygone era: real linen sheets, headed notepaper, even your name on a card in a little brass slot on the door. The food is anything you want, from classic French toast, waffles, muffins, fresh fruit, bagels and cream cheese to Chinese congee – Hong Kong was home for Seth; Eastwood spent many years there.

Walnut House B and B

1350 Walnut St. • 739-6941

In their craftsman-style house on Kits Point, Liz Harris and Mike Graham serve magnificent breakfasts. The main course might be a cream cheese and smoked salmon soufflé or roasted red pepper and asparagus frittata. Often on the menu are pancakes or Harris's legendary gingerbread waffles, blueberry and orange scones, or upside-down cranberry-walnut bread pudding. The romantic bedrooms have fully stocked bookcases. The Treetops room boasts a view of the city skyline and stencilled trees on the walls.

FOOD AND WINE CLUBS

If you're nuts about food and wine, few occasions are as pleasurable as getting together with like-minded (and like-spirited) people. Want to find fellow restaurant junkies? Eager to sip rare vintages? Just want to learn as much as you can about the wines of a certain region? Join the club.

Note: Guests (some clubs allow them) normally pay a bit more than members.

John B Wine Club
John B Neighbourhood Pub
1000 Austin Ave. • 931-2337
Of the approximately 15 events per year hosted at this lively venue, about a third are for "complete and utter neophytes." Wine tastings range from a basic introductory class to high profile tastings of fine Bordeaux. The appetizers are matched to the wines. Annual membership of $25 gives you a discount on tastings and wine, and a two-for-one discount on food in the pub before or after the tastings. Tastings range from $15 to $125, with most averaging $25 to $35.

Vancouver American Wine Society
7831 Tweedsmuir • 274-2534
This is the biggest wine society on the continent, says John Levine, who founded this highly active and education-based club. The $30 annual membership lets you attend 25 tastings a year — the charge for each ranges from $18 to $23. As its name suggests, the club's focus is on labels from California, Washington, Oregon, Idaho and New York. Join, and you'll learn about wine appreciation, different varietals and individual wineries (often from the winemaker concerned). Picnics and BBQs, too.

The Australian Wine Appreciation Society
Jim Forbes • 736-1134
John Schreiner • 980-5964
Real amateur or real keener — your level of wine knowledge doesn't matter at this decidedly unstuffy society. Held about once a month, usually at the Coast Plaza Hotel, tastings feature 8 to 10 wines from Down

Tour B.C.'s Wine Country
Planning to visit the Okanagan or Vancouver Island? The British Columbia Wine Institute produces a touring map that directs you to a number of leading wineries. For a free copy, check your nearest L.D.B. store or tourist information centre, or write to: The B.C. Wine Institute, 1193 West 23rd Ave., North Vancouver V7P 2H2

Home Wine Making and U-Brews

Whether you make it in your basement or have it made elsewhere, this is a huge trend. The reason for many is price — a bottle of drinkable plonk averages under four bucks. For others, it's the fun of making your own wine, pure and simple: tinkering with formulae, trying new recipes and — what the heck — if it fails, you'll have a lifetime supply of vinegar. The government keeps stuffing loopholes, so if you want to keep your cellar filled, get going.

Under and a speaker — often a visiting winemaker. Annual dues are $30 per person, $50 per couple. Wine tastings range from $20 to $35.

The Cape Wine Society
Lance Berelowitz • 683-4733
There's growing interest in South African wines. This society offers up to eight tastings a year, which may include ports and fortified wines as well as regular wines. Tastings often include mature varieties that are not otherwise available. Annual membership is $30 per person, $50 per couple. Tastings cost $20 to $30 and are held at Seasons Restaurant.

Chaîne des Rotisseurs
Dr. Gerald Korn • 876-9288
An international organization dating back to 1248, this is the grandaddy of all food clubs. To join, you must attend two dinners before applying for membership, be nominated by two members and have your application approved by a committee. Initiation fee is around $400 — more if you're a professional. Annual dues are about half that. The Chaîne hosts six or seven functions annually, a third of them formal. Dinners range from $60 to $125 and include wines from the club's own cellar which are billed at their original cost rather than replacement value.

Les Chevaliers des Vins de France
Jim Davidson • 985-5407
Affiliated with the French Trade Commission, this club offers a broad range of wine possibilities, from famous Burgundies to wines from the less-known regions. Initiation is $65 and dues are $45 annually. Of the eight or nine tastings a year, two or three are dinners held at such venues as Lumière, Le Gavroche, the Sutton Place Hotel and, most recently, the Metropolitan Hotel. Dinners are in the $65 to $70 range. Tastings average $25.

Les Dames d'Escoffier International
878-1846
This worldwide society of professional women in the fields of food, fine beverage and hospitality is

dedicated to supporting and promoting the achievement of women in the culinary professions. It does so by organizing educational and charitable activities which fund scholarships and grants. Membership is by invitation only but the public can attend fundraising dinners and classes organized by "Les Dames."

The German Wine Society
Marion Johnson • 224-6813

We all know Black Tower and Blue Nun, but those are only the tip of the German wine iceberg as members of this society well know. Specially imported wines are brought in for dinners about nine times year. The dinners are held at various restaurants and golf and country clubs. Initiation is $27, or $44 for a couple, and dinners average $35. A summer social is catered by the club's committee.

The Grapevine Wine Club
737-2006

Run by noted noses Michael and Memory Walsh, who define their corporate mission in these words: "To encourage wine enthusiasts to enjoy the pleasures of a wine culture including food, travel and vineyards." Club perks include wine tours to noted regions like Burgundy and Champagne, extensive wine courses (the Walshes are both Certified Wine Educators with The Society of Wine Educators) and the opportunity to purchase specially selected wines by the case. Membership fee: $45/ couple annually.

Advanced Wine Clubs
Once you're into the wine scene, you'll hear about other clubs around town, highly specialized organizations that focus on the vintages of Bordeaux or Burgundy. These usually have a very small membership, not for snobbish reasons but simply because the clubs can often only obtain a magnum or a couple of bottles for tasting purposes. When you're ready to graduate to the highest level of wine knowledge, ask to be put on the membership waiting list.

All Hail, the Glorious Pud!

The idea originated in the U.K., traditional home of the pudding. The Pudding Club is now a phenomenon across the Atlantic and has caught on in the "colonies," too. Every so often, local restaurant The Hart House (6664 Deer Lake Ave., Burnaby, 298-4278) hosts a special evening where classic puddings are the focus of the night. After a prime rib dinner, staff parade in with a number of puddings such as sticky toffee pudding, "spotted Dick" and several others. Those in attendence sample the lot and vote for their favourite. Pudding Club nights are usually sold out well in advance.

International Wine and Food Society
Gordon Wilcox • 872-8621

The largest gourmet organization in the world, this London-headquartered society is geared towards amateurs and has 105 members in Vancouver, mostly couples keen to improve their food and wine knowledge. Initiation fees are $45, plus $65 annual membership. Attend the five to seven events a year — cooking demos, wine tastings and master classes — and you'll learn about everything from working with chocolate to gourmet tricks with muskox.

The Opimian Society
Lorna Porter • 732-1517

The oldest wine club in Canada, with 10,000 members across the country, the Opimian celebrated its 25th anniversary in 1998. Members range from "newly legal drinkers to the geriatric." A wine purchasing co-operative, the club brings in at least 250 professionally selected wines a year from around the world (even places like Macedonia). It tells you about their background and whether the wine is to drink now or to put under the bed. Old favourites, new discoveries — the wines range from $8 to $60 a bottle. Initiation is $65 and membership annually is $60, which includes a subscription to *Wine Tidings*, Canada's wine magazine, and access to wine tours. Tastings and dinners tend to be informal — a fireworks dinner and cruise was one recent example. There are also winemakers' dinners at restaurants. The club provides a yearly update so you know where your cellar stands.

The Vancouver Mycological Society
878-9878

Anyone who likes grubbing around in dank forests in search of chanterelles and other exotic mushrooms will find the search made easier as a member of this society. Membership is $15 a year for individuals or families. Highlights are the Mushroom Show (where you can bring your own for identification) and a potluck Survivors' Banquet in January. The society meets on the first Tuesday of most months at the VanDusen Gardens. Newsletters six times a year relay news from around the world. The Mushroom Hotline provides details on upcoming forays.

Vita e Vino Italian Wine Society
Maria Tommasini Robertson • 926-0379

Proving that there's more to Italian wine than chianti, this society works closely with the Italian Trade Commissions in Toronto and Montreal to introduce a wide range of wines. The club is as suitable for amateurs as experts, says Robertson, who runs it. Producers' dinners (usually held at large hotels) and festival-style tastings twice a year add up to about seven events annually. Membership is $50 a year ($80 for a couple). Dinners are normally $50 to $70. Videos and slide shows are on the agenda for the future.

EIGHT WAYS TO A WINNING DINNER

Why do some restaurants leave you muttering "never again" while others signal the start of a lifelong relationship? The secret, as in love, is invariably one of communication.

1. Choose the right place. Asking friends for recommendations, reading current guidebooks or picking the brains of a hotel concierge will increase the odds of success considerably. Bear in mind, too, that any restaurant worth its imported sea salt will read you a few dish descriptions over the phone, or fax you a menu.

2. Pick the right time. Restaurants are at their most frantic mid-evening Fridays and Saturdays. Go earlier, book later or dine out on a Tuesday — the day after the chef's day off, when he or she is fresh, relaxed and raring to go.

3. Make reservations *and keep them*. Showing up on time is polite, showing up ten minutes late is excusable, showing up not at all — without canceling — isn't.

4. Something to drink? "Martinis are fun but they kill your palate," says one sommelier whose personal choice — and recommendation — for an aperitif is a crisp white wine.

7. Feel free to grill your server about the menu — especially when it comes to deciphering dish descriptions. The "beet jus" listed among the menu prose may not be the vast crimson lake you imagine, but just itsy-bitsy polka dots around the plate rim.

8. Tipping is a reward for good service. Fifteen percent is normal but if your every whim has been catered to, a little extra won't hurt.

SPECIAL OCCASIONS

Your younger sister's birthday, a barbecue with your buddies on the first warm Saturday of the summer, a special dinner with friends you haven't seen in eons – there are so many reasons to celebrate during the year, and food plays a major role in all of them.

It's what goes on our plates, the care we take, the effort we make, that makes the difference between a run-of-the-mill day and a special occasion. Not only that, but the dishes we cook – our Mom's Christmas pudding or an aunt's turkey dressing at Thanksgiving – are traditions that link us back to earlier generations.

Here in Vancouver, food can connect us with other things too: with the farmers who grow what we serve at our table, with the flavours and rituals of other cultures, and with annual events that help those in need.

It's all cause for celebration.

CATERERS & PARTY PLANNERS

"Actually," you say to your friends, "I'm not cooking myself, I'm having the dinner catered." Gosh, how posh. Well, maybe it used to be, but it's not anymore – and nor is it viewed as the cheat's way to entertain. When you're working like a maniac, calling in the experts may be the only way you can make time to feed your friends.

Catering is a scary word but all it really means is having someone else do the work. It can be the death-defying chocolate cake or lemon tart you order from the specialty bakery for dessert. It might be a couple of dozen tiny Jamaican patties to serve before supper. It can be a spectacular knock-the-socks-off-your-visiting-cousin sit-down dinner for four, a buffet for 20 of your dearest friends or your wedding reception.

If you get all quivery at the thought of hiring someone to take over the reins, remember the guidelines. Plan as far ahead as you can. Good caterers get booked up fast, especially around Christmas. Be upfront about how much you want to spend so there are no nasty surprises. Depending on your budget, you may want to have a caterer look after everything: food, wine, servers, tables, chairs, cloths, plates, cutlery and flowers (there's a lot to think about). Have some idea of the kind of food you'd like. After that, it's your party, so relax and enjoy it.

NORTH VANCOUVER

Reel Appetites
2-123 Charles St. • 929-5443

The company that fed the X-Files can feed you. While most of their business involves getting up at the crack of dawn to make breakfast for movie crews, Reel Appetites also caters weddings, parties and everything from dinner for two to a BBQ for 3,000. Trucks with self-sufficient kitchens let them go anywhere. They've cooked on a football field in Squamish for a corporate client, helicoptered food to a glacier and served meals on boats. On the less glamorous side, they send lunches to downtown offices.Choices range from basic to eclectic to crazy, with a focus on West Coast cuisine. Their breakfast burritos are famous.

People Who Cater

Catering companies aren't the only people who cook in Vancouver. Ask if your favourite restaurant caters outside events. Often, they do. Hotels are experts at feeding other people and offer the added bonus of party rooms and staff right on the spot.

VANCOUVER:
Chef's Secret Service
4434 West 10th Ave. • 222-9800
Colourful and zingy, flavourful food (you can taste it in the small restaurant) best describes what this West Side catering company offers. Appetizers include such delights as prawn and chicken gyoza with serrano chili sauce or Brie and blueberry phyllo purses. Main courses can be casual — how about a prosciutto, spinach and cheese strudel — or white-linen formal, such as a butterflied leg of lamb stuffed with herbs and wild mushrooms. Deliciously homey desserts.

Chez Cuisine
730-5545/266-5752
Connie Papin was the Catering Manager of "Tomato to Go" for two years. Ruth Laxton has cooked for some of the city's top caterers. Together, they offer Chez Cuisine — basically, lunches and dinners that they prepare and serve in your home. They will also come to your home, make supper for tonight and leave you three "corner cupboard" dishes to tide you over. Dishes are along the lines of Moroccan-inspired vegetable stew, pesto lasagna, Tuscan chicken with orzo. For cocktail parties, they offer hors d'oeuvre platters — everything from wild mushroom strudel to salmon gravlax on blinis with crème fraiche — to salads, sandwiches and desserts.

Kitchen to Kitchen
1279 Pacific Blvd. • 899-8909
Catering with a health bent: no oils, low salt, and mainly vegetarian and seafood dishes. "The trick is to do it as fresh as possible," say Roger Racette and chef Catherine Potin, who hails from the Paris area. Their corporate and private clients sometimes specify organic vegetables. Kitchen to Kitchen has even catered all-vegan weddings. Typically, they're asked for whole stuffed squash and whole decorated salmon, but they do serve the occasional roast beef sandwich.

The Lazy Gourmet
1605 West 5th Ave. • 734-2507
Okay, she didn't actually invent it (see page 208) but

Parties on the Cheap
Costco is one of the best places for one-stop party shopping that won't make you wince when you get to the cash desk. Huge slabs of brownies and Nanaimo bars, sausage rolls and assorted hors d'oeuvres by the tray to heat and serve, humongous pies, whole Bries, sacks of potato chips: what's available varies — go with an open mind. Check your local Safeway or Canadian Superstore, too. Many now carry "warehouse-sized" lasagnas and desserts.

Behind the Eight-Ball?
If you're stuck with organizing the annual office bash, check out Commodore Lanes & Billiards (838 Granville St., 681-1531) as a possible venue. Funky 1930s atmosphere, free entertainment — and space for up to 300.

owner Susan Mendelson was unquestionably the person who raised the Nanaimo Bar to cult status. She also created that cocktail party standby, the pastry-wrapped Brie. Since 1977 — her first gig was the Vancouver Children's Festival — the high-energy Mendelson has been feeding folks around town. In the early days, she served salmon Wellington. Today, she and her crew offer a world's worth of dishes. A buffet may include "new wave" Caesar salad with red chile croutons, classic poached salmon, coconut curry chicken, thyme-scented mixed rices and green beans with a Japanese sesame dressing. Chef-attended "theme" stations let your guests roam from a Mexican taco and fajita bar to others serving West Coast seafood, Asian stir-fried dishes, pasta or Mediterranean tapas. Desserts, such as the mini white chocolate bombe or the double fudge chocolate cake, are deservedly popular.

Lesley Stowe Fine Foods
1780 West 3rd Ave. • 731-3663

Rather than supplying her elite list of customers with "tick off the boxes" menus, Stowe creates dishes specifically for the occasion. From dinner for 10 to events for 1,000, she's done the lot, including some high profile events such as the opening of the Vancouver Public Library. Once she even flew a dinner of B.C. foods to Newfoundland.

Liliget Feast House
1724 Davie St. • 681-7044

Dolly Watts is the first name people think of for First Nations cuisine in Vancouver. This is authentic regional food. On her dinner menus you'll see dishes like alder-grilled salmon with juniper sauce, fiddleheads and sea asparagus, and wild rice salad. For a buffet event, she might suggest warm buffalo "smokies" or clam fritters or smoked duck sausage with wild Saskatoon berry sauce. Bannock, the traditional bread, is a must.

Major the Gourmet

102-8828 Heather St. • 322-9211

For years, New Zealander Nicky Major has been catering for some of the top names in the city. Weekdays, you can sample some of her dishes at M.T.G., a small restaurant on the premises. In 1997, Major won an award for "Best Catered Event in Canada" for two 700-person parties she catered on consecutive nights. A sit-down dinner for 500 is nothing – or a dinner at $400 a head, the ultimate for an L.A. law firm – but she also handles far smaller private parties. Signature dishes are her hors d'oeuvres: the mint-cured salmon, the sundried tomato and cream cheese platter, and the addictive one-bite flans she's been making since she first launched her business in 1973.

Meinhardt Fine Foods

3002 Granville St. • 732-4405

Otherwise known as "food heaven" this gourmet grocery store specializes in providing party food for groups of up to 100 (although one customer orders a dinner, almost weekly, for six). Menus are created in consultation with the client. Drawing from global influences, dishes lean towards the big-flavoured and colourful. Sea bass is seasoned with cilantro and ginger or tandoori spices. A salad combines roasted eggplant, garlic and tomato. For appetizers, Chef Tracy Rowand might suggest appetizers of beef tenderloin on rye bread with horseradish mayo. When it comes time to choose dessert, remember Meinhardt Fine Foods has its own pâtissier on staff.

The Menu Setters Fine Food & Catering

3655 West 10th Ave. • 732-4218

Most Vancouverites know this tiny store as the place for superb cheese, but mother-and-daughter team Alice and Alison Spurrell are also ace caterers who specialize in smaller home parties. Their crab-and-artichoke lasagne and the cannelloni – stuffed with chicken or vegetables – are famous. For casual "dos"

Lotsa Coffee

Got a large gang coming over? Most Safeway stores can lend you a party-sized coffee urn. It's a free service (though they do need a deposit).

Call 1-800-SAFEWAY and they'll arrange it.

the Spurrells can put out platters of cheese, fresh fruit, smoked salmon or grilled Mediterranean vegetables. A typical buffet dinner includes cold salmon with sorrel mayonnaise, chicken with mushrooms, wild rice pilaf and various salads and desserts.

The Peake of Catering
4501 Main St. • 872-8431

Former chef to the Sultan of Brunei, owner David Peake caters in your home or wherever you want: "What works best for your needs." He also caters for Alaskan cruises and private jets. Dinner might include smoked-salmon-wrapped snow peas, goat cheese crêpes, sea bass with an oriental glaze — elegant, sophisticated food.

Tastebuds
4255 Arbutus St. • 731-7232

Stop by to sample some of Tastebuds' wares at their retail store in the Arbutus Shopping Centre and you can pick up a catering menu at the same time. Their forté is fresh uncomplicated dishes like seafood-stuffed gougeres, Mediterranean meatballs with saffron sauce and Vera Cruz chicken stew. Their spinach bread and Tex-Mex dips are good for parties.

Wieland's Home Cooking
5637 Cypress St. • 320-8486

When Yaletown was still a gleam in an architect's eye, chef Markus Wieland opened up Alabaster, a restarant that served exemplary northern Italian cuisine. What panna cotta! What veal! The bad news is that Alabaster folded. The good news: Wieland still cooks for private customers, in their homes. A sample menu might kick off with Dungeness crab salad with sautéed artichoke hearts and cucumber vinaigrette. This might be followed by oven-roasted quail on mushroom risotto with aceto balsamico glaze, then cranberry and lime granitato with fresh mint to clear the palate, then seared Ahi tuna on asparagus and lemon grass with baby nugget potatos and a light lemon butter sauce. To finish: a tarte tatin of spiced Anjou pears and vanilla ice cream.

Help for Non-Profit Organizations

Safeway has community cookers — basically large barbecues — and tent canopies for use by non-profit organizations. Send a letter of request to Mark Stortz, Director of Public Affairs, Canada Safeway Ltd., 7280 Fraser Street, Vancouver, V5X 3V9.

As well, Buy-Low Foods (3151 Arbutus St., 738-5255) offers free use of a room to any local, non-profit organization. Coffee and cookies included.

Throwing a Party

Maybe you'll have it catered, maybe you won't. Maybe, instead, you'll throw a gazillion chicken wings on the barbie or make the biggest pot of chili that Vancouver has ever seen.

Some folks you might want to invite along for the fun include:

People who bring basic necessities:

Pedersen's Party Rentals
8739 Heather St.   •   324-7368
Wine glasses, plates, cutlery, napkins, table cloths, tables, chairs, canopies for your yard, candelabras — everything you need, barring the food, for a hassle-free party. You can pick up or have it all delivered.

People who bake fabulous cakes (check the bakery listings as well, and where it reads "desserts" think "birthday cake"):

Pacific Institute of Culinary Arts
1505 West 2nd Ave.   •   734-4488
Special-order birthday cakes cost around $18. Open 9:30 a.m. to 4:30 p.m. weekdays only.

Vancouver Community College
250 West Pender St.
You can only make orders in person, and you'll need to schedule your event around term-time, but it's worth it for the deals you get on birthday and wedding cakes.

That's Entertainment!
Parties or dinners can go like clockwork provided you've got everything organized, as Vancouver's catering professionals are well aware. Let guests help, says Caren McSherry. "Have serving platters set out with little pieces of paper saying that the herbed cheese appetizers go here, the blue corn fritters there…"

"Set your table well ahead of time," advises Lesley Stowe. Instead of poinsettias at Christmas, "Bunch up some beautiful fabric. Arrange tons of different sized candles on it — all one colour — then wind ribbon among the candles."

Nicky Major the Gourmet's idea? "Hire your son's or daughter's friends to help keep things tidy during, and after, the event so you can enjoy your guests."

NANAIMO BARS

by Marg Meikle

Everyone knows what a Nanaimo bar is supposed to look and taste like: the rich, slightly chewy base of chocolate, graham crackers, coconut and nuts; the smooth, yellowish, creamy-custard middle; the hard, semi-sweet chocolate top. Weighing in at over 5,000 calories per baking pan, the Nanaimo bar is as irresistible as it is deadly to a Special K waistline.

True aficionados debate at length whether the bars should be eaten freezing cold or at room temperature. Then there's the perfect size: should it be two or three healthy bites or a lasagna-sized chunk? But nothing beats the debate over the correct name. Over the years, the triple-layered confection (with only slight variations) has been known as New York dream bars, London fog bars and a dozen other names. Such diverse places as Saskatoon, Mississauga and Wisconsin have claimed them as their own.

By any name, they are a legend — but in the West we know that they really are Nanaimo bars. All you have to do is ask the 52,000-odd citizens of Nanaimo, B.C., which takes its name from the Salish Indian word "syn-ny-mo," or "big, strong people." The local chamber of commerce is asked constantly about the dessert's true origins. The commonly held story is that a Nanaimo housewife entered a recipe for chocolate squares in a contest, under the title "Nanaimo bars," and the popularity of the bars — and the name — spread from there.

Wherever the first recipe came from, and when — some claim they came from London in the 1880s, others cite New York in the 1930s as the source — word spread quickly about this easy-to-make (there's no baking involved), great-tasting square. By 1960, there was a recipe on the can of one of the essential ingredients, Bird's Custard Powder. However, it wasn't until the late 1970s that someone realized people would pay money for this favourite childhood treat. Susan Mendelson, a Vancouver caterer, was one of the first to market Nanaimo bars. Today, Mendelson's Lazy Gourmet store sells several variations on the original recipe. You can find them frozen and ready-to-eat in your local supermarket, or buy a mix that lets you bake your own.

Still, the best Nanaimo bar remains the one you make from scratch in your own kitchen. And, despite the current preoccupation with fat content and cholesterol, when a plate of Nanaimo bars is passed around, eyes continue to light up in recognition as that first custard-and-chocolate bite slides sinfully down the throat.

MARKETS AND FESTIVALS

Eating and celebrating are as closely linked as burgers and buns or bacon and eggs. Imagine Christmas without mincemeat pies, Thanksgiving without turkey or your birthday without a birthday cake. It just wouldn't be the same.

In Vancouver, food is central to a huge number of special events, ethnic festivals, arts festivals and fundraising events. It seems every month offers a new reason to go out and eat. In a smaller way, we also celebrate food on a daily basis. Who among us doesn't get a small surge of pleasure tasting the first local strawberries or crisp stalks of asparagus? Who hasn't devoured a half-dozen Okanagan peaches at the peak of their amazing coral-skinned golden-fleshed ripeness? One summer we grabbed an entire flat of local raspberries from the market. Jam was the idea, but the reality was different: We ate the lot!

To Market, To Market

For hundreds and hundreds of years, "market day" was – and, in many parts of the world, still is – the high point of the week. Off you went, basket over your arm, to see what you could find. Even today, when many markets offer foods from around the world year-round, there's still that sense of anticipation. What will you discover today?

Indoor Markets

NEW WESTMINSTER:
Westminster Quay Public Market
810 Quayside · 520-3881
Lots of fresh produce, pies from the Farm Cottage Baking Co., exotic condiments from Here's the Garlic and great cheeses from Cheese Please Plus. Not just for locals. A fun Sunday afternoon SkyTrain excursion.

NORTH VANCOUVER:
Lonsdale Quay Market
123 Carrie Cates Court · 985-6261
Many of the same stall-holders as Granville Island

and an equally good selection of meat, seafood and produce. Downtown foodies can ride the SeaBus over on their lunch break, pick up fresh fish for tonight's dinner and stash it in the lunchroom fridge.

RICHMOND:
Richmond Public Market
8260 Westminster Hwy. • 821-1888
Stores here cater to the surrounding Asian population, which means great produce, fresh fish, Chinese pastries and more.

VANCOUVER:
Granville Island Public Market
Granville Island • 666-5784
Whether you want the ingredients for a quick sandwich (or a quick sandwich itself) or everything you need for a blow-their-socks-off dinner party for 24, you'll find it here. Fresh salmon, superb meats, a vast selection of cheeses, breads, chocolate croissants and fresh pastas – the list goes on.

Robson Public Market
610 Robson St. • 682-2733
West Enders drop by on their way home for fresh fish, veggies and baked goodies. Standouts here are RB's Meats, where owner Ron Burridge sells grain-fed lamb raised on his farm in the Fraser Valley, and the Blue Ribbon Deli – the rotisserie chicken is a must. Highly recommended is Dabne's for spices.

Outdoor Markets

Here's where you come closest to the people who grow what they sell. In fact, most farmers' markets make that a condition. Something else you notice: a lettuce that was picked a few

Granville Island Secret
Finding a place to ditch the Honda can be hairy — especially on weekends. Unless your parking karma's exceptionally strong, get there a bit before 8:30 a.m. on a weekend morning and you'll find it's mostly just you and the stall holders. Browse around, have a coffee, buy what you want as the stalls open, and as you leave, wave cheerily to those lining up to get on the Island.

Summer's bounty at a farmers' market

hours ago lasts far longer than a tired and weary vegetable that's spent three days on the road.

COQUITLAM:

Coquitlam Farmers' Market
Coquitlam Rec Centre, 633 Poirier • 730-0450
At this small (but growing) market held Sundays through the summer, you can buy veggies and fruits, all direct from the farm, as well as prepared foods and crafts.

LANGLEY:

Pioneer Farmers' Market
McBurney Plaza • 534-6314
Saturdays June through October you can shop for fruits, vegetables and home-baked goodies.

SURREY:

Surrey Farmers' Market
N. Surrey Rec Centre, 10275 135th St. • 591-4289
Head out to the heart of the Fraser Valley on a summer Saturday and pile your basket with the fruits and veggies sold by local farmers. Check out the crafts stalls, too.

VANCOUVER:

Capers Farmers Market
1675 Robson St. • 687-5288
Held Thursdays from mid-July to Labour Day, this downtown outdoor market lets you meet the folks who grow the amazing organic vegetables sold at Capers. Nugget potatoes from Pemberton, beets, squash, carrots, kale and sweet Chilliwack corn, extraordinary peppers, tomatoes and blueberries, and arugula, tatsoi and all the other greens we've come to know and love – they're all here.

East Vancouver Farmers' Market
Trout Lake Community Centre, 3350 Victoria Dr. • 879-3276
Started in 1996, this has already become a popular place for Saturday shopping. Here's a chance to meet the people who grow what you eat. From the May long weekend until Labour Day, the market brings

new delights every week. Intensely flavoured straw-berries. Wonderful toma-toes. Big heads of or-ganically grown lettuce. Also scones and muffins baked that morning, bedding plants, fresh flowers by the bunch and crafts. A backyard table lets locals get rid of that vigorous zucchini crop.

Fresh fruit from the Okanagan

Granville Island Farm Truck Sales
Granville Island, public market parking lot • 666-6477
In the summer season, watch for the weekly truck market held in the parking lot to the east of Granville Island Public Market. Wonderful corn, exceptional tomatoes and luscious table grapes — you'll come upon some real gourmet treats.

Festivals

Get the calendar off the kitchen wall now, and mark in the dates of these events so you don't miss a single one of them. Here's a season-by-season rundown:

SPRING: March, April, May

VANCOUVER:
Dining Out for Life
682-5992
One evening each March, more than 100 Vancouver restaurants donate a considerable percentage of their food revenues to Dining Out for Life. Funds raised go to Aids-related charities. Check local newspapers for lists of participating restaurants.

Granville Island Market After Dark
Granville Island Public Market • 730-0450
Normally the market aisles are silent in the evening, but one night a year in early May they swarm with

Festive Breads for Easter
Ecco Il Pane (238 West 5th Ave., 873-6888; 2563 West Broadway, 739-1314) makes traditional gubana, a sweet bread with pinenuts and raisins soaked in marsala and grappa, as well as crescia — a claypot-baked cheese bread — and sweet rosemary and raisin buns. At the Broadway Bakery (3273 West Broadway, 733-1422), you'll find Greek bread called tsouraki with a red-dyed egg at its centre.

eager eaters and drinkers. At this fundraiser for FarmFolk/CityFolk, bakeries, wineries, pizza makers, produce growers and the B.C. salmon people offer info and tastes. A major draw are cooking demonstrations by some of the city's star chefs.

Taste of the Nation
691-7764

Presented by "Share Our Strength" (SOS), North America's largest non-profit fundraising association for anti-hunger, anti-poverty charities, this annual dining event is held one day each year in April or May in over 100 cities across North America. Vancouver's event puts together 60 or so of the region's finest restaurants and beverage suppliers. It's a great opportunity to taste new wines. Not overly dressy (unless you want it to be), it's probably the year's best dining bargain. Watch for announcements in the media.

Out of Town Wine Festivals
Alpine Wine Festival at Whistler: September (1-604-932-3210);
Fall Okanagan Wine Festival: October (1-250-861-6654);
Cornucopia Food & Wine Festival, Whistler: November (1-604-932-3210);
Pacific Northwest Wine Festival, Victoria: (1-250-592-5081);
Kamloops Art Gallery Wine Festival, March: (1-888-537-6218);
Spring Okanagan Wine Festival, April/May: (1-250-861-6654).

Vancouver International Wine Festival
Vancouver Trade and Convention Centre
999 Canada Place • 872-6622

Held in late April/early May, this festival began as a small fundraiser for the Vancouver Playhouse and has grown to become one of the most exciting wine events in North America. At this mega-event, experts can mull over the fine differences between Bordeaux vintages, and even the rawest beginner can learn an enormous amount. Most instructive of all are the tastings, which let you taste hundreds of different wines from virtually every wine-growing country — and talk to the men and women who make and sell them. Many of the wines are unavailable in B.C., but for this occasion you can buy them on the spot. BC Transit, advisedly, usually offers free passes for attendees.

The Wellness Show
Vancouver Trade and Convention Centre
999 Canada Place • 661-7373

Usually held in March, The Wellness Show amply proves that healthy living and zippy flavours needn't be mutually exclusive. Cooking demonstrations by well-known local chefs and the opportunity to sample products are only two reasons to visit.

SUMMER: June, July, August

STEVESTON:
Salmon Festival
Steveston Community Centre, 4111 Moncton St. • 277-6812
Mark July 1st on your calendar if you want to taste salmon – red spring salmon from Bella Coola usually – barbecued over alderwood fires. Chinese, Japanese and Greek traditional dishes, too.

VANCOUVER:
Brewmaster's Festival
Plaza of Nations • 290-4268
The first was held in 1993. Since then, local microbreweries have popped up all over the place. This June weekend happening lets you taste your way through lagers, ales, stouts and pilsners, and pick the brains of the brewmasters. Seminars cover topics such as cooking with beer.

Canadian Barbecue and Chili Festival
Westminster Quay Public Market • 520-3881
Usually held on the B.C. Day long weekend, this heated affair has drawn a bigger crowd each year since it was first launched in 1987. Discover chili, beef brisket, pork ribs and other good smoky, spicy dishes. Contestants compete in over 150 categories.

Caribbean Days Festival
A July event organized by the Trinidad and Tobago Society of British Columbia. Live and recorded music set the scene for limbo contests, costume parades and island food. Feast on Jamaican rice, roti or jerk chicken, washed down with a glass of Ting. Check newspapers for exact dates.

FraserFest
Westminster Quay Public Market • 520-3881
Salmon barbecues and pancake breakfasts are part of the fun at this waterside festival held mid-July. Includes

Market Mania
A friend calls it vegeholic-ism — and we're all suspectible. Enchanted by the sheer ripeness and profusion of a farmers' market, it's easy to go stark raving nuts. A big bag of this, a huge bag of that, and suddenly there's enough food in your fridge to feed an army. If it's fruit, eat it fast. Two healthy adults can work their way through a flat of raspberries in a couple of days. Strawberries on your corn flakes, straw-berries with your lunchtime bagel, strawberries for dessert with ice cream.

Vegetables are more of a problem. Produce wilts. Here's what to do with that fridge drawer bursting with produce:
- Shred greens and add to chicken stock, along with noodles and a dash of soy sauce for instant Asian soup.
- Add chopped raw spinach to bottled pasta sauce.
- Purée tomatoes — skin, seeds, the whole shebang (okay, maybe take out the core) — and freeze in baggies for use in pasta sauces and soups.
- Cook green beans, drizzle with vinaigrette and use as a marinated salad.
- Roast red peppers under the broiler, stick in a plastic bag to cool, then remove skin, core and seeds. Drizzle with olive oil. They'll keep in the fridge for a week and work well in omelettes and pasta sauces.

workboat parade and marching mascot parade.

A Marriage Made in B.C.
1-800-811-9911

This union of wild B.C. salmon (through the B.C. Salmon Marketing Council) and B.C. pinot blanc (through the B.C. Wine Institute) is a highly successful one. Around mid-July to the end of August, restaurants around the city create vibrantly exciting salmon dishes which are specially paired with B.C. wines. Check the media, or your local L.D.B. or private wine store for news of who's participating. Usually over three dozen restaurants are involved and local chefs go to enormous lengths to synchronize the complexities of food and wine. One year, staff at the John B Pub created a curried apple crisp topped with frilly red lettuce called lollo rosso, a dash of lime mascarpone and cardamom-marinated salmon. The spice's clean sweetness and the Granny Smith apples were specifically chosen to work with the tropical fruit nuances of Wild Goose pinot blanc. Another time, the Hotel Vancouver's 900 West had two dishes on offer. A little potato pancake held smoked Roma tomato and a chunk of salmon and was ringed with crème fraîche and a razor-sharp lemon marmalade made from the zest, flesh and juice of the lemon plus a tiny bit of sugar. Beside it, a salmon "lasagna" featured smoked Campbell River Chinook layered with pasta, and was sauced just before serving with a ragout of white beans, fava beans, bean-size lengths of asparagus, tiny cubes of tomato, mussels and clams. O'Doul's served up salmon as tartare and as escalopes with a citrus cilantro vinaigrette. The Salmon House on the Hill devised a fusion rice roll that incorporated smoked fish and Saskatoon berries mixed with mirin and rice vinegar. Hart House treated their salmon simply, laying it gently on a bed of mesclun and topping it with a feather-light sabayon flavoured with roasted shallots and maple syrup. Dishes are different every year, which is why the event is a "must" on the gourmet calendar.

Easter Treats

For the kids, try Tinker's Hatch bakery (4894 MacKenzie St., 261-4484) for hand-decorated Easter cookies. Make Chinese marbled eggs for adults. Hard-boil eggs as per usual, crack gently all over, then simmer with tea leaves 20 minutes. Let them cool in the water, shell and serve in wedges.

Powell Street Festival
Oppenheimer Park, Powell St. • 739-9388
Traditionally held during the B.C. Day long weekend, this celebration by the Japanese community has been around since 1977. As well as checking out the crafts and martial arts displays, it's a chance to taste "homestyle" Japanese foods such as takoyaki — bits of octopus wrapped in dough and grilled.

Vancouver Folk Music Festival
Jericho Beach Park • 602-9798
Dig out your tie-dyed caftan, kick off your shoes, let down your hair. This is the place to do it. It's also the venue for exceptional food. This is one July event where it doesn't make sense to bring a picnic. While tie-dye-hards mourn the disappearance of the Egg McBuddah (a scrambled egg patty with green onions and bean sprouts) there's plenty of other great nosh to make up for it, including Hornby Island pizza, home-made lemonade, Ethiopian food from the Nyala African Hotspot and other global cuisine.

FALL: September, October, November

<u>ALDERGROVE:</u>
Feast of Fields
Fraser Common Farm
1374 256th St. • 734-0450
The nearest that Vancouverites get to a harvest festival is this September event held at a farm in the Fraser Valley, a fundraiser for FarmFolk/CityFolk. The farm is an absolute joy — rolling acres green with growth. Chickens squawk, cows moo, barns dot the horizon — it may be real country, but the food is real gourmet. Leading chefs present dishes made on the spot and

Festive Breads for
Harvest Time

Terra Breads (2380 West 4th
Ave., 736-1838; Granville
Island Public Market,
685-3102) makes pane all'uva,
studding the grapes tic-tac-
toe style into the dough.
Concord grapes go into the
schiachatta baked at Ecco II
Pane (238 West 5th Ave., 873-
6888, 2563 West Broadway,
739-1314).

served on leaves or inside miniature pumpkins.
Growers of tomatoes, peppers and greens offer
samples. Orchardists introduce you to Cape
gooseberries or luscious purple grapes.

NEW WESTMINSTER:
Queensborough Urban Farmers Fall Fair
Queensborough Community Centre, 920 Ewen Ave.
• 525-7388
Shopping at the farmers' market, entering the
spaghetti-eating contest and enjoying a corn feed are
just some of the fun activities at this September event.

RICHMOND:
Cranberry Harvest Festival
Richmond Nature Park, 11851 Westminster Hwy •
273-7015
October marks an entire day that revolves around the
tangy deliciousness of cranberries. Tour a cranberry
farm and the Ocean Spray plant, hunt for wild
cranberries or buy fresh cranberries to take home.

VANCOUVER:
Apple Festival
UBC Botanical Garden, 6804 SW Marine Dr.
• 822-9666
At the turn of the century in North America, you
could have bitten into more than 1,800 apple varieties.
These days, you'll find maybe a half dozen types for
sale at your local supermarket. Since 1991, the UBC
Botanical Garden has been doing what it can to raise
apple awareness at its annual October festival, which
is presented by The Friends of the Garden. In a typical
year, it offers over 35 varieties for buying, more than
60 kinds to taste (for a nominal fee) and over 40
varieties of trees to take home and plant in your own
backyard. Watch demonstrations of grafting and cider
pressing. Taste apples you've never heard of, such as
Maiden's Blush, Sweet June and The Lady (a favourite
of the ladies-in-waiting at the court of Louis XIII).

B.C. Food and Beverage Month
666-3921

Further evidence that Vancouverites are a greedy lot is an entire month — September — dedicated to eating and drinking (and officially proclaimed so by the Lieutenant Governor, no less!). An annual salute to the quarter of a million B.C. people involved in the food and wine biz. Look for special promotions in the supermarket and special menus at your favourite restaurant. With markets filled to bursting with Fraser Valley-grown vegetables, it's no hardship to support the local economy by choosing local foods.

Festival of Flavours
Vancouver Trade and Convention Centre
999 Canada Place • 526-9356

This October event at the Vancouver Trade and Convention Centre celebrates B.C.'s booming food and beverage industry. It's a "don't miss" event for foodies who want to spend a happy couple of hours wandering around exhibitors' stalls and sampling everything from chutneys to specialty breads. High notes are the cooking demonstrations which usually feature some of the best chefs in the city. There's also the annual chocolate and truffle competition. Keep your eyes on the local media for exact dates.

GVRD Farm Open House Day
432-6339

All kinds of farms open their doors to the public during this one-day event, usually held the weekend before Thanksgiving. Touring a working farm really brings home the link between field and fork. Farmers are on hand to answer questions and you can often sample or purchase what you see growing.

Hadassah Bazaar
257-5160

Its longtime home at the P.N.E. Food Building has bitten the dust, and it hasn't found a permanent new one yet. But the date of this popular rummage sale-cum-fundraiser stays the same — the first Wednesday in November — and so does the array of superb dill pickles, cheesecake and tons of good home-baking.

Cheap Trip to Hong Kong

Few visitors to Hong Kong leave without spending a few hours in one of the famous night markets, a heaving mass of shoppers till late in the evening. Vancouver now has its own version — smaller and a lot less crowded — which takes place on weekend evenings during the Summer. Shopping, eating and free entertainment are all part of the fun. To catch the action, head for East Pender and Keefer Streets between Main and Gore.

Living Naturally Fair

1675 Robson St. (Capers parking lot) • 687-5288

Expanded to a two-day event in 1998, this popular September country fair (in the heart of the city) raises funds for A Loving Spoonful, the non-profit organization that provides free meals to people living with HIV and AIDS. As well as filling your basket with organic fruits and veggies direct from the growers, you'll find fresh-baked goods, the latest natural products and supplements, and entertainment.

Moon Festival

The Chinese Cultural Centre, 50 East Pender St. • 687-0729

Harvest time in the Chinese community means the eating of moon cakes whose flaky pastry exterior conceals a mixture of egg yolks, lotus seed paste, walnuts or watermelon seeds. The Chinese Cultural Centre celebrates the Moon Festival (which occurs in late September) with music, storytelling and other entertainment. Events vary from year to year.

The Mushroom Show

Van Dusen Botanical Garden, 5251 Oak St. • 878-9274

Is it a gourmet treat – or a lethal weapon? It's a good idea to find out before you sauté what might be a chanterelle but maybe isn't. Hosted by the Vancouver Mycological Society (878-9878) in October, this is an excellent opportunity to learn from experts how to identify those weird funghi you find in the woods.

Xclusively BC

Vancouver Trade and Convention Centre
999 Canada Place • 641-1448

Made up of some top B.C. chefs, this organization is devoted to raising funds to supply bursaries to British Columbians pursuing careers in food or wine. Once a year, they host the foodie event to end all. Every ingredient, every wine, every detail is grown or produced here in British Columbia. Seven or eight chefs are involved, and to say that there's gentle competition is an understatement. The result: a staggeringly exciting dinner.

WINTER: December, January, February

B.C. Wine & Oyster Festival
739-7801
Major slurping and sipping are scheduled each January at this annual fundraiser for the B.C. Children's Hospital Foundation. Virtually all of B.C.'s leading wineries are on hand. An Oyster Shucking Challenge and a Raw Oyster Eating Contest add to the fun.

Bacchanalia
Sinclair Centre, 757 West Hastings St. • 299-7851
Sippers oust shoppers when the Burnaby Association for the Mentally Handicapped hosts its annual Bacchanalian Wine Festival fundraiser in Sinclair Centre. If it's a northwest Pacific wine, chances are good you can sample it here. Various restaurants provide the munchies. Check for dates — this was formerly a fall event but scheduled later in the year in 1998/1999.

Have a Happy (Vegetarian) Christmas
Traditional mincemeat contains suet — the fat around an animal's kidneys — which is something vegetarians don't even want to think about. Around Christmas time, Uprising Breads Bakery (1697 Venables Street, 254-5635), carries vegetarian mincemeat.

THE SECRET SIDE OF
GRANVILLE ISLAND PUBLIC MARKET

Dussa's for a wedge of ripe Brie, fruits and veggies from your favourite stand, a bag of crusty buns — shop at Granville Island regularly and you can almost do it with your eyes closed. But did you see those local Okanagan melons? The organic wild rice? The chili pepper plants?

Seasonal food from local farmers is one of the unexpected plusses. Farmers have priority for day table space, and priority also goes to seasonal food that you won't find in any supermarket. Such as:

- "Transparents," the first local apples
- Organic baby potatoes from Pemberton
- Asparagus from the Sunshine Coast
- Unusual apples from Denman Island – Bramleys, Belle de Boscoop, Cox's Orange Pippins – as well as crabapples and quinces, all certified organic
- Melons from the Okanagan
- Heritage apples
- Table grapes
- Tinned venison from Mayne Island: pâté, medallions of venison in black currant gelée, venison with mushrooms and burgundy
- Chili sauces and chili pepper plants
- Organic wild rice
- Locally grown walnuts and hazelnuts
- Certified organic cherries, plums and apricots from the Okanagan
- Homegrown produce from the Fraser Valley
- Organic salad greens and vegetables from a farmers' co-operative
- Japanese pastries such as green tea cake and bean paste cake

Days and seasons vary. When the crop is ripe, the farmers come to town. If you'd like to know exactly when, contact the Market Office at 666-6477.

TO EVERYTHING THERE IS A SEASON...

(by permission of the East Vancouver Farmers' Market)

Apples: August-June
Apricots: July-August
Basil: July-September
Beets: July-October
Blackberries: August-October
Blueberries: July-September
Broccoli: July-October
Brussels sprouts: October-December
Cabbage: July-February
Carrots: July-November
Cauliflower: June-November
Celery: July-October
Cherries: June-July
Chinese vegetables: June-September
Chives: April-October
Cilantro: June-October
Corn: August-October
Cranberries: October
Cucumbers: July-September
Currants: August-September
Dill: mid-July-September
Garlic: July-October
Grapes: September-October
Green beans: July-September
Hazelnuts: September-October
Kale: mid-August-November
Kiwi: October-February
Lavender: June-October
Leeks: July-November
Lettuce: June-October

Marjoram: June-October
Melons: August-September
Mushrooms: Year-round
Nectarines: July-August
Onions, green: June-September
Onions, red: October-January
Onions, yellow: September-March
Parsley: May-October
Parsnips: October-March
Peaches: July-September
Pears: August-April
Peas: June-July
Peppers: July-October
Plums: August-September
Potatoes: June-October
Radishes: May-October
Raspberries: July-September
Rhubarb: April-July
Rosemary: Year-round
Sage: Year-round
Salad greens: June-October
Shallots: August-September
Spinach: April-September
Strawberries: June-September
Summer squash: July-August
Swiss chard: July-October
Tomatoes: July-October
Thyme: June-November
Turnips: May-February
Winter squash: mid-September-December

Picnic Time Suggestions

• Sausages, from your favourite butcher, are great cold. Grill them just before you go on the picnic. All you need to round out the meal are steamed new potatoes left to cool, a dipping sauce of half mustard and half mayo, and a green salad.

• Barbecued chickens from Safeway, take-out coleslaw, crusty bread.

• Salad Nicoise which you make on the spot. Take along washed greens, tomatoes, cooked green beans, black olives, hard-boiled eggs, a can or more of tuna, a container of homemade vinaigrette and an *enormous* bowl.

STAR-STRUCK FOOD

Vancouver astrologer Jef Simpson's monthly dinners at Monterey Lounge & Grill (1277 Robson St., 684-1277) are famous. As far as the well-known Vancouver astrologer knows, he was the first to develop the sign 'n' dine connection, and, since 1993, he's been putting theory into practice.

Each menu is different, created from the list of vegetables, grains, nuts, fish and meats ruled by a particular birth sign. Filling a room with Virgos (or any other sign) makes interesting viewing. "Gemini and Sagittarians love to party," says Simpson, "so everybody talks and nobody listens. At an Aries dinner, there is a common energy in the room: they're confident. Scorpio and Capricorn are both into control and power. They're very sceptical."

Here is Jef Simpson's analysis of each sign's eating habits and tendencies (courtesy of Jef Simpson at the Cosmic Data Bank, Vancouver B.C., 669-7501):

ARIES (MARCH 21-APRIL 19)
Ariens have a high metabolic rate and tend to eat their food too quickly. Food prepared quickly or cooked at the table suits their love of speed. Baked or barbecued food is appropriate. Lamb, venison and goat are all ruled by this sign.

TAURUS (APRIL 20-MAY 20)
This sign appreciates good food. They relish plain and simple dishes but will never refuse rich sauces. Food from almost any country or region is served at the Taurean dinner table. According to an 11th century Persian astrologer, the Taurean's love of food excels that of any other sign.

GEMINI (MAY 21-JUNE 21)
As an impatient and versatile sign, Gemini is associated with all dishes that take minimum time to prepare and eat. They especially like food that can be eaten while walking down the street or on the move.

CANCER (JUNE 22-JULY 22)
The sign of the mother and homemaker, Cancers cook meals that are both lavish and wholesome. They enjoy eating at places on or near the water and love a classic romantic setting.

LEO (JULY 23-AUGUST 22)
Cordon bleu cuisine is the ideal fare for Leos, whose foods are traditionally lavish, rich and well presented. The true Leo is more concerned with what food looks like and how it tastes than whether it is healthy.

VIRGO (AUGUST 23-SEPTEMBER 22)
Virgoans are more involved in the day-to-day preparation of food than any other sign except Cancerians. Often fussy about their diets, they favour plain, healthy food in small portions.

LIBRA (SEPTEMBER 23-OCTOBER 23)
Librans like to frequent fashionable eating places or those close to cultural centres. They are famous for their love of sweet things. Ideally, Libran food should be light, pleasantly presented and easy to digest.

SCORPIO (OCTOBER 24-NOVEMBER 21)
A love of the truth means that people born under this sign are likely to be concerned about the real nature of the food they eat and especially alert to the perils of suspicious chemical additives.

SAGITTARIUS (NOVEMBER 22-DECEMBER 21)
This wanderer of the Zodiac prefers a restaurant with a view and a fireplace. Sagittarians like to eat quickly or perform some other activity while eating. They prefer grilled, toasted, baked or barbecued foods.

CAPRICORN (DECEMBER 22-JANUARY 19)
Capricorns are fond of food and will eat almost anything. They are known for their love of traditional feasts. Some use food to make a statement about personal success, status and wealth.

What's Your Sign?
Several years ago, a typographical error enchanted the food lovers among the readers of a certain local paper. The typo resulted in the creation of a "new" astrological sign: Spagittarius (the pasta gatherer, presumably).

AQUARIUS (JANUARY 20-FEBRUARY 18)

The true Aquarian is an experimenter and innovator willing to try any new dish, however modern or exotic, however strange the combination of ingredients. Some revive ancient recipes while others are happier with the latest developments.

PISCES (FEBRUARY 19-MARCH 20)

Piscean chefs produce some of the most exotic and inventive dishes. This sign is fond of anything unusual or exotic which stimulates their artistic imagination. They are prone to food fads and tend to be vegetarians. At the opposite extreme, others ruled by this sign become gluttons.

FOOD PEOPLE

Making a living through food — growing it, harvesting it, importing it, selling it, cooking it, serving it, doing anything with it — is a wonderful way to spend your days. The people who do so are a very special breed.

Think about it for a minute: Whether they're up with the lark checking the crops, or on the phone to faraway places tracking down the latest shipment of imported mustards, or cooking away till the wee hours, their ultimate goal is to bring pleasure to the rest of us.

I've heard organic salad growers speak of "nurturing people's bodies and souls," watched chefs devote hours to a special dish that disappears in minutes, listened to them explain why they only use the best ingredients, and talked to the folks who supply them.

What's common to them all? Passion. Dedication. Joy. They genuinely love what they do.

Come and meet some of them...

NUTRITIONISTS AND DIETICIANS

Gold and crunchy deep-fried fish and chips. Bouncingly fresh salad greens. Slurpy noodles. Chocolate bars. Sushi. Aaargh! So many choices, so little time. If you feel fit and you're happy with the number you see on the scales, you're probably eating healthily. If you're not, or you have specific health problems or food allergies, you may need professional help. Your doctor, local hospital or health unit can link you to a registered dietician or nutritionist.

VANCOUVER:

Dial-a-Dietician
1060 West 8th Ave. • 732-9191

Available weekdays 8 a.m. to 5 p.m., this free service offers nutritional advice in English, Cantonese, Mandarin and Punjabi. Primarily funded by the B.C. Ministry of Health, it is staffed by registered dieticians who can answer virtually any nutrition question over the phone. If you're a recently diagnosed diabetic, or you're worried about cholesterol or hypertension, you're not alone. About half the 30,000 calls the service receives annually concern medical-related questions. Moms call in to ask how to cope with their newly vegetarian teen. Others want to be guided towards low-fat options (read, lose weight by eating more healthily). If callers need ongoing help, dieticians can tell them about programs and services available in their neighbourhood.

FitFood
736-5615

No matter how devoutly you promise yourself you'll stick like Krazy Glue to Canada's nutritional guidelines, the first evening you're too bushed to cook usually finds you calling out for pizza. Tapping into FitFood is a better alternative. Capers, that wellspring of wholesome ingredients, offers a FitFood program that delivers healthy dishes right to your door. The menu changes weekly. Choices for a typical day's worth might include a breakfast of blueberry pancakes with low-fat whipped yogurt and maple syrup, Greek-style chicken pita for lunch and baked salmon fillet with

---

Hospital Food

Gourmet cuisine may be the last thing on your mind as you emerge from the throes of the anaesthetic. It's the only thing on your mind thereafter. According to hearsay, St. Paul's and Vancouver Hospital will never make it into the Michelin guide; Lions Gate is marginally better. Voted best because it offers a choice of three cuisines — Chinese, Indian and Canadian — is Mount St. Joseph's.

vegetables for supper, plus fruit salad and samosa snacks. Program organizer Angela Bissett is endlessly flexible. If you just want dinner or lunch, fine – daily, weekly, whatever. Deliveries can be made to your home or office, Monday through Friday. Call for a faxed menu and detailed price sheet.

FOOD STYLISTS AND PHOTOGRAPHERS

That salad you've just tossed, that platter of antipasto and those roast potatoes, are never going to be absolutely perfect. You can have the best culinary skills and ingredients in town, but there's still no way that your cake or casserole will look as mouth-watering as that luscious full-colour page in the magazine. Why? Because dishes in print are like supermodels. They're not real. Before they appear for the public, they're groomed by experts and immortalized by photographers who know every trick in the book. Here's how it all happens.

The Secrets Behind a Star Burger

If you think that White Spot Triple O burger that you see on the poster or your TV looks a lot more glamorous than the one you get at the drive-in, there's a reason. It's called "the food stylist."

Nathan Fong's job is to make food look beautiful for print and film advertising. Lights, camera, action...whoah! It's not just any old burger that gets its moment in the limelight. In fact, as the photographer sets up the shot, he doesn't work with the star, he works with a stand-in.

Meanwhile, Fong is carefully examining 10 dozen buns. "They're specially baked for me," he reveals, "and specially selected in-house. I'm getting the cream of the cream. From those I pick half a dozen perfect tops and bottoms." In real life, the buns are toasted – which shrinks them a little. In the advertising world, that "toasted" look comes from a mixture of water and Kitchen Bouquet carefully applied with a brush. Fong then waxes the buns with paraffin to stop them absorbing the sauces.

He next re-forms the meat patties to make them look extra thick. (This isn't false advertising; they still contain the same amount of meat served in any Triple O.) "Next I fry up the burgers," says Fong, "at least a dozen, and then I cover them with vegetable oil to keep them from oxidizing, which makes them look dark in colour. You want them to have that just-grilled look."

Building the burger is an art in itself. "On the bottom of the bun, I put a little bit of cardboard or foam core," Fong reveals, "then some paper towel, so that the patty doesn't press into the burger. Then I take a nice burger patty and position it so it shows its best angle. Then I put a little bit of foam core and paper towel on the top of the patty." Because the Triple O's trademark is a burger cut in half, he next takes the perfect top and halves it with an electric knife. Two toothpicks are carefully positioned to help the top halves stay in place. Small pieces of paper towel or cardboard are inserted here and there so that, from the photographer's viewpoint, bun halves and burger are perfectly parallel.

Relish and White Spot's famous Triple O sauce are supplied in litre containers. Fong gets rid of excess relish liquid by placing it in a paper towel-lined strainer. He applies the Triple O sauce with a syringe, and uses a tiny palette knife to add relish underneath the top bun half. Scissor cuts in the burger patty and bottom bun create the illusion the bun has been completely halved.

"The important thing is the pickle," says Nathan Fong. "They are specially made for White Spot. I go through dozens to find the best-looking ones, then I dry them and put them on top of the bun, at right angles to the cut. Finally, I take a fine brush, dip it in oil, and oil the pickles and burgers to give them a gloss."

Putting together a Triple O takes about an hour. Order lettuce, onion or cheese and that takes even longer. Picture-perfect in every way, the burger that goes before the camera is known — what else? — as the "hero."

Making the Picture Perfect

John Sherlock has shot the lot — White Spot Triple O's, B.C. salmon, *Bishop's: The Cookbook* — in fact he figures 85 percent of his projects are food-related. Of all the "stars" that sit patiently in front of his camera, the most challenging, says Sherlock, are Yves Veggie Cuisine hot dogs. "They're essentially colourless extruded protein re-formed and spiced,"

Dust Your Desserts
Pies and crisps look even more scrumptious if you shake a little fine powdered sugar over them just before you serve them.

he says somewhat clinically of a vegetarian dish that has won fans around the world.

"It has a short life in front of the camera. A lot of food, you can undercook. Some you can paint to make them 'live' in front of the camera for a long time. Yves' products are very delicate." On your plate, that's not a problem, but when it's kept in the open air for a couple of hours, any hot dog can understandably start to wilt. Also making it more challenging is the "lyrical flow of mustard" that's become a visual signature along the tops of these particular hot dogs. "We assemble it, place it on a bun and shoot. We do this over and over until we get the right one."

Persistence pays off, but photographers and stylists sometimes have to resort to out-and-out fakery. Steam in a photo is usually the real thing but "smoke" is made from a special solution then fanned to diffuse it. Often the food itself is cold or at room temperature.

Contrary to popular belief, photographic lighting isn't "hot" and doesn't melt food, but a scoop of ice-cream starts to lose its shape in seconds. That is, if it's real, which it usually isn't. "All stylists have different recipes," says Sherlock. "Generally, icing sugar, shortening, corn syrup, food colouring and various other ingredients." They look great, but you wouldn't want to eat them. "One sundae sat on my studio windowsill for six months and never changed."

On with the show: Using a stand-in, Sherlock arranges positioning and lighting. The product has to fit the layout of the ad or magazine; space may have to be left for type to be superimposed. Once the "hero" product appears, it's action time. "I like to shoot as quickly after that as we can," he says. "You can artificially induce the food to last longer — for instance, you can chemically treat greens so they don't wilt — but, for the most part, I like a more naturalistic presentation."

Sherlock admits that if he's photographing an extreme close-up of a dish, "it has to be ultra-perfect. So much of our perception is visual. That's all you have to go on." The big question, in his mind is: "If I look at it, does it make me want to eat it?" And if it does, he's done his job.

Giving Food the Professional Look

For under a dollar, a plastic squeezie bottle is one of the best deals around.

Try a Zorro-like slash of sour cream across homemade borscht, or a squiggle of pesto on pasta — friends can mix it in themselves.

Fill a squeezie bottle with chocolate sauce and you can draw hearts, flowers or zig-zags on a plate, then sit a scoop of ice-cream on it. Top it off with a sprig of mint.

FROM THE GARDEN TO THE RESTAURANT:

Herbs at Bishop's

Walk through the door of Bishop's, one of Vancouver's most highly praised restaurants, and you will be gently escorted to a linen-draped table. Sit down and, soon after, a server will offer you house-made breads baked that morning – perhaps a wedge of focaccia aromatic with rosemary or a herb-speckled slice cut from a wholewheat loaf. To accompany the bread there is a meticulously shaped triangle of butter, adorned – always – with a single perfect basil leaf or a small sprig of thyme.

Herbs in the bread and herbs in the butter are just the beginning. "We use a lot," says Bishop's Executive Chef, Dennis Green. Frequently showing up as a garnish, the herbs reflect the restaurant's emphasis on fresh, regionally grown ingredients – and echo what's in the dish. Herbs that aren't quite as photogenic as others, says Green, find a home in sauces.

"Whatever you use has to be appropriate," he emphasizes. "Woodier varieties are better cooked, whereas, in the summer, we would use whole leaves of fresh basil." Summertime is when Green makes herbs into vinegar (he estimates he has about four gallons of chive flower vinegar stashed away). "We've also been playing with herb-infused oils such as basil or dill," he says, revealing that blanching the herb for 10 seconds, then puréeing it in the oil helps retain its fresh green colour.

He's a firm fan of the alchemy that herbs can work in his kitchen: "They add so many different elements to food. Thyme almost has a salinity to it. You find you can cut back on salt." One of Green's favourite combinations is rosemary with lamb, "and lemon thyme on fish is a personal preference of mine." (Bishop's menu sometimes features local clams steamed with lemon thyme, Chinese black beans and roasted garlic.) Professional tips? Be careful not to overpower a delicate food with an herb. "You wouldn't poach sole with sage but we have served grilled salmon with a rosemary-infused oil."

Traditionally, parsley has been the poor relation of the herb family but Green uses it in a dazzling sauce to accompany salmon, and kitchen staff know it as a reliable way to pump up the colour of pesto. Basil is an obvious match with tomatoes, says Green, but at Bishop's this popular summer herb shows up at dessert time too. Customers go ga-ga over the pears poached in a red wine sauce with basil.

Dennis Green especially likes to double an herb's impact by including it in a marinade, and then incorporating a small amount of the same herb in an accompanying sauce. A keen home cook, he often places rosemary branches on his coals and a few leaves on the chicken he's barbecuing. His garden also grows creeping marjoram, different kinds of thyme, tarragon and variegated sage. And then there's that big sage bush. Green smiles. "I've transplanted it from house to house." Any herb-lover will understand.

FEAR ITSELF

Eyes pop, sweat beads the brow, hands reach unsteadily for the jug of ice water. There's nothing like a really incendiary hot sauce. Once upon a time, there was chili sauce. Then came salsa. Now, we can find dozens of varieties of "hot," ranging in strength from tame to ones that will blast the top of your head off. Among the latter is a Vancouver-made brand called Fear Itself.

Andrew Scott has been working as a chef since the late 1970s. Trained in Banff, Alberta, he ricocheted back and forth across the country before eventually settling in Vancouver. Everywhere he went, he delved deeper into his passion for spicy food. In 1994, an old hand in the hospitality business by the name of Justin Joyce hired Scott to work at the Ouisi Bistro, which specializes in Louisiana and other hot cuisines. Along with his chef's hat, apron and knives, Scott brought along a secret weapon: his specialty habanero sauce.

"People would come in and say 'you can't make it hot enough for me,'" Joyce remembers. Nothing like a challenge. Scott began tinkering with his hot sauce, adding more and more habeneros, spiking it with East Indian spices, experimenting with proportions, always aware that the challenge is to create extremely intense heat with flavour.

Happy with the final recipe, Scott and Joyce offered it in little ramekins on the sides of customers' plates. "Can we get some to take home?" they were asked with increasing frequency. "I spoke to Justin," says Scott, "and he was the first person to listen when I said, 'I think we should market this stuff!'"

They started making small batches in the Ouisi kitchen. Next came the label. Backtrack to Scott's early teens when he owned a snake he called "Fear Itself." All along, it had seemed like a suitably scary name for a hot sauce. Besides, "It's not just fearfully hot," they say, "it's fearfully delicious."

Scott can take unbelievable amounts of heat. Joyce has trained himself to tolerate high-decibel hot sauces. "Ours is painful but it's still an enjoyable sensation," he says, pointing out that some sauces now available use pepper extract — the equivalent of pepper spray for your tongue.

Fear Itself fans have found a multitude of uses for the sauce. Eggs? That's for raw beginners. Some users mix it into hot chocolate, others sprinkle it on watermelon or swirl it into yogurt and relish the fire-and-ice contrast. At Ouisi Bistro, it's shaken into Bloody Caesars, is a primary ingredient in curry and, once in a while, is used in a chicken marinade. Say Scott and Joyce: "If you have good flavour components in a hot sauce, you can put it into anything."

The Fear Itself label advises: "Use a little 'til you need a lot!!"

WHERE THE CHEFS SHOP

Richard Zeinoun and **Lisa Gibson** of Habibi's buy their vegetables from New Apple Farm Market (2856 West Broadway, 739-6882), as well as Chinatown and Granville Island. Spices come direct from Lebanon, and tahini, beans and pickles direct from Tony's Imports in Montreal.

Carol Chow of the Beach Side Café loves roaming around Japantown, especially the Sunrise Market (300 Powell St., 685-8019) — "The fruit's really good" — and anywhere in Chinatown. "The fish you see down there, like eels or periwinkles, you don't see at places like Granville Island."

"Find me the best cannoli in town!" said **Noel MacDonald**, food nut and researcher with Business in Vancouver. The consensus is that the award goes to — roll of the drums, please — Pasticceria Italia (2828 East Hastings St., 251-6800).

"I buy bread from La Baguette et L'Echalote (1680 Johnson St., 684-1351). If I have time, I go to Steveston for fresh prawns."

— **Robert LeCrom**, Executive Chef, Hotel Vancouver.

Karen Barnaby of The Fish House in Stanley Park generally buys her meat at Arctic Meats (1714, Commercial Drive, 255-1301). "The pork there is really good, and so are the free-range chickens, and, given notice, they'll roast a duck for you in the roaster." For fish, Barnaby heads to the T and T Supermarket at 1st and Renfrew.

In the market for goat? Local goat doesn't cut it, says **Assefa Kebede** of Nyala African Hotspot, who features goat on his menu. "It's tough and has no taste. Goat has to come from Australia. It needs to feed on desert, which makes it leaner."

"At the East Vancouver Farmers' Market and on The Drive. For bulk stuff, I love Famous Foods. For price

What's in that Triple O Sauce?
It's one of the big culinary puzzles around town: Exactly what does White Spot put in their famous Triple "O" sauce? According to legend, the sauce came into being when a customer wanted a triple helping of relish and mayo. Nah, it couldn't be that simple. White Spot isn't telling, but a few people were willing to give it their best guess…

"Mustard-pickles, a jar of Heinz Chili Sauce in the blender but the mayo is made separately, and they do something different to it."
— Kerry Moore, *Vancouver Province*.

"Mayonnaise, onion, garlic, pepper and probably a really mild chili sauce."
— Judi Lees, Travel Writer

"Mayonnaise, ketchup and a drop of Worcestershire Sauce — I was told that in all confidence."
— Herb Barbolet, FarmFolk/CityFolk

"Ketchup and mayonnaise, but probably a certain brand of mayonnaise. I used to work with someone who had worked at White Spot and that's what they said it was."
— Karen Barnaby, Executive Chef, The Fish House in Stanley Park

"It's a combination of red relish and mayonnaise specially made for White Spot."
— Anonymous

and selection, they're second to none. Also T and T for seafood. The one at Renfrew and lst Avenue has a great special: four small containers of Chinese food for $10. You cook the rice at home – and the food is better than in many Chinese restaurants."

— **Andrew Skorzewski**, Rainforest Café

Fresh Fraser Valley duck legs for confit de canard can usually be found at Mah Roy Markets (290 Keefer, 682-4071). Demand is high so check availability first.

"I buy my meat at Seafair Meats in Richmond," says **Michael Noble** of Diva at the Met. "It's a classic butcher's shop. They make great smoked ham and their own corned beef. There's a lot of love put into what they do." (12-8671 No. 1 Rd., Richmond, 274-4740.)

"Every Saturday morning when it's on, I go to the East Vancouver Farmers' Market, and if I don't find what I want, I head down Commercial Drive. Bosa's sometimes (562 Victoria Dr., 253-5578), Bonanza (265 East Hastings St., 688-6824) and T and T (100-2800 East 1st Ave., 254-9668) for Asian ingredients. I like Old Town Market in Yaletown. They carry good products like Avalon milk and Terra Breads. It's my neighbourhood."

— **Barbara-jo McIntosh**, Barbara-Jo's Books to Cooks

"I love basmati rice and the best I've ever had in my life – and the best pizzas – are at Zagros (1326 Davie St., 689-5999)."

— **Richard Toussaint**, Café de Paris

Karen Barnaby favours La Grotta del Formaggio for Cecco pasta – although "Del Verde" can be good too" – and for olive oil. La Grotta del Formaggio (1791 Commercial Drive, 255-3911) import specialty Italian cheeses – tallegio, buffalo milk mozzarella, and there's a cheese called burra which has butter inside. They also sell incredibly long pine nuts. You can see them in the window. And it's the only place to go for a mortadella sandwich.

"Calabria Meats at 37th and Victoria is the place for Italian sausage – the spicy is best."

— **Julio Gonzalez Perini**, Villa del Lupo

Elizabeth Iachelli of the Italian Chamber of Commerce of B.C. goes to Bosa (562 Victoria Dr., 253-5578) for pasta, coffee, "and Italian ingredients you can't find elsewhere." Among them, sardines which she uses to make a version of a famous Palermo dish called pasta con lasarde. Just chop up onion, fry it in olive oil, add the can of sardines, heat through and serve over pasta. Other favourite ingredients: "I buy panna cotta mix from Bosa. Just add milk. People rave about it. Also, I always use Coricelli Olive Oil."

Alex Martyniak of the Italian Chamber of Commerce of B.C. buys back bacon at Polonia Sausage House (2434 East Hastings St., 251-2239). He also buys Riomare Brand canned tuna at Bosa foods, which he puts in a risotto along with barbecued salmon from Superstore. His favourite pasta brands: Barilla and La Molisana. You can also buy good Italian cheese at Canadian Superstore, he says.

"Serge Gutman at Freden (1529 East Pender, 251-2277) sells excellent sausage. They have good prices on Camembert, too."
— **Hervé Martin**, the Hermitage

"For meat, I go to Jackson's Meats. For seafood, Chinatown is the cheapest and the best."
— **Richard Toussaint**, Café de Paris

"The Union Market (known for years as the Gomes Market) located at Union and Hawks in Strathcona (810 Union, 255-5025) was bought by a new generation of Portuguese owners a few years ago and is run by hard-working Gloria and Andy — short for Hannibal — Bernardino. They've kept up the reputation of their predecessors and, in my opinion, even improved on a good thing. Many of their offerings are rooted in Portuguese cuisine but they have just about everything that you could want packed into about 400 square feet. The bakery in the back produces fresh breads and pastries as well as other deli-type food items (fabulous pizzas) every day. Their specialty is Portuguese corn bread (both yellow and white) and I could eat a loaf a day! Their croissants

Tour de France
A ticket to Paris out of the question? This is the next best thing. Every year since 1989, Hervé Martin of the Hermitage (1025 Robson St., 689-3237) has hosted his own gastronomic Tour de France. Starting the first Monday in February, and lasting six weeks, the culinary ramble takes in a number of regions famed for their food and wine. The journey begins in Alsace, then heads west to Champagne (coinciding with Valentine's week) before going on to Burgundy, Provençe, Perigord, and winding up in Brittany/Normandy. You can sample the cuisine of each region from the special à la carte menu and match your choice with appropriate wine. Vive la France!

The baguettes served at Provence (4473 West 10th Ave., 222-1980) are flown in frozen from Toronto and baked in the restaurant. You can buy them there.

are revered by even my French friends. Cinnamon rolls are very lightly sweetened and made from a very nice dough, not those overly gooey boobytraps you often get! Other interesting things on the shelves include a great selection of dried and canned beans, especially those typically found in Mediterranean cuisine, like fava, lupini, black and kidney beans. In the freezer you may find sardines imported from Portugal and unusual fish like sticklebacks. They also have a small but good and very reasonably priced selection of grapeseed and olive oil. Things like Nutella and marmalade in the plastic square containers recall visits to the local grocers on past European trips."

— **Victoria Pratt**, public relations consultant to the food, beverage and hospitality industry

Karen Barnaby suggests Superstore for ethnic items like chapati flour and the big oriental vegetable section, and "President's Choice olive oil can be really good."

A favourite of **Sharon Speirs**, from Raintree at the Landing, is Annie's Shiitake Mushroom Sesame Vinaigrette, which she finds at Choices. "We grill veggies, toast sesame seeds and toss it all together."

"Apart from flying to Winnipeg?" says cooking teacher **Sylvia Molnar** when asked the best source of Ukranian sausage. In her opinion, you'll track it down at Polonia Sausage House (2434 East Hastings St., 251-2239). "They have wonderful fresh meats, too. I also like the Mennonite sausage from Dussa's (Granville Island Public Market, 688-8881). I use it in soups. It has a wonderful smoky flavour and isn't too fatty."

Stephen Wong's Chinatown Finds:
- "The dried shrimp you find in Chinatown are a great way to beef up the flavour of a bisque."
- "Pender Seafoods (284 East Pender, 687-5946) has great live shrimp, black cod, sea bass and skate."
- "A Chinatown store called Cheong Lee (there's no English name on the sign, the address is 260

East Pender) is one of the best places for lemongrass and a favourite stop for banana leaves."

- "As well as chicken cut every which way, Lekiu Poultry (256 East Pender, 681-1012) has fresh duck eggs. Mix them with chicken eggs and they make a dynamite omelette, almost nutty-tasting."
- "Man Cheong (250 East Pender, 685-4333) is one of the few places in Chinatown where you can get enoki mushrooms and fresh baby corn."

For produce, **Carol Chow** likes Kin's Farm Market in Park Royal South, in West Vancouver. "Great stuff and good prices."

Fleuri's **Kai Lerman** buys most of his supplies at Granville Island but this Richmond resident willingly treks across the Lions Gate Bridge to The Black Forest Delicatessen (Park Royal South, 926-3462) for meat and sausage, where he zeros in on schinkenspeck "like proscuitto but better" and Neurberger sausages. "They're like a bratwurst, very juicy and tasty."

"The Greek yogurt from Parthenon Supermarket (3080 West Broadway) reminds me of Winnipeg sour cream."
— **Sylvia Molnar**, cooking teacher

Julio Gonzalez Perini of Villa del Lupo is a fan of Capers for produce. He shops at La Grotta del Formaggio (1791 Commercial Dr., 255-3911) for cheese, and Granville Island Public Market for fish. "I go to Roberto Meat Market on East Hastings for veal, beef, sausages and free-range chicken — they're all good. I come from Buenos Aires, so meat is a must."

Chef, cookbook writer and food consultant **Bill Jones** recommends these winners:
- Mediterranean Specialty Foods (2768 Kingsway, 483-4033) for "the cheapest pasta in town — Italian brands from a dollar a package. Good olive oil from Greece and Portugal, and a good selection of olives."

The merguez served at Provence (4473 West 10th Ave., 222-1980) comes from Freden Fine Foods (1529 East Pender St., 251-2277). You can buy it there, or at some Safeways and IGAs.

- Kings Supermarket (5818 Victoria Drive, 301-1225) has "some of the freshest Chinese produce in Vancouver, a great selection of hard-to-find vegetables and a huge selection of sauces, seasonings and dry goods. The in-store BBQ and take-out section boasts some of the tastiest and cheapest food around."
- Park May Guy Foods Ltd. (5763 Victoria Drive, 327-7922). "Great frozen dim sum — the pork and shrimp dim sum are particularly good. The take-out counter and sit-down restaurant offer Hong Kong specialties at very reasonable prices."
- Happy Family Dim Sum (4129 Fraser St., 873-2232). "The pan-fried pork dumplings are excellent, along with the shrimp dumplings and green onion pancakes."
- Que Pasa Mexican Foods (1637 West 5th Ave., 730-5449) is great for its "variety of whole and ground chilies. Green achiote paste — which is difficult to find — is available along with a great selection of fresh tortillas."
- National Cheese (7278 Curragh, Burnaby, 438-8561). "A good selection of domestic and imported cheeses at reasonable prices."
- Dussa's Ham and Cheese (Granville Island Public Market, 688-8881). "Friendly staff, and an excellent source of hard-to-find cheese. The place for David Wood's Salt Spring Island cheese, and unpasteurized French Camembert, when available."
- A. Bosa and Co. (562 Victoria Drive, 253-5578) for Italian foods, "and they carry an extensive collection of stovetop espresso makers."

Guys and Grills

If the scent of burning charcoal finds you racking your brains for new ideas, Vancouver chefs have some lickety-spit solutions:

"Sardines, head on!" exclaims Hervé Martin of L'Hermitage. Fresh, of course, and he finds them in Chinatown. "A little bit of Provençal herbs or a bit of fennel inside the tummy, a drop of olive oil and a drop of freshly squeezed lemon juice just before you serve them."

Fruits and vegetables, recommends Karen Barnaby of the Fish House in Stanley Park. "Fresh figs. Halve, grill, splash with balsamic and add a little bit of mascarpone. Serve with lamb or for dessert." Even thinly sliced carrots aspire to backyard greatness when grilled and sprinkled with an orange-zest-and-rosemary gremolata, says Barnaby.

Chris Johnson of RainCity Grill favours boneless Fraser Valley quail alongside brochettes of morels, cherry tomatoes and fingerling potatoes (the potatoes parboiled so everything is cooked at the same time.) "Simply serve on a bed of arugula and maché."

Food writer Jurgen Gothe likes to sling a bunch of sausages on the barbecue: "Wild boar or venison from Windsor Meats," or smoked pork loin which is already cooked, "but gets little tire tracks on it." On the side: halved pitted peaches with a dash of butter and sugar.

Pasta on the barbie? "Si," says Umberto Menghi. While it cooks in a pot, throw tomatoes on the grill drizzled with olive oil and sprinkled with oregano, pepper and salt. The scooped-out tomato flesh goes on the pasta, plus chopped fresh basil, garlic and parmigiana.

VANCOUVER'S CHEFS:

What Do They Eat at Home?

"Bruschetta is so easy and so good. Just rub slices of stale bread — good bread, not the supermarket kind — with garlic and toast them on both sides under the broiler. Drizzle with really good olive oil and some aged balsamic vinegar, and sprinkle with sea salt and cracked pepper."

— *Caren McSherry, Caren's Cooking School*

"I bone a chicken and stuff it with a bit of brioche, sun-dried tomatoes, prosciutto, fresh chives, onion and sage. Tie it up and slowly roast it with a bit of olive oil, rosemary and cracked black pepper. Make a jus from the pan juices. Serve it with mashed potatoes and green salad."

— *Julio Gonzalez Perini, chef, Villa del Lupo*

"I like to marinate rabbit with Dijon mustard, herbes de Provençe, olive oil, sea salt and pepper, then barbecue it. It gives it a nice colour, a crispy golden brown, and flavour. It works with chicken, too."

— *Jean-Francis Quaglia, chef, Provençe*

"I do a lot of German cooking at home. Buy a can of Hengstenberg sauerkraut, wash it a little bit. Sauté finely sliced onions and apples — two-thirds onions, one-third apple — in butter or pork fat. Add the sauerkraut and season with salt and pepper. Make a spice bag containing a clove of garlic, thyme, bayleaves, peppercorns, coriander seeds and juniper berries, all crushed. Add a little white wine and some chicken stock. Bring to the boil and put in the oven for half an hour. The sauerkraut should still be a bit crunchy. You can also add sautéed, diced bacon to it. Sausages, nice mustard and bread — that's all you need."

— *Kai Lerman, Executive Chef, Sutton Place Hotel*

"I combine olive oil, a little bit of chopped onion, some basil powder and garlic powder. Sauté those ingredients. Add some white wine and a Knorr vegetable-, beef- or chicken-stock cube. Crush a 28 ounce tin of tomatoes, and add that and some salt and pepper – very little salt, though, because there is salt in the stock. Cook for half an hour. It's enough for one kilogram of pasta, elbows or shells or penne – all types of pasta. When the pasta is done, the sauce is ready. It's very plain and cheap. Not even six dollars to feed six people with a good plate of pasta. Add a piece of bread and some salad – that's a complete meal. If you can afford a glass of wine, it's even better."

   – Susan Renzullo, Bianca-Maria Italian Foods

"On my nights off, I eat at home. I like cooking. I go to Granville Island Market and buy ingredients like nice, new white potatoes. I slice them, cook them and make a hot potato salad with a little bit of mustard, chives, raspberry vinegar and olive oil in the dressing. I put some salmon in the frypan. No seasoning, just salt and pepper and maybe a couple of prawns or scallops on top. I always like to open a bottle of wine and smoke my pipe afterwards."

   – Robert LeCrom, Executive Chef, Hotel Vancouver

"Try fresh garlic, a little chili, a little chopped Italian parsley, salt and pepper on pasta. It's great if you add fresh crab."

   – Julio Gonzalez Perini, chef, Villa del Lupo

"Here's a great marinade for steaks and roast beef. You need the juice of one lemon, one bountiful tablespoon of dried basil, a teaspoon of pepper, three tablespoons of soy sauce, and six cloves of finely chopped garlic. Add one cup of canola or vegetable oil, and one cup of water or leftover wine. Mix it all together and place in a jar (this makes enough for about four meals). Pour the marinade liberally over the meat and marinate overnight up to 36 hours. Grill or roast as usual."

   – Brian Jackson, Jackson's Meats

"This is a Lebanese dish called foule. Soak baby fava beans overnight. Cook them until soft. Crush garlic, add lemon juice, salt, olive oil and dried mint. Add to the drained beans. Eat warm or cold with pita. If you want to make this dish ahead of time, keep the beans in the fridge and put the sauce in the fridge separately, adding the lemon juice at the last moment."

    — Richard Zeinoun and Lisa Gibson, chef/owners, Habibi's

"Asian spices are great. They're so flavourful. Just put soya sauce, sesame sauce, chopped cilantro and maybe some chili sauce together — it's good for barbecued anything except maybe beef. Allow a couple of hours marinade for chicken — then just toss it in with prawns at the last minute."

    — Carol Chow, chef, Beach Side Café

Executive Chef Michael Noble (l) and Restaurant Chef David Griffiths of Diva at the Met

Chef's Tip

"When you have beautiful New Zealand spinach, or any spinach or greens, don't cook them in water. Sauté them in butter. You may have quite a volume. Just add more greens as they wilt."

    — Michael Noble

"We do a lot of pasta. The kids love that. This one is a summer pasta. In the blender I put three almost over-ripe tomatoes, cores removed and cut in chunks, three garlic cloves and a handful of fresh basil. I dump in some balsamic vinegar and a good whack of extra virgin olive oil, plus salt and pepper. Blend and put on pasta with some parmesan. It's just gorgeous. Sometimes we add sausage, grilled and cut in chunks."

    — Michael Noble, Executive Chef, Diva at the Met

"Cut an eggplant, a bell pepper and a potato into chunks. Pan-fry them, then add a teaspoon of garam masala, a teaspoon of cumin, salt and pepper. Add a little water, cover and cook over slow heat until vegetables are cooked. It's called a sabji — a medley of vegetables — and you can serve it with plain yogurt and some Indian bread."

    — Vikram Vij, chef/owner, Vij's

"Sauté chopped garlic in olive oil, and embellish it with roasted red peppers and parsley. Serve over pasta. Simple and quick."

    — Maria Tommasini Robertson, Vita e Vino, Italian Wine Society

"Here's my grandmother's recipe for potato salad. Sauté diced onions and bacon until they're cooked but not brown. Deglaze the pan with vinegar and put it in a bowl. Add mustard, sunflower oil, salt, pepper and hot chicken stock. At the same time, cook Yukon Gold potatoes — leave their skins on — in salt water with parsley and caraway seeds. Peel them, slice them 1/4-inch thick and put them in the warm marinade. Swirl the bowl around lightly. You don't want to break up the potato. Let it sit and it sucks all the marinade up. Add some parsley, and that's it."
  — *Kai Lerman, Executive Chef, Sutton Place Hotel*

"I freeze puréed fruit to make fruit fools. Take it out, add whipped cream. Instant dessert."
  — *Barbara-jo McIntosh, chef/owner, Barbara-Jo's Books to Cooks*

"It's nice to sauté scallops with a little lemon thyme, chives, extra virgin olive oil. Grate on top some really super Parmesan cheese, add salt and pepper."
  — *Umberto Menghi, restaurateur*

"Sprinkle pork ribs on both sides with the juice of one lemon, then sprinkle them with oregano, salt and pepper. Let sit two or three hours before they go on the barbecue. Once you've tasted that on ribs, you'll never want anything else."
  — *Brian Jackson, Jackson's Meats*

"When I first moved to Vancouver, I took a Japanese cooking course at the Dunbar Community Centre taught by a dynamo named Ron Suzuki. Week after week we learned not just sushi and teriyaki but wonderful homestyle dishes, too. One became known, in our house anyway, as 'Mrs. Suzuki's Pork and Pickled Vegetable Dish.' It comes originally from Clara Suzuki, has been modified by her son Ron, and is extremely easy to make and thoroughly delicious:
"Pork and Fukujinzuke": Cut two pounds of boneless pork into thin strips, about 1 x 1/4 inch, and place in a heat-proof bowl. Fold in a clove of sliced, crushed garlic, and four slices of ginger root. Mix in a half to a whole can of fukujinzuke (Japanese pickles), two

Chef's Tip

"Try to buy things on a daily basis. Don't buy asparagus just because it's on sale for $1.99 a pound and keep it for two weeks. Pay a dollar more a pound and enjoy it fresh. Keep things simple."
  — Carol Chow, Beach Side Café

tablespoons of mirin (Japanese sweet cooking wine) and 1/4 teaspoon of cayenne pepper. Mix well and press the mixture to the sides of the bowl. Place the bowl in a saucepan containing one inch of cold water. Cover and bring the water to a boil. Cook for three to four minutes, then lower heat and let pork steam for 25 to 40 minutes. Serve with hot rice or steamed vegetables."

— *Angela Murrills, food columnist and author*

"Many people overlook the benefits of a marinade. A simple marinade of lemon juice and olive oil flavoured with rosemary and garlic is great for pork chops, veal chops and lamb leg. A marinade of ginger, lemon, teriyaki sauce, sherry, garlic, shallots and soy sauce will greatly enhance the flavour of Chilean sea bass, flank steak and chicken breast."

— *Bruno Born, Sausi's Bar & Grill*

"Here's how to prepare a ham. Remove the skin, diamond-score it and put cloves in the centre of each diamond. Make a mixture of dry mustard, brown sugar and beer, like a thick paste. Put double tinfoil down in your roast pan, put the ham in and spread the paste liberally all over the ham. Cook it for 10 minutes per pound at 300 degrees. During the cooking, in between swigs (all chefs have to have a swig) pour more beer over the ham — every 20 minutes or half an hour depending on the size of ham. It comes out lovely and moist."

— *Brian Jackson, Jackson's Meats*

"Sauté fennel in a hot cast-iron pan with a bit of garlic for 10 seconds, and add a little pepperoncini. Brown the fennel, serve it with veal scallops or red snapper."

— *Umberto Menghi, restaurateur*

SNAPSHOTS OF SOME SPECIALISTS:

Catering to Cravings

GAME FOR A CHANGE?

Bison? Alligator? Many of the more exotic meats on restaurant menus come from Hills Foods Ltd. (109-3650 Bonneville Pl., Burnaby, 421-3100), whose Wild Ideas listing each week details what's on offer and/or in season. Fresh or frozen and flown in from Quebec, foie gras is a constant. Lined up in their "regular" shopping list are elk, wild Arctic caribou and wild boar (available whole, in pieces, even – think Christmas – with a head for display), not to mention skinned and coiled rattlesnake, alligator burgers, frog legs, turtle meat, ostrich and Hawaiian sea vegetables. Minimum $100 order and you pick it up. Give Hills a buzz first to check that what you want is in stock or to have their lists faxed to you. For smaller (and frozen) quantities, check your local supermarket or specialty butcher.

ICE-CREAM DREAMS

Vince Misceo leaves Baskin Robbins at the starting post. At La Casa Gelato (1033 Venables St., 251-3211) he has built up a repertoire of some 150 different flavours, all made from natural ingredients. You'll usually find about 60 of them for sale. Death by Mango streaked with raspberry purée is magnificent, and the strawberry variety is like sticking your face in a bowl of ripe berries. Ginger has a zingy freshness, so does lemon, and the peach apricot yogurt is a lush treat. Watermelon sorbetto is simple, cleansing – and 100 percent fat-free. They're all magnificent, but that's not Misceo's claim to fame. Simply put, he's known for varieties that border on the downright weird. Occasionally, he whips up a batch of curry or garlic ice cream; in December, he makes pine needle sorbetto. Wasabi ice cream is a strange mix of hot and cold, and the avocado is outstandingly rich. A whisper of cardamom signals the nut kulfi ice-cream. A red bean version has an interesting mealy texture and a pleasant taste. The oddest flavour of all is durian, made from a huge knobby Asian fruit that looks like a medieval instrument of torture (and smells like a festering cabbage). Of all the containers in the store, this is the only one with lid always on.

BEYOND BAGELS

Solly's makes terrific bagels — plain, speckled, wholewheat, multigrain or a slew of other flavours, including a terrific pumpernickel and, during October, a pumpkin variety — but just as many people stop by for the cinnamon buns, which are huge, their tops dark brown and as sweet and sticky as toffee. They have many more coils than most buns of their type, which means more hiding places for butter and sugar. Solly's is also famous for its authentic Jewish pastries. Rugoleh is a rich dough spread liberally with jam, spattered with raisins or sweet poppy seeds or chocolate, then rolled up and sliced. Roly Polys are made of finely chopped oranges, raisins, walnuts, coconut and real Turkish Delight. Mandelbroit is biscotti-like almond bread, and babka is a loaf rolled with fudgy chocolate. You'll also find knishes — fat little pastry cushions stuffed with spinach and mushrooms, potato and onion, or sweet cheese — plus "salty twists" and lokshen kugel made with noodles, cream cheese, raisins and cinnamon.

Yoka Vandenberg

ROAST-AROMA

On weekends you take your chances, but every weekday for sure, Yoka Vandenberg roasts the coffee beans she sells at Yoka's (3171 West Broadway, 738-0905). The smell is something you'd like to bottle and unleash under your nose a nanosecond before the alarm goes off. Big hessian sacks of green beans are ranged along one wall. On the counter — and under it — are the 25 or so varieties of beans and blends that Vandenberg measures out on an old-fashioned scale. Mocha Java and Dark Roast are the most popular.

OLIVE ONE OF THOSE

The olives at the Parthenon Supermarket go way beyond the pimento-stuffed variety (though they carry those, too). Made in-house and addictive beyond reason, the Sicilian spicy olives are marinated with lemons, oregano, a hefty whack of chili peppers, garlic and allspice. Jalapenos and sundried tomatoes infuse the Lebanese spicy kind. Throubes are olives dried in the Greek sun. The "Christmas mix" is some of these, some of those, mingled with sundried tomatoes, peppers and lemon. Sampling encouraged.

Kyriakos Katsanikakis at the Parthenon Supermarket

Where to Get that Garlic Fix

- **Skordalia**, an addictive mashed-potato-and-garlic dip is sold "to go" at Minerva's Mediterranean Deli (3207 West Broadway, 733-3954).
- Check Indian and Asian grocery stores for garlic poppadoms.
- **The Epicure's Cupboard** (5633 West Boulevard, 264-8200) carries locally made Roasted Garlic and Onion Jam.
- **Everything Garlic** (Lonsdale Quay Market, North Vancouver, 988-0003). The name says it all.
- **The Stinking Rose** (2830 Bainbridge, Burnaby, 420-7730). When the restaurant first opened, garlic ice cream was on the menu. "It didn't go down well," says owner John Venditti, "and nor did the garlic wine." What does sell is the potato-garlic soup, the baked garlic Brie, the 40-clove garlic chicken, and prime rib with its garlic demi-glas. Here, the garlic even comes free. Sit down and you can dive right into the roasted garlic on the table and the garlic pizzaiola sauce.
- **Wild Garlic** (2120 West Broadway, 730-0880). The most frequently ordered dish is the slow-roasted candied garlic. You might then move on to fried jalapenos stuffed with garlic and Asiago, elephant garlic chips with lemon aioli, or smoked garlic and eggplant spread. Garlic shows up in a sauce that accompanies gnocchi and duck breast, or mixes in with mashed yams. Dessert? How about a white chocolate candied garlic hazelnut terrine.
- An **Annual Garlic Festival** is held at the Matsqui-Sumas-Abbotsford Museum (853-0313). Cookbooks, demonstrations, a garlic peeling competition and your chance to be Mr. or Ms. Garlic Festival.

FOOD ORGANIZATIONS

FarmFolk/CityFolk
208-2211 West 4th Ave. • 730-0450

Its logo — a garden fork and a table fork — symbolizes what this Vancouver-based organization aims to do, which is to remind us of the direct connection between what grows in the fields and what ends up on our plate. FarmFolk/CityFolk is committed to the development and maintenance of a just and sustainable food system, and one of its major goals is to reconnect people with their food sources. Its information services can help you buy direct from a farmer, tell you where you can take the kids to a farm for a day, or answer your questions on certified organic food. It supports the development of farmers' markets, community kitchens, allotment gardens and demonstration farms. FarmFolk/CityFolk hosts two major celebrations a year: Granville Island Market After Dark (see page 213) and Feast of Fields (see page 217) — tasty ways to experience the quality and variety of local foods — and the creativeness of local chefs. Annual membership includes a lively newsletter that keeps you up to speed with what's happening locally, nationally and globally to the food we eat.

Foodrunners
311 East 6th Ave. • 889-4018

Ever wonder what restaurants or catering companies do with their surplus food? Many donate it to Foodrunners, which in turn distributes it to soup kitchens, shelters, missions and other places around the city.

Vancouver Food Bank
311 East 6th Ave. • 876-3601

The Greater Vancouver Food Bank Society feeds about 7,000 people a week — 2,500 of them children. Numbers rise annually, and so does the need. Adding an extra item or two to your grocery list doesn't cost much (and you can usually leave your donation right there in the Food Bank bin in your supermarket). What the Food Bank needs most are non-perishable foods such as canned meats, canned beans, peanut butter, powdered milk, macaroni and cheese, baby food, formula and pablum, canned fruits and vegetables, rice, canned stew, pasta noodles and sauces, and canned and packaged soups. Tax deductible contributions are also welcome — and necessary. The Food Bank can also use volunteers.

KIDS AND FOOD

Just because you're curious and passionate about what you eat doesn't mean your kids will be — but the chances are definitely higher. Taking them with you on culinary rambles around the city is one way to do it. Show them live crabs in Chinatown. Figure out together all the names of the various greens — and take a bunch or two home to try them out. On summer Saturdays, skip breakfast and go straight to a farmers' market for fresh-baked muffins and lovely drippy peaches from the Okanagan. It's a great way to introduce your child to fresh, natural foods.

Children and restaurants used to be mutually exclusive. Not anymore. Almost all places welcome kids, provided they don't disrupt other people's meals. If you need a high chair, book it with your reservation. For a happy few years, between eight and twelve years old, kids are usually well-behaved and happy to join you for lunch or dinner anywhere. After that..."Uh, Mom, some of my friends might see me with you."

The best destinations are ethnic restaurants. Dim sum at a Chinese restaurant is enormous fun — what's inside those little baskets? So is learning to eat with chopsticks. Shrimp dumplings are usually a treat with small fry. Sticky rice, too, because unwrapping it is like opening a present and inside it's sticky. Other times of day, try gentle noodle dishes that are messy like spaghetti. Lemon chicken is usually a safe bet. Tell them it's like McNuggets but tastes sweeter.

Children aren't supposed to like spicy food but if you've ever left your eight-year-old alone with the taco chips and salsa, you'll know lots of them do. Tandoori chicken at an Indian restaurant is almost always a huge hit. So is calamari at your favourite Greek eatery (with baklava for dessert).

Don't discount Japanese restaurants, either. One of the nicest New Year's celebrations we ever had was when our daughter Kate was two-and-a-half, and the three of us spent a happy few hours in our own private tatami room. Sushi rolls, noodles, teriyaki, tempura — apart from sashimi, there's practically nothing on a Japanese menu that kids don't like.

Look Mom, Free Cookies
It's not just an urban myth.
Any kid who goes to a
Safeway store only has to ask
for a cookie at the bakery
counter and he or she will be
given one free.

Where Chefs Take Their Kids
"They love Uncle Herbert's in
Ladner," says Michael Noble of
Diva at the Met. "It's always
very good. The ambience is
English pub style and the food
is good, too."

McDonald's at Your Place
Kids inhale soft drinks. If you
have a large number of little
thirsts to quench, consider
McDonald's Orange Bowls. $8
plus tax gets you concentrate,
100 cups and free Orange
Bowl rental (there is a $40
refundable deposit). Call your
local McDonald's for info.

DINING OUT: Kid-Friendly Places

Earls
Various locations
"Kids love things that even surprise their parents,"
says the company. "They just eat it in smaller
quantities." They like children here, they really do.
And, though there's no specific kids' menu, Earls does
offer half orders of its more junior-friendly dishes such
as Caesar salad, margarita pizza, tomato-basil linguine
and fettucine alfredo. The big burger is the ideal size
for two kids. So is the rack of ribs. Guaranteed to
please even the fussiest eaters are Earls wings or
chicken tenders and fries.

BURNABY:
Rainforest Café
4700 Kingsway • 433-3383
This chunk o' the jungle in Eaton Centre is terrific
for kids of all ages. You may want to warn little ones
that there's a realistic thunderstorm every 22 minutes.
Life-like, animatronic elephants and gorillas, real
macaws and a ceiling that drips with tropical foliage
provide the setting for surprisingly tasty food. Ribs,
pizzas and pasta are all good bets — as are the desserts.

VANCOUVER:

Isadora's Co-operative Restaurant

1540 Old Bridge St., Granville Island • 681-8816

One of the first "family" restaurants in Vancouver, this Granville Island fave has it all: a kids' menu, space to play inside, the Water Park outside for summer days – and crayons.

Mark's Steak and Taphouse

2486 Bayswater St. • 734-1325

Half-price pizzas Tuesday nights. Paper tablecloths and crayons.

Stretch their Culinary Horizons

All of these are warm welcoming places where you can have a good meal and your kids can try something new – or familiar. See "Restaurants" (pages 161 to 189) for more about each establishment.

Fatzo's
Hachibei
Habibi's
La Bodega
Las Margaritas
The Lazy Gourmet
Ouzerie
Provence
Rasputin
Sophie's Cosmic Café
Stepho's
Templeton Restaurant

Party Time at McDonald's

The easiest of all parties — everyone loves the food and you don't have to clean up afterwards. A flat rate of $5.95 plus tax includes Happy Meals, a gift for the birthday girl or boy, goodie bags, games, activities, what McDonald's calls "reserved access" (which means your own party area) and the services of a host or hostess. Call 268-0333 for info.

BUFFETS FOR KIDS: Eat as Much as You Like

"Wow, you mean I can eat anything I want – and then go back and get some more?!!" Kids love buffets, and parents do too, because they know that if little Roman or Julie has picked out everything on the plate, he or she is likely to eat it. Try these places:

LANGLEY:
Mongolie Grill
1-6233 200th St. • 533-3135
Strictly speaking not a buffet, but close. Choose what you want from the chicken, marinaded beef, prawns, two kinds of noodles, vegetables and sauces. Have it weighed and give it to the cook.

RICHMOND:
Knight & Day
3631 No. 3 Rd. • 244-8858
(see also: Surrey; Vancouver)
Family food at bargain prices. Sunday brunch plus themed dinner buffets – seafood, continental, international – Fridays through Sundays.

Mongolie Grill
100-8400 Alexandra Rd. • 276-0303
(see: Langley)

SURREY:
Knight & Day
9677 King George Hwy. • 588-7575
Family food and Sunday brunch buffet.
(see also: Richmond; Vancouver)

VANCOUVER:
Fleuri/Sutton Place Hotel
845 Burrard St. • 682-5511
A very elegant restaurant with a chocoholic buffet every Thursday, Friday and Saturday. The buffet comprises about 30 feet of dessert: Pies, tarts, tortes, cakes, brownies, bits of fudge to fill in the cracks and crêpes which your little sweeties can garnish with all the chocolate chips and chocolate sauce they want. Just this once, skip supper and go straight to dessert.

Tours for Tots
Store tours that take in the bakery are popular at Safeway with daycare kids and kindergartens. Call 1-800-SAFEWAY to set one up.

"Freeze homemade baby food in ice cube trays. Then store in freezer bags."
— Andrew Skorzewski, Rainforest Café.

Griffins/Hotel Vancouver
900 West Georgia St. • 662-1900
Buffet heaven: Breakfast, lunch, appetizers at dinner — there's a special children's menu in the evening — plus a dessert buffet. Any kid with a brain will want to live at the Hotel Vancouver permanently. Saturdays, they can tackle the Mediterranean buffet (which includes pizzas). Sunday brunch includes a special child's buffet with neat-looking desserts they can garnish with Smarties, gummy bears and other good stuff.

Incendio Pizzeria
103 Columbia St. • 688-8694
The draw here is all-you-can-eat pizza on Sunday evenings for one set price. The only stipulations: a compulsory beverage purchase, no food fights and no doggy bags. In return, you and yours can take a whack at any or all of Incendio's 22 pizza varieties. The Siciliana includes capers, onions, anchovies and black olives. The Capricossa piles on ham, salami, artichokes, mushrooms and so on. A little more restrained is the pesto pizza, which features the obvious plus onion and chicken. A seafood variation contains shrimps, calamari, baby clams, mussels and Asiago cheese.

Knight & Day
3684 Lougheed Hwy. • 299-7701
(see also: Richmond; Surrey)

Mongolie Grill
467 West Broadway • 874-6121
Strictly speaking not a buffet, but close. Choose what you want from the chicken, marinaded beef, prawns, two kinds of noodles, vegetables and sauces. Have it weighed and give it to the cook.

Bishop's for Kids

"You take a boneless, skinless chicken breast, sear it in a pan, grill it and leave it to cool. Then slice it on the bias and cut into bite-size pieces. Then you take two ripe Roma tomatoes and cut them lengthwise into eighths. Dice a rib of celery and add that too. Squeeze over it the juice of a lemon, and a couple of tablespoons of really good olive oil. A little pepper, you need hardly any salt. It's a wonderful summer salad and kids love it."

— John Bishop

Real French Fries
Introduce older kids to the best French fries in town at Café de Paris (751 Denman St., 687-1418).

259

One Mean Machine

If they're sci-fi addicts, your kids will get a kick out of watching the automatic sushi maker at Sushi Robo (1709 Robson St., 682-7155). Out comes a mat of rice, next a non-robotic human lays on the tuna or salmon, and then, like some medieval instrument of torture, metallic "jaws" clamp the whole shebang together.

Power Breakfasts and Lunches

Extremely good boys and girls of a suitable age can be taken to the Four Seasons Hotel (791 West Georgia St.) for a meal. The Garden Terrace is probably a more appropriate choice than Chartwell. Both offer a terrific kids' menu geared to the 3 to 12 age group. Breakfast dishes are junior favourites — dishes like mini pancakes with maple butter, cereal with bananas. Lunch or dinner offerings include macaroni and cheese, a Whamburger or Whizburger, fish and chips, chicken fingers, hot dogs and other kidstuff, with a choice of Bibb salad or chicken noodle soup. The back of the menu has puzzles and pictures to colour. Prices for junior meals, parents will be happy to hear, are more than reasonable.

LEARNING TO COOK

Peanut butter. White bread. Any kid can slap together a sandwich. For many, that's as far as it goes. Here are some places that make it fun to learn a bit more.

VANCOUVER:

Barbara-Jo's Books to Cooks

1128 Mainland St. • 688-6755

This jewel of a cookbook store occasionally holds cooking sessions specifically for kids. You'll find junior cookbooks, too. Store owner Barbara-jo McIntosh recommends: *Fanny at Chez Panisse* by Alice Waters (HarperCollins); *Beaver the Baker* by Lars Klinting (Douglas & McIntyre); *The Truffle Hunter* by Inga Moore (Milestone Publishing); and *The Magic Spoon Cookbook* (which comes with its own spoon) by Suzanne Gooding (Klutz Press).

Community Centres

various locations

Some offer cooking courses for kids as young as four years old. Contact your nearest Centre for information or keep your eyes open for the "Recreation Guide" flyer usually distributed with community newspapers.

Cookshop at City Square

555 West 12th Ave. • 873-5683

During the summer holidays, you can sign up your 10- to 13-year-old for a series of four hands-on classes. All are held during the same week. At the end of it, your kid will know how to make "junk" food (that isn't junk), pies, picnic fare and dinner dishes such as beef fajitas and cashew chicken stir-fry.

Contributors

JAMES BARBER is Canada's best known food personality, and the host of *The Urban Peasant*, the internationally acclaimed TV cooking series.

Author of the bestselling *Chef on the Run* cookbook series, DIANE CLEMENT is a partner in Vancouver's highly popular Tomato Fresh Food Café.

Keen cook and gardener DUNCAN HOLMES writes frequently on the pleasures of the palate, and is the author of several books.

Gourmet and bon vivant JAMIE MAW is food editor of *Vancouver* magazine.

Creator of the "City" series, writer/broadcaster MARG MEIKLE is author of *Dog City: Vancouver*, and is currently at work on *Garden City: Vancouver*.

The photographs in *Food City: Vancouver* were taken by Peter Matthews, with the exception of the following:

page 11   courtesy of James Barber.
page 149   courtesy of Whitecap Books.
page 168   courtesy of the Metropolitan Hotel.
page 190   photo by Tim Pelling.
page 192   photo by Rob Melnychuck.
page 246   courtesy of the Metropolitan Hotel.

Index

ANGELA MURRILLS was born in Bury St. Edmunds, England, and studied at Concordia University in Montreal. She has lived in Vancouver since 1980 and is a regular restaurant reviewer and Food Editor for *The Georgia Straight*. She is also co-author of *Farm Folk/City Folk* (Douglas and McIntyre, 1998).

Please let Angela know about any omissions, additions, deletions or comments for the next edition of *Food City: Vancouver*. Write to her at:

Angela Murrills
c/o Polestar Book Publishers
PO Box 5238, Station B
Victoria, BC
V8R 6N4

BRIGHT LIGHTS FROM POLESTAR BOOK PUBLISHERS

Polestar Book Publishers takes pride in creating books that enrich our understanding of the world. We support independent voices that illuminate our history, stretch the imagination and engage our sympathies.

The City Series: Definitive Guides to Your Favourite Pastimes in Your Favourite Cities
These comprehensive guides present a dynamic way of experiencing favourite cities and popular urban pastimes. Here is indispensable and intriguing information for real people who live, work and play in and around major Canadian urban centres. Follow your dog's lead with *Dog City*; grow a green thumb with *Garden City*; dine out on *Food City*.
The City Series: Discover new worlds in your own backyard.
Watch for: *Garden City: Vancouver* (Spring 1999)

Dog City • Vancouver: The Definitive Guide for Dog Owners in Vancouver and the Lower Mainland
by Marg Meikle
With an introduction by Stanley Coren, author of *The Intelligence of Dogs*
Explore the world of the urban canine! Journalist and dog owner Meikle has the inside scoop on finding, caring for and enjoying life with your dog in the Lower Mainland.
1-896095-38-0 • $18.95 CDN • $14.95 USA • b&w photos and illustrations throughout

Non-Fiction
From Farm to Feast: Recipes and Stories from Saltspring and the Southern Gulf Islands
by Gail Richards and Kevin Snook
Here is the most valuable kind of cookbook: one that renews our relationship with healthy food while revelling in the delights of fine cuisine.
1-896095-43-7 • $29.95 CDN • $24.95 USA • full-colour photos throughout

The Garden Letters *by Elspeth Bradbury & Judy Maddocks*
"...lively and humorous writing about the labours of life and gardening." — *The Guardian Weekend*
1-896095-06-2 • $19.95 CDN • $15.95 USA • illustrations throughout

The Real Garden Road Trip *by Elspeth Bradbury & Judy Maddocks*
Longtime friends Elspeth and Judy trek cross-country to find "real gardens and real gardeners."
1-896095-35-6 • $24.95 CDN • $19.95 USA • photographs throughout

Fiction
West by Northwest *edited by David Stouck & Myler Wilkinson*
A brilliant collection of short fiction that celebrates the unique landscape and culture of BC. Includes stories by Bill Reid, Ethel Wilson, Wayson Choy, George Bowering, Shani Mootoo and others.
1-896095-41-0 • $18.95 CDN • $16.95 USA

Fresh Tracks: Writing the Western Landscape *edited by Pamela Banting*
"A diverse gathering of over 40 writers, this is an entertaining and thoughtful exploration of how the western landscape influences all aspects of human life and creativity." — *Quill and Quire*
1-896095-42-9 • $21.95 CDN • $18.95 USA

Polestar titles are available from your local bookseller. For a copy of our catalogue, contact:
POLESTAR BOOK PUBLISHERS
PO Box 5238, Station B
Victoria, British Columbia
Canada   V8R 6N4   http://mypage.direct.ca/p/polestar